The Fisher

THE FISHER

Life History,

Ecology,

and Behavior

Roger A. Powell

UNIVERSITY OF MINNESOTA PRESS
Minneapolis

Library of Congress Cataloging in Publication Data

Powell, Roger A.
  The fisher.

  Bibliography: p.
  Includes index.
  1. Fisher (Animal) I. Title.
QL737.C25P66   599.74'447   81-14775
ISBN 0-8166-1053-3   AACR2

5-18-01   c. 2 gift

599.74

Pow

To ThaCho
   Because I like to think you made it
And to Uskool
   Because I am sorry
I loved you both

Contents

Preface

On 17 April 1974 my wife Consie reached in to the nest box of a captive wild fisher and took out two gray, squirming, little bodies (the female fisher had been closed out of her nest box for the removal of her kits). Thus began two years of experiences that will stay with me for a lifetime.

I remember being scared, excited, nervous, and awed as Consie removed the kits from the nest box. We were taking on a responsibility that turned out to be much greater than we had imagined. It was absolutely necessary that we take the responsibility, however; I had to have two fishers that I could handle in order to complete my research. Hand raising kits was the only way I could get fishers that could be handled and taught to run on a treadmill as adults, and this was the biggest bottleneck in my research for my doctoral degree. In order to determine the energy expenditure of the radio-tagged fishers that I followed in the woods in Michigan's Upper Peninsula, I had to know the metabolic rates of fishers running at different speeds. I would do this by incorporating a treadmill into a metabolic chamber and running adult fishers on the treadmill. The two kits were my future adult fishers.

Consie and I named the two kits (a female and a male) ThaCho and Uskool. The names mean "fisher" in the Chippewayan and Wabanaki languages. ThaCho and Uskool had been born on 29 or 30

March 1974 in a wooden nest box lined with straw. Their mother had been fed a more than adequate diet of road-killed mammals and birds and had been taking excellent care of her kits. We placed the kits in a cardboard box lined with wool rags and heated with an electric heating pad. They requested their first meal by squealing and squirming about three hours after being removed from their mother. We bottle-fed them *Esbilac* (a simulated bitch's milk manufactured by Borden's) every three hours, night and day, for the next week. It took a while for us to get used to feeding baby fishers and for the fishers to get used to being bottle-fed, but everything worked out fine. Consie and I took turns getting up in the middle of the night so that each of us only had to get up once each night.

I was perhaps too worrisome a guardian for the kits. At any sign of diarrhea, reduced appetite or excessive activity I would be on the phone to the veterinarian, who was exceedingly patient and gave me much wise advice—such as using *Kaopectate* for the kits' diarrhea. Probably ThaCho's and Uskool's greatest feat was surviving me!

When ThaCho and Uskool were about three and a half weeks old, we changed their feeding schedule to every four hours. This meant that Consie and I could trade nights of feeding the kits; one of us could stay in bed all night. The nighttime feedings were completely discontinued when the kits were four and a half weeks old.

ThaCho and Uskool taught us many things about themselves and about raising baby animals. Most important, they taught us to pay attention to what they were trying to tell us. ThaCho became a very fussy eater when she reached about eight weeks of age. Was she getting too much to eat? Was she sick? No—she was getting ready for food of a more solid consistency than liquid formula. At first we would rub ThaCho's and Uskool's tummies with a piece of facial tissue before feeding them. This stimulated them to urinate. By the time they got to be a few weeks older, though, we were going through a lot of tissue. I cannot remember who struck on the idea, Consie or I, but we began holding them over the toilet when we stimulated them. Then all we needed to do was a little bit of cleanup.

By far the biggest cleanup came when the kits were weaned. We fed them a puree of *Esbilac* and finely ground raw venison. They loved it. They also made total messes of themselves. They were not content with putting the food in their mouths but insisted on getting it all over their faces, paws, and tummies as well. Cleaning a squirming fisher kit with a damp washcloth is almost impossible, but letting our female Newfoundland dog clean up the mess was easy. Kaloosit, the Newfoundland, loved the job: she got a rare treat of venison and *Esbilac* puree. In addition, the kits did not squirm much while being cleaned with her tongue.

ThaCho and Uskool stayed in a variety of places during the time they lived with us. At first, they went through a graduated series of cardboard boxes; then they went on to a gable in my upstairs study and then to our front porch. I set up a treadmill on the front porch so that I could train them. ThaCho and Uskool would perch with their paws on the front door, looking inside the house and hoping I would come out and play with them. They soon learned how to distinguish whether I was coming out to play with them or to run them on the treadmill. ThaCho discovered that she could hide in places I had trouble reaching—such as under a cage or on top of the curtains in a corner. While the fishers were living on the front porch, there was more than an occasional "bump in the night."

Finally, ThaCho and Uskool moved to the pen where I kept my captive wild fishers. This pen was approximately 6 by 12 meters, had a sagging wire-mesh top, and was out in the woods away from people. ThaCho and Uskool had individual cages with nest boxes. After September 1974, I did not leave them together because of the spats they had over food. I traded access to the big pen back and forth between them every other day, and they learned my ritual. Each day when I came to the pen, both fishers were out of their nest boxes and running back and forth, excited to see me. I climbed in to the pen and played with whichever fisher was out and then closed that fisher in to his or her cage. That was the trick. They quickly learned to recognize when I had decided it was time to stop playing and to close whoever was out in to his or her cage. I learned how to trick them into getting back inside their cages. With both fishers in their cages, I let one fisher out to play. When the playing was finished, I gave the fisher in the pen food when that fisher was to be fed. I sometimes wonder who really played. I believe I played as much as they did, or more.

In early April 1975, my cousin flew ThaCho, Uskool, and me to Dick Taylor's laboratory at Harvard University. It was there that I collected the actual data on metabolic rates and running speeds. ThaCho and Uskool balked on the treadmill and did not like living in concrete runs, and they told me so: Uskool (by this time weighing well over 5 kilograms) gave me a solid warning bite by taking my whole nose firmly between his canines. (My cuts healed quickly, but the bruises lasted for weeks and the scars are still there.) Nonetheless, the fishers gave me the data I needed, and the results were better than I had hoped.

When I returned to Upper Michigan in mid-May 1975, I was in a quandary. The work for which I had raised ThaCho and Uskool was finished, and yet I did not want to let them go. I continued to make observations of their killing techniques for snowshoe hares, and I collected scats for my work on the fisher's digestive efficiency with different types of prey, as I had done before I went to Harvard for the metabolic studies. I persuaded myself that I needed to keep them in captivity.

On 19 July 1975, Uskool died of an unknown cause. I took his body to one of my favorite places in the woods and left it there. Scavengers came, and so he gave someone a free meal and was put to good use. Still, I wished that I had let him go before he died.

I kept ThaCho, though. In March of 1976, Tom Sterling, a wildlife filmmaker, took many rolls of motion film of ThaCho in her pen. Tom was able to disguise her pen so that ThaCho appeared to be free-living, and ThaCho, in turn, performed like a star. But, like all of us when we have a good thing, Tom wanted more. He pressed me to make a decision about what I would do with ThaCho. I decided to let her go. Then, he pressed me to set a date, so that he could film the release. The date was set for 10 April 1976.

In early April, I gave ThaCho a live porcupine in her pen for the first time. Although it took her a few days to get hungry enough to brave the quills, she eventually killed the porcupine. I know of only one other eyewitness account of a fisher killing a porcupine. While he was doing research for his doctorate, Mal Coulter of the University of Maine at Orono once observed a female fisher killing porcupines.

ThaCho did exactly what I had expected from Coulter's account. She circled the porcupine, looking for an opportunity to attack its face. Then, she jumped in, bit the face, and jumped back away before the porcupine had a chance to hit her with its tail. Killing a porcupine is not easy, and it took ThaCho a long time before she did it. She eventually pulled the top off the porcupine's head with her final, killing bite.

When 10 April came, I was ready to let ThaCho go. I knew that she could kill hares and porcupines, the two main live prey for fishers in Upper Michigan. Tom, Consie, and I took ThaCho to an area in the woods where there is little human activity and let her go. Tom went through more rolls of motion film, and I went through rolls of slide film as ThaCho snooped about in the manner of a well-fed, hand-raised wild animal. We watched her for about three hours. At one point, she loped up to me and climbed up on top of my head; this had been one of her favorite tricks during the preceding two years. Then ThaCho disappeared into the woods. After waiting about half an hour, we started back toward my truck. Tom decided that he wanted to film a hillside with young aspen and spruce and set up his camera. As though on cue, ThaCho came snooping down the hillside, flushed a snowshoe hare, and took off after it. That was the last I saw of ThaCho, and Tom got it all on film.

For the next two months, I left food for ThaCho, but she only came back to take it once. Either she learned to survive on her own, or she died of an accident soon after her release. I like to believe that she survived, but her death would only have been natural. ThaCho still lives as the finale to Tom's film, "Superior, Land of the Woodland Drummer," which has been shown around the country on Audubon, National Geographic, and other lecture circuits.

I did not mean for this book to be an account of my experiences with, and attachments to, ThaCho and Uskool. I have actually tried to keep their names and personalities out of the body of the book. But they were an important part of my research, and they deserved to be acknowledged.

In writing this book I have tried to walk a fine line. On the one side, there is the public's increasing interest in wildlife and nature. People are interested in knowing about what animals do and how they fit into the scheme of nature, and they are demanding accurate information. The weasels are certainly a fascinating family of mammals. The fisher especially has broad appeal because of its beauty and its ability to deal with porcupines and their quills. But much of the literature about the members of the weasel family has been filled with myths, misinformation, and anthropomorphisms that do not accurately portray these predators. Many people have a very inaccurate image of weasels, minks, martens, fishers, wolverines, and the rest. Therefore, I have tried to write a book that would have appeal to the general public and at the same time accurately deal with the biology of one member of the Mustelidae.

On the other hand, in the scientific literature there is a dearth of information on members of the weasel family, and this is especially true of the fisher. Most of the studies done on the fisher during recent years (since 1950) have been master's and doctoral theses, and most of the knowledge and information gained from these studies has not found its way into the circulating scientific literature. Consequently, in this book I have tried to gather the information included in unpublished theses, the information available in the scientific literature, and the information gained from my own research on fishers. My goal has been to provide the scientific community with a book that covers comprehensively what is known about the fisher. Obviously, as soon as the book is published, it will already be out of date. I hope it will be a source of background information for subsequent work.

My study was done between 1972 and 1976. Most of my fieldwork was done in the Ottawa National Forest, which is located in the far-western tip of Upper Michigan. Although I made observations of fishers' tracks over much of the forest, I concentrated my work in an area a little over 100 square kilometers in size in the southeastern corner of the national forest. I also kept several fishers in captivity for various lengths of time, and I studied the fisher's energetics in the laboratory. My study area is sometimes mentioned in this book, and this reference is to the area of my concentrated fieldwork in the Ottawa National Forest.

Acknowledgments

Numerous people have been of tremendous help to me while I was doing my research and while I was writing this book. It is impossible to name every one of them or to describe how they helped, but I would like to make an attempt. Bob Brander ignited the first spark and made the first contact that initiated the work on this book. Monte Lloyd and Dave Mech provided valuable help with my research, and Monte, because of his editorial experience and ability, deserves much of the credit for anything good that I put in writing.

George Kelly, Mark Clem, Slader Buck, Curt Mullis, and Rich Leonard all provided unpublished data, some of which were incorporated into their own theses and some of which were not. Len Radinsky supplied me with a collection of endocasts of brains for many representatives of all but one genus in the family Mustelidae. T. J. Dunn gave me calm advice on how to deal with the confusing signals I received from ThaCho and Uskool when they were kits.

The Department of Biology at the University of Chicago provided me with office space, library privileges, and a visiting scholar position while I was writing the rough draft for this book.

In addition, the following people provided important help to me at various times and places: Richard Abel, Ron Alderfer, Stuart Altmann, Steve Arnold, Prassede Calabi, the Camp NoBuck trappers Leo and Barney, Bonnie Clements, Rich Earle, Ruth Gronquist,

Kim Iles, Phil Jensen, Les Johnson, Ross Kiester, Faye McLamb, Nancy Martin, the students of North Central College, the North Central Forest Experiment Station of the U.S. Forest Service, Lew Ohmann, Catherine Owens, Rick Prestbye, George Rabb, Vicky Rountree, Roy Settgas, Jerry Sutherland, Dick Taylor, Craig Wickman, Walt Winturri, and Phil Wright.

Numerous state agencies generously provided data on the distributions of fishers in response to a survey conducted by Wendell Dodge. Wendell willingly provided me with the results of his survey.

My parents gave me support while I was working on this book, though they did not know that I was writing a book. I regret that my mother did not live long enough to sit back and read this book. She would have loved it, no matter what its quality.

My wife Consie has lived through my frustrations and joys as I have worked with fishers and worked on this book. With her has been the responsibility of bringing me up when I am down and keeping me up when I am up. She has done a wonderful job. She has also done a wonderful job with many of the illustrations in this book. Without her artistic abilities, this book would have looked very different.

I believe that it is appropriate to acknowledge the contributions of nonhuman animals, too. My Newfoundland dog Valor's Ottawa Kaloosit CD was a priceless help in many aspects of my work, besides cleaning fisher kits. During two winters of fieldwork, Kaloosit hauled all of my gear in to and out of the woods on a toboggan and hauled fishers out of and back into the woods. She was a companion while I was tracking fishers, a hand warmer on cold days, a safety factor in the woods, and a listener when I had troubles with my research and writing. At eight years of age, she is still working with me in front of toboggan and travois, and she loves it.

And, of course, nothing would have been the same without ThaCho and Uskool.

The Fisher

Chapter 1

The Fisher Itself

The first time I saw a fisher I was driving a beat-up, army-surplus jeep down an old logging road in the Superior National Forest in northeastern Minnesota. A black animal appeared in the vegetation at the edge of the road, paused, streaked across the road, and then disappeared. I did not even have time to think "fisher." Since then, all of my spontaneous observations of wild fishers have been like the first. I suppose the secretiveness of the fisher has been a factor in my interest: a rare and exceedingly beautiful animal that is relatively unknown can be almost irresistibly fascinating.

But I have not studied the fisher only because of its beauty and allure. Members of the weasel family, like the fisher, are keenly adapted predators that have been very successful. By studying them we gain a better understanding of the ecology and behavior of predatory and prey species. Members of the weasel family have many anatomical and behavioral characteristics that have changed very little since the time of the Miacidae, the ancestors of all living carnivores. Thus, the study of these animals can help us to understand how primitive predators may have lived. Fishers are the only predators that consistently prey upon porcupines. To do this fishers have evolved unique hunting and killing techniques. Studying these techniques provides a better understanding of the evolution of predator-prey relationships. Finally, the natural history of the fisher lends itself to population and energy-budget models that are of interest in investigations of predator-prey relationships. In many ways, the fisher is an excellent predator to study.

Name

No one knows for certain how the fisher acquired its name, a seemingly inappropriate one since it does not fish. The animal's other common names—pekan, pequam, wejack, and Pennant's marten—are more suitable. The names black cat and fisher cat are sometimes applied to the fisher, but they also are misleading since the animal is not related to members of the cat family. Perhaps the best name given to the fisher was tha cho, which means "big marten" in Chippewayan (Coues 1877). The fisher is very similar to the American marten, but it is much larger. Other American Indian names for the fisher were uskool (Wabanaki), otchoek (Cree), and otschilik (Ojibwa). The last two names were turned into the name wejack by fur traders. The relationships between the various Indian tribes and their languages have been described by Spencer and co-workers (1965).

Some people have concluded that, in order to have acquired the name fisher, fishers must have raided traps baited with fish or taken fish being used as fertilizer in fields (Coues 1877; Hodgson 1937). It is also possible that the fisher was confused with the otter, an expert fish catcher. The most likely possibility is that early settlers noticed the fisher's similarity to the European polecat, or fitch ferret, which is a bit smaller than a female fisher but also dark colored and of the same body build. Trevor Poole (1970) included fitchet, fitche, and fitchew (derived from the Dutch root *visse*, meaning "nasty") among the other names for the polecat. The pelt of the polecat is called *fiche, ficheux,* or *fichet* in French (Dodge 1977). The similarity of these words to the name fisher is striking. The early American settlers may have believed that the fisher was the same animal as the polecat they had known in Europe, or they may have given the fisher its name because of its physical resemblance to the polecat.

Figure 1. Adult female fisher with snowshoe hare she killed.

Description

The fisher is a medium-size mammal and the largest member of its genus (Anderson 1970). It has the general body build of a stocky weasel and is long, thin, and set low to the ground (Figure 1). Adult male fishers generally weigh between 3.5 and 5.5 kilograms, and adult female fishers weigh between 2.0 and 2.5 kilograms. (See Table 1 and Figure 2.) A male fisher that weighed 9.13 kilograms was reported to have been found in Maine by Blanchard (1964); the animal apparently was the heaviest fisher recorded. Adult males average a little less than twice the weight of adult females (Table 1). The weights of adult females are more constant than those of adult males over the species range.

The significant sexual dimorphism in body size apparent in weight is also seen in length. Sexual dimorphism in weight is more pronounced, though, because weight increases roughly with the cube of increases in the linear dimension. Lengths of male fishers range from 90 to 120 centimeters, and those of females range from 75 to 95 centimeters.

There are no published records of heights of fishers. Therefore, the height and the length of fishers cannot be compared as a measure for

Figure 2. Sexual dimorphism in body size of fishers. The fisher on the left is a 2.1-kilogram female; the fisher on the right is a 5.7-kilogram male. (Both fishers were sedated when the photograph was taken.)

fisher elongation. Hall (1974) found that the hindlimbs of a weasel are barely more than half as long as its body (excluding its head and tail) but that the hindlimbs of a carnivore of average build (such as a raccoon) are roughly the same length as its body. The forelimbs of weasels are correspondingly short. Sokolov and Sokolov (1971) reported that the hindlimbs of European pine martens are relatively longer than those of weasels; the same should hold true for fishers.

Another measure of an animal's elongation is its length divided by the cube root of its weight. The fisher's elongation on this measure is slightly less than that of its near relatives the weasels but considerably greater than that of other members of the weasel family, such as skunks and badgers (Powell 1979b).

The fur of fishers varies among individuals, sexes, and seasons. Males have coarser coats than females. On prime, early winter coats the hair is dense and glossy, ranging in length from 30 millimeters on the stomach and chest to 70 millimeters on the back. The color appears almost uniform black from a distance, especially in contrast to snow, but it actually ranges from deep brown to black, with very light-colored hairs around the face and shoulders. Coulter (1966) re-

Table 1. Average Weights (± Standard Deviation) of Fishers
in Several States and Provinces

Location	Male	N	Female	N	Source
California	4.08 ± 0.64	2	2.34 ± 0.26	3	Grinnell, Dixon, and Linsdale 1937
California	3.81 ± 0.53	5	1.83 ± 0.30	3	Buck, Mullis, and Mossman 1978
Maine	4.49	51	2.35	44	Coulter 1966
Maine[a]	4.91 ± 0.78	36	2.43 ± 0.34	32	Coulter 1966
Maine[b]	3.48 ± 0.43	15	2.12 ± 0.24	12	Coulter 1966
Michigan[c]	4.98 ± 0.80[i]	15	2.22 ± 0.28	10	Powell 1977a[d]
Minnesota[e]	3.98 ± 0.57[i]	34	2.25 ± 0.22	13	Irvine 1961, 1962
Minnesota	4.04 ± 0.56	9	2.22 ± 0.21	6	Clements 1975 and Mech (personal communication)
Minnesota[f]	3.89 ± 0.69	50	2.20 ± 0.37	38	Wisconsin Dept. Natural Resources, unpub. files
New Hampshire	4.30 ± 0.65	39	2.14 ± 0.18	21	Kelly 1977
New York[g]	3.71 ± 0.75	26	2.06 ± 0.40	41	Hamilton and Cook 1955
Ontario[h]	3.94 ± 0.75	147	2.11 ± 0.35	154	Clem 1977

[a]Adults only.

[b]Juveniles only.

[c]Including three male fishers captured in the adjacent Nicolet National Forest, Wisconsin.

[d]Including nine weights from the Michigan Department of Natural Resources and the Wisconsin Department of Natural Resources.

[e]Released in the Ottawa National Forest, Michigan, 1961 to 1963.

[f]Released in the Nicolet and Chequamegon National Forests, Wisconsin, 1962 and 1963.

[g]Estimated from weights of skinned carcasses.

[h]Estimated from weights of skinned carcasses, according to Hamilton and Cook (1955) and Kelly (1977).

[i]Significantly different, $p < 0.01$, Student's t test (see Chapter 9).

ported that young fishers in Maine tended to be darker than adults and that females tended to be darker than males, but this relationship does not hold over the continent (Max Bass, personal communication; Powell, unpublished data). The tail, rump, and legs are glossy black. The face, neck, and shoulders usually have a hoary gold or silver color that comes from tricolored guard hairs (Coulter 1966). These hairs begin at the eyeline on the face and extend backward along the top of the neck to the shoulders and at times as far back as the rump. They are dark brown to black, tipped with a straw-colored, blond, or silver subterminal band. The proximal section of the guard hair from the body to the point where the hair protrudes from the underlying fur is gray. Much of the color variation of fishers is due to the distribution of the tricolored guard hairs. The undersurface of fishers at all seasons is a uniform brown, except for white or cream patches of no predictable size or shape on the chest and in the underarm region and around the genitals.

Spring and summer pelage is more variable in color than winter pelage. The entire coat may gradually lighten, occasionally so much as to make the fisher almost strawberry blond (Figure 3) because of the loss of the terminal part of the tricolored guard hairs. Fishers may begin to shed as early as April, but the single yearly molt generally occurs during late summer and early autumn (Coulter 1966; Grinnell, Dixon, and Linsdale 1937; Powell, unpublished data). I raised two fishers that both lost localized patches of hair during April and May of two successive years (Figure 4). During September and October, the guard hairs are noticeably shorter than during the rest of the year, giving a sleeker than normal appearance. At this time, the fisher's normally bushy tail may be almost ratlike. The molt is finished by November or December, and at this time the fur is very soft and glossy. "The flesh side of prime pelts is creamy-white indicating that color pigments have been fully absorbed from the skin" (Coulter 1966, p. 41). Juveniles have acquired the general color of adults by four months of age (Coulter 1966; Powell, unpublished data). (See Figure 5.)

Fishers have five toes on all four feet. Their claws are retractable but not sheathed. Fishers are plantigrade animals (walking on the whole foot; see Figure 6), and their feet are very large, presumably for walking on snow. There are pads on each toe and a central pad on each foot. From the central pads to the heels of the hindpaws, there

Figure 3. Adult female fisher showing light-colored spring pelage. The black tips of the tricolored guard hairs have been lost, giving her a strawberry-blond coloration.

Figure 5. Juvenile male fisher, five and a half months old, showing adult pelage. Juveniles acquire the general coloration of adults by four months of age.

Figure 4. Adult female fisher with bare patch of skin on her chest in April. Fishers may begin to shed as early as April, though the yearly molt generally occurs during the late summer and early autumn. Sometimes small patches of hair, as shown here, are lost during the early molt.

Figure 6. Fisher showing plantigrade foot posture. Fishers walk on their entire feet, rather than on their toes as candids and felids do. Note the position of the back right foot.

are coarse hairs covering tough skin. Retractable claws, pads, and tough furred hindpaws give fishers excellent traction on the ground, in the trees, and on logs, rocks, and other surfaces in their woodland habitat. The small, circular patches of very coarse hair on the central pads of the hindpaws appear to be associated with glandular activity and carry an odor distinctly different from other fisher odors (Figure 7). These small patches of coarse hair may, of course, have multiple functions.

Fishers run in a fashion typical of members of the weasel family. The forelimbs move together, with one slightly in front of the other; the same is true of the hindlimbs. The forepaws leave the ground slightly before the hindpaws land, allowing the hindpaws to fall into the same place as the forepaws. This leaves a characteristic track in the snow—two footprints right next to each other but slightly out of line. Figure 8 shows a fisher running, and Figure 9 shows a typical fisher track pattern in the snow. In very deep snow, fishers may be forced to walk rather than use their normal gait (Cahalane 1947; Grinnell, Dixon, and Linsdale 1937; Powell, unpublished data). Fishers may also walk on a thin snow crust, which would break under the force of their normal gait (Figure 10).

Figure 7. Small circular patches of coarse hair on the central pads of the hind-paws of a nine-week-old fisher. These whorls of hair appear to be associated with glands, since the patches on adults carry an odor distinctly different from other fisher odors.

Trappers' accounts and early scientific reports claimed that it was possible to determine a fisher's sex by its track size. Coulter (1966) measured the hindpaws of 38 male fishers and 27 female fishers. The lengths ranged from 8.6 to 12.5 centimeters in females and from 10.0 to 13.5 centimeters in males. Even though the distributions of the lengths of back feet were different for the two sexes, the lengths overlapped, except at the extremes. Thus, it is not possible to determine positively a fisher's sex from its foot length or track size unless the foot length is less than 10 centimeters or greater than 12.5 centimeters. This occurs in only about 15% of fishers.

Classification

The scientific name for the fisher is *Martes pennanti*, a reference to Thomas Pennant, one of the first people to describe the fisher in the scientific literature (Pennant 1771). However, Pennant's descriptions of the fisher appear to have been the source of about 80 years of confusion concerning how many species of fishers there are. In 1765 Buffon wrote the first scientific description of the fisher, des-

Figure 8. Fisher running. The fisher's running gait is typical of members of the weasel family. The front legs move together as do the back legs, and the back feet fall into the prints left by the front feet.

Figure 9. Typical fisher track pattern (upper half of photo) showing that one foot is slightly in front of the other both front and rear and that the back feet fall into the prints left by the front feet.

Figure 10. Tracks left by a fisher walking on a thin snow crust. Had the fisher run with its typical gait, it would have broken the crust.

cribing it from a specimen in a collection in Paris (Buffon and D'Aubenton 1765); Buffon called the animal the *Pekan*. In 1771 Pennant described Buffon's *Pekan* but gave a new scientific description of what he called the *Fisher*, using the same specimen Buffon had used for the basis of his description. Pennant apparently was unaware that his *Fisher* and Buffon's *Pekan* were descriptions of the very same specimen.

Audubon and Bachman (1845), among others, were responsible for reducing the taxonomic status of the fisher to one species (Hagmeier 1959), although they still included it in the genus *Mustela*. Coues (1877) was the first person to determine the root of the classification problems. Nomenclature varied until the late 1800s, when it was acknowledged that the correct species name was *pennanti* (Hagmeier 1959); and by the first part of this century it was acknowledged to be in the genus *Martes*.

The fisher is classified in the order Carnivora, the family Mustelidae, subfamily Mustelinae, and genus *Martes*. There are seven families in the order Carnivora: Mustelidae, Canidae (dogs, wolves, foxes), Ursidae (bears), Procyonidae (raccoons, pandas), Viverridae (mongooses, civetcats, genets), Hyaenidae (hyenas), and Felidae (cats).

The family Mustelidae is divided into five subfamilies. Mustelinae includes the weasels, ferrets, polecats, minks, martens, wolverines, and tayras. Mellivorinae has a single species, the ratel, or honey badger. Mellinae includes all the other badgers. Mephitinae includes all the skunks (Radinsky [1973] has suggested that it should also include the stink badgers). And Lutrinae includes the otters.

The genus *Martes* has seven extant species, which are divided into three subgenera: *Pekania, Charronia,* and *Martes* (Anderson 1970). The fisher is the only living member of the subgenus *Pekania*, which includes three extinct species. The only living member of the subgenus *Charronia* is the yellow-throated marten, *Martes flavigula* (Figure 11), which is found in eastern Asia and southern India. Yellow-throated martens have large, yellow throat patches, contrasting light and dark colors on their faces, and dark brown to black feet, legs, and tails. The subgenus *Martes* includes the other five extant martens: the beech, stone, or house marten, *M. foina*; the European pine marten, *M. martes*; the sable, *M. zibellina*; the Japanese marten, *M. melampus;* and the American pine marten, *M. americana*. These five species all have yellow or orange throat patches and are rusty red-brown in

Figure 11. Yellow-throated marten. Yellow-throated martens are found in southeastern Asia and southern India. *(Brookfield Zoo, Chicago Zoological Society)*

Figure 12. American pine marten. American pine martens are in the same subgenus as European pine martens, sables, and Japanese martens and closely resemble them.

color; the color is darker on the tail and legs (Figure 12). They have relatively large, rounded ears and bushy tails. The beech marten is the largest (Anderson 1970; Jensen and Jensen 1970); and the American pine marten, the smallest. There is no question that the beech marten, which is sympatric with the European pine marten, is a distinct species; but Anderson (1970) and Hagmeier (1955, 1961) have hypothesized that the other four may be members of a single circumboreal species. They are very similar in morphology, habits, and habitat and are allopatric. The species ranges of these four species are shown in Figure 13.

Three subspecies of fishers were recognized by Goldman (1935): *Martes pennanti pennanti, M. p. pacifica,* and *M. p. columbiana.* It is questionable whether recognition of subspecies is warranted. Goldman stated that the subspecies were difficult to distinguish, and Hagmeier (1959) concluded from a more extensive study that the subspecies were not separable on the basis of pelage or skull characteristics. Coulter (1966) felt that there are too few specimens from different parts of the fisher's range to determine conclusively whether there are any subspecies.

Evolution

The evolution of the fisher is difficult to trace, because its ancestors appear to have been small, arboreal, forest-dwelling carnivores that did not leave a clear fossil record. All modern carnivores evolved from the Miacidae (Colbert 1969; Ewer 1973; Romer 1966). The miacids were the first mammals to evolve the flesh-shearing dentition

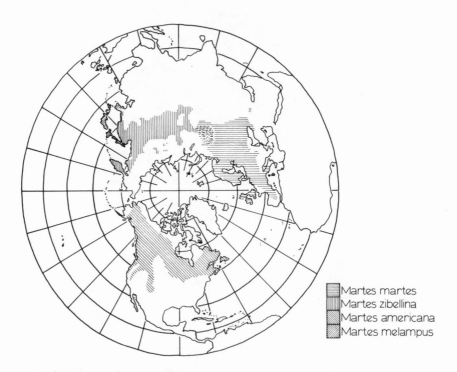

Martes martes
Martes zibellina
Martes americana
Martes melampus

Figure 13. Species ranges of the European pine marten, sable, American pine marten, and Japanese marten. It has been suggested that these four species may actually be one circumpolar species. Note that the ranges are completely nonoverlapping, except for a small area in northern Asia. This area of possible overlap of European pine marten and sable ranges is in an area that has been little studied and for which there are contradictory statements about species ranges. (*Adapted by C. B. Powell from Anderson 1970 and Hagmeier 1955*)

characteristic of modern carnivores (Colbert 1969; Ewer 1973; Romer 1966). This dentition was well suited to the evolution of the extreme adaptations to the flesh-eating habits of some modern carnivores. The miacids gave rise to two major groups of carnivores, the Canoidea and the Feloidea, in the late Eocene or early Oligocene (Figure 14). Mustelids may represent a basal lineage of the canoids (Romer 1966), from which the canids, ursids, and procyonids evolved. Although it is difficult to distinguish between the early viverrids, canids, and mustelids in the fossil record, it appears that other canoids quickly diverged from the mustelids (Anderson 1970; Ewer 1973). Small, elongate carnivores with short, stocky legs and five toes on each foot, the mustelids have maintained many characteristics of the miacids (Anderson 1970; Colbert 1969; Ewer 1973; Romer 1966). The dentition of the mustelids reflects their carnivorous habits, and their reduced number of molars indicates that they are more carnivorous than the miacids were (Anderson 1970; Colbert 1969).

Between the late Eocene (the time of the divergence of the rest of

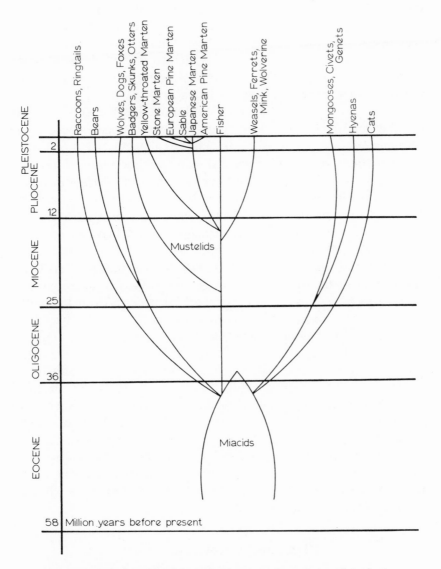

Figure 14. Evolution of the fisher. Also shown are the evolution of the families in the order Carnivora and details on the evolution of members of the weasel family and the genus *Martes. (Adapted by C. B. Powell from Anderson 1970 and Ewer 1973)*

the Canoidea from the Mustelidae) and the Miocene, the adaptive radiation of the Mustelidae was wide and often short-lived. This gave rise to a confusing fossil record, but by the end of the Miocene the five subfamilies recognized today were distinguishable. Most members of the subfamily Mustelinae have retained primitive features: small size, carnivorous dentition, and forest habitat. Several marten-like fossils from the Miocene have been found, but it is not certain whether they were true martens (Anderson 1970). Some Pliocene mustelids were intermediate between *Mustela* and *Martes*, but by that time there were true martens living in Asia. *Martes palaeosinensis* and *M. anderssoni* lived in China during the Pliocene and were probably ancestral to the fisher; both species have been placed in the subgenus *Pekania*, along with the fisher (Anderson 1970). All three subgenera of *Martes* are distinguishable in the Pliocene fossil records.

The first true fisher found in North America was *Martes divuliana*, dated from the middle Pleistocene. It is probable that it came to North America via the Bering Bridge, since relationships to *M. palaeosinensis* and *M. anderssoni* are strongly indicated (Anderson 1970, Kurtén 1971). *M. divuliana* was slightly smaller than *M. pennanti* and was probably semiarboreal. Anderson (1970) hypothesized that *M. divuliana* preyed on squirrels of the genera *Sciurus*, *Glaucomys*, and *Tamias*, since remains of these animals have been recovered from the same deposits as fossil remains of *M. divuliana*.

Remains of the modern fisher, *Martes pennanti*, are first found in late Pleistocene deposits, and the species probably is not directly descended from *M. divuliana*, which is only known from middle Pleistocene remains (Anderson 1970). There is no overlap of the fossil record for *M. divuliana* and *M. pennanti*, and no fossil fishers have been dated between the fossils of these two. Present-day fishers show no morphological differences from the late Pleistocene fossil fishers. However, the distribution of fossil sites indicates that fishers once lived in areas farther south than they have occupied during recent times (Anderson 1970). This is undoubtedly related to the climatic changes associated with glaciation.

The Fisher's Ecological Niche

The food webs of which fishers are a part are complex. It is a difficult task to identify all the relationships among all the organisms that are somehow associated with the fisher. However, within all food webs it is possible to identify a small number of trophic levels: the first trophic level contains the producers (the green plants), the second trophic level contains the primary consumers (the herbivores that eat the plants), the third trophic level contains the secondary consumers (the carnivores that eat the herbivores), and the fourth trophic level contains the tertiary consumers (the higher carnivores). It should be noted that the classification of organisms by trophic level is a classification by function and not by species. Therefore, one species can occupy more than one trophic level.

The fisher, as a predator, must be placed in the third or fourth trophic level and actually fits in both. Most of the fisher's prey are herbivores (snowshoe hares, mice, porcupines) and so the fisher is a secondary consumer. Occasionally, however, fishers eat berries and other carnivores; this makes the fisher both a primary and a tertiary consumer as well.

In the community of organisms living in the northern forests of North America, the fisher most clearly takes the role of a predator on small- to medium-size mammals and birds. In this role, the fisher is a competitor with other predators. Depending on the specific community, fishers can be in competition with coyotes, bobcats, lynx, foxes, martens, wolverines, and weasels. However, the fisher has little competition with other predators for the porcupine, and as such the fisher takes a unique role in many northern communities. As far as is known, adult fishers are not themselves subject to predation.

Study Techniques

Techniques used to study the ecology and behavior of mammals fall into two broad categories, which I call direct and indirect study methods. Direct study methods entail the direct observation of a mammal as it goes through its everyday routine. Indirect study involves gaining information from secondary sources, such as tracks in the snow and animals in captivity. There is actually a broad continuum of techniques of which direct and indirect methods are extremes. Direct experimental manipulation of certain aspects of an animal's biology within wild populations utilizes both direct and indirect methods.

Direct observation is the best way to gain accurate information about a mammal, at least as an initial step before experimental manipulation is used to test hypotheses generated by direct observation. However, direct observation cannot be used with some mammals because such observations are impossible or would affect the mammals' behavior. Both of these factors limit the direct observation of fishers. Thus, all studies of fishers have used the various means of indirect observation.

Before the studies of deVos (1951, 1952) and Quick (1953a), almost all source material for articles about the fisher's ecology and behavior came from trappers. Trappers were the first white people to spend extensive amounts of time in the forests where fishers were present, and they are still the only people who get in to certain areas of Canada. Trappers were and are interested in fishers because of their valuable pelts. Steel traps, devices that when triggered cause a set of steel jaws to spring closed and hold an animal's foot firmly, are the predominant tool used to trap fishers. Traps are set in those places and baited with those substances that are believed to increase the number of fishers caught. Some trappers use quick-kill traps for fishers, but such traps are used less frequently than they could be because they are bulky and because some trappers believe they are difficult to set. Trappers have always been interested in making observations about the natural history of the animals they trap. Much of the information gathered is used to increase the number of animals trapped, and all of it is gathered from incidental observations and not through strict data-gathering techniques. Thus, the information provided by trappers has been valuable because it has been the first information gathered, but it has not always been completely accurate. Trappers were the first to report that fishers are the only predators consistently able to prey upon porcupines. They were also the first to report that fishers can be very agile in trees. On the other hand, trappers have also been the source of misinformation; for example, that fishers flip porcupines over to kill them and can walk along the bottom sides of branches; that fishers are the most agile of all mammals in trees; and that fishers are so strong that they habitually fight with and kill other predators, including bobcats and lynxes. Each of these pieces of misinformation has at least a grain of truth in it, but exaggeration has often overcome truth. At least, trappers can be credited for their lively imaginations.

deVos and Quick used trappers' observations as supplements to information collected from observations of fishers' tracks in the snow and from carcasses of fishers killed by trappers. Since these reports, tracking has become a major source of information about the fisher's natural history. The combination of information obtained from fisher carcasses and information obtained from tracks has provided much of our present knowledge about the distribution, diet, habitat, and reproduction of fishers. One limitation of using information from tracking is that individual fishers usually cannot be identified. Also, tracking and carcasses can only provide data about the fisher's winter habits.

With the development of radiotelemetric techniques in the 1960s and the continued refinement of these techniques since then, new information has been collected on many species, including the fisher. Radiotelemetry involves placing a small radio transmitter on an animal; in studies of fishers, the transmitter has been mounted in a collar placed around a fisher's neck. Each transmitter has a different frequency, and so individual fishers can be identified. The transmitters' signals are monitored by using a radio receiver tuned to the frequencies of the transmitters on the animals being followed. The transmitters that are most commonly used issue beeping signals with a constant pulse rate and provide location data. Transmitters with variable pulse rates have been used to provide activity data (activity increases the pulse rate). Transmitters with continuous signals can also be used to obtain activity data because there are slight frequency changes whenever the radio-tagged animal changes the angle of the transmitting antenna with respect to the receiving antenna: active animals change direction often and so create small frequency changes. Other types of transmitters have been used to gather data on body temperature, heart rate, and other physiological functions in animals other than the fisher. Different types of transmitters have different limitations, and the transmitters used in a study must fit the questions being asked and the specifications imposed by working conditions. For example, the transmitting range for a transmitter depends not only on its battery power, but also on the topography of the animal's environment and the height of the receiving antenna. In order to increase the transmission range, many workers have mounted receiving antennae on trucks, towers, and small planes. Radiotelemetry has greatly increased the information that can be obtained about an individual's movements and the social organization of a species.

Radiotelemetric data complements data gathered from other sources because data can be gathered during the entire year. Although the new knowledge of the biology of the fisher gained from radiotelemetry has been extensive, there is still much to learn.

Finally, some studies have used observations and experiments on captive fishers to supplement information gained from tracking, studying carcasses, and radiotelemetry. The secretive nature of fishers captured in the wild and the small number of fishers accustomed to humans has limited the studies. Much information can be obtained from captivity studies, however, and much of the work on the fisher's energetics and predatory behavior has depended on captive animals.

Chapter 2

Anatomy

Fishers show no special skeletal or muscular adaptations not common to the other carnivores. Therefore, this chapter will not be a detailed description of bones, muscles, and systems. A general discussion of the carnivores' anatomy can be found in *The Carnivores* by R. F. Ewer (1973), and more detailed analyses can be found in the works cited in this chapter.

Post-Cranial Skeletal and Muscular Systems

Because they are predators, fishers must be able to perform a wide variety of movements. Prey must be sought, captured, killed, and eaten; and these activities vary with the type of prey. Therefore, fishers cannot be specialized for only one type of movement but must be able to run for long distances, sprint for short distances, climb trees, dig, and do even more. The fisher's skeleton is not extremely specialized (Ewer 1973; Leach 1977a, 1977b). The body is characteristically elongate in that the fisher is a member of the Mustelidae, but the body is not as elongate as the bodies of members of the genus *Mustela*. Fishers' limbs are relatively short with respect to their body length when compared to other carnivores such as dogs and cats. Their tails are relatively long and are used for balance in climbing, jumping through ground brush, and turning quickly. Undoubtedly, having an elongate body is to a fisher's advantage when it

23

goes through hollow logs or down holes, but the elongation has not been taken to such an extreme that it poses limitations on a fisher's other abilities.

The comparative morphology of the postcranial skeletons of members of the genus *Martes* has been studied by Anderson (1970), Joliceous (1963a, 1963b), Leach (1977b), Leach and Dagg (1976), Ondrias (1960, 1962), and Sokolov and Sokolov (1971). All these researchers concluded that the appendicular skeletons of these mustelids are not specialized in an extreme form for any manner of locomotion. Sokolov and Sokolov (1971) did conclude that the postcranial skeleton of the European pine marten is more specialized for arboreality than that of the European polecat. However, the polecat is more adapted to a ground-dwelling mode of life, is a less-generalized mustelid than the European pine marten, and has skeletal morphology and musculature closely resembling that of other members of its genus.

Leach (1977b) and Leach and Dagg (1976) tried to find distinguishing features of fisher and American pine marten appendicular skeleton bones that would allow identification of individuals by species and sex. They found that species and sex could only be distinguished from morphometric data. In their samples, no overlap occurred in the measurements taken on fisher and marten bones, and there were several measurements that could be used to distinguish between the sexes within each species. However, their samples came entirely from the Algonquin District of Ontario. Table 1 Chapter 1 shows that there is considerable range in weights of male fishers across the continent. Consequently, the distinctions they found among their fishers and martens may not hold for other areas of North America.

The running gait of mustelids is always associated with a slight strengthening of forelimb muscles due to the shock-absorbing role of these limbs at the end of the suspended phase of the gait (Gambaryan 1974). Leach (1977a) found this to be the case with fishers. During the support phase of the gait, the greatest load on the forelimbs is borne by the extensors of the shoulders and elbow, by the flexors of the carpus (forepaw), and by the muscles of the forelimb joints (Gambaryan 1974). All of these muscles are well developed in the fisher. The serratus ventralis and pectoral muscles, which act to prevent abduction of the upper limb and to transfer the weight of the body to the limbs during the stance phase, are particularly well developed. In vertical climbing these muscles are used along with the latissimus dorsi, triceps brachii, and biceps brachii, which are also well developed (Leach 1977a). Leach (1977a) concluded that small, agile animals adapted to running over rough ground could use similar modes of progression in trees without extensive changes in limb structure. He believed, therefore, "that the existence of the musculature development needed for cursorial locomotion in marten and fisher potentiates a secondary function of arboreal locomotion" (1977a, p. 40).

Fishers (and other martens) may exhibit a small adaptation for climbing. This adaptation is taken to extreme form in the Ursidae. The scapulae of bears have a wide flange, the postscapular fossa, on the upper part of their posterior margins (Figure 15). The subcapularis minor muscle arises from this fossa, runs along the scapula, and inserts in the head of the humerus (Davis 1949). The reason for the unusual development of this muscle in bears appears to be that bears climb by pulling their heavy bodies up with their forelimbs. This method of climbing exerts forces that are the exact opposite of those created during normal quadrupedal locomotion and tends to pull the humerus out of the glenoid. The enlarged scapularis minor functions to oppose this pull. The scapulae of many carnivores do not have a postscapular fossa (Figure 15), and those animals that do have this fossa are at least partially arboreal. Fishers and other martens (Figure 15) do have this fossa (Leach 1977b), though a large subscapularis minor is not developed (Leach 1977a). Since fishers are considerably smaller than bears and since much of their arboreal activity is jumping and running along branches, it is to be expected that the development of the postscapular fossa would be less than that occurring in bears. However, when climbing vertical tree trunks, fishers do pull their bodies up with their forelimbs; this activity correlates with the development of the postscapular fossa. The postscapular fossa is larger in fishers than in American pine martens (Leach 1977b).

In fishers, as in most carnivores, the forelimb is used for a variety of purposes. In contrast, the hindlimb is used almost exclusively for locomotion and has fewer adaptations beyond those for locomotion. Fishers and martens, however, are among the very few carnivores that have tremendous mobility of the ankle joints. They are able to

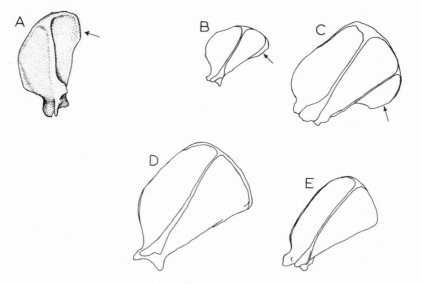

Figure 15. Scapulae of several carnivores. (A) Fisher, (B) raccoon (*Procyon*), (C) bear (*Ursus*), (D) large felid (*Panthera*), and (E) canid (*Canis*). Note the large postscapular fossa on the scapula of the bear (arrow) and the small postscapular fossae on the scapulae of the raccoon and the fisher (arrows). The postscapular fossa in an attachment for muscles used in climbing by species that must pull themselves up with their forelimbs. D and E are shown for comparison. (*Redrawn by C. B. Powell from Leach 1977b [A] Davis 1949 [B-E]*)

rotate their hindpaws through almost 180° degrees and to grasp branches exceptionally well with their hindpaws. Fishers are able to descend trees head first (Figure 16) and to hold on with their hindpaws. This observation was made by Grinnell, Dixon, and Linsdale (1937, p. 224):

> The fisher was up about forty feet. When it saw us it started down, head foremost like a Douglas squirrel. Its hind legs and claws were used in exactly the same manner as a squirrel uses its rear legs and feet in descending a tree. When it got to within fifteen feet of the ground and clear of limbs it stopped and began scolding the dog just as a big gray squirrel would do. Like a squirrel it pounded with one forefoot and then the other on the tree, all the while hanging there head downward.

No work has been done on how fishers use their limbs during locomotion, but work has been done on the beech marten (Gambaryan 1974) and members of the genus *Mustela* (Gambaryan 1974; Hildebrand 1974). Because of the elongation and increased mobility of their spines, mustelids flex and extend their spines to accelerate

Figure 16. Twelve-week-old fisher descending a tree headfirst. Fishers are able to turn their hindpaws through almost 180 degrees and to grasp branches with their hindpaws.

their trunks during locomotion on the ground. "Flexion and extension of the spine is best achieved with simultaneous pushing away or suspension of the limbs, and therefore the Mustelidae developed the bound, in which the hindfeet push away together and the forefeet land together" (Gambaryan 1974, p. 254). Actually, most mustelids use the halfbound, in which the forepaws land alternately but the hindpaws land more or less in unison (Hildebrand 1974).

Some of the locomotory characteristics of fishers can be traced from footprints in the snow. The front feet land with one slightly in front of the other and the backfeet land in approximately the same places as the front feet. The forceful extension of the spine as the forepaws are lifted from the ground imparts acceleration to the trunk and promotes extended flight. When mustelids run, their bodies are suspended for a relatively long time while in the extended position. Because the hindpaws land close to, and not in front of, the forepaws, flexion of the spine while the body is supported only by the forepaws is by inertia. Figure 17 shows the stages in the halfbound of the beech marten.

Baculum

Wright and Coulter (1967) examined approximately 75 bacula of juvenile and adult male fishers from Maine to determine whether bacula could be used to determine the ages of fishers. The bacula of adults are more than 10.00 centimeters long, have an enlarged proximal end and a splayed distal tip with a small oval or round foramen, and commonly weigh more than 2.00 grams. Fully mature bacula

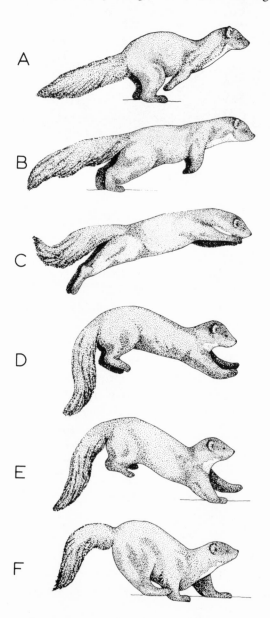

Figure 17. Beech marten going through the stages of the half-bound. (A) Beginning phase of support by back legs, (B) ending phase of support by back legs, (C) beginning phase of free flight, (D) ending phase of free flight, (E) beginning phase of support by front legs, and (F) ending phase of support by front legs. (*Drawn by C. B. Powell from photos in Gambaryan 1974*)

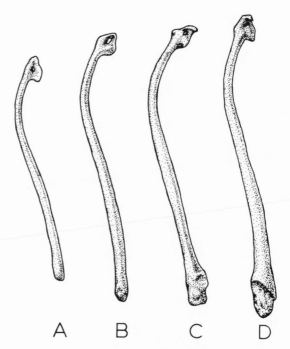

Figure 18. Fisher bacula (distal ends upward) showing progressive changes with age. (A and B) Bacula from juveniles trapped on 12 October and 5 January, respectively; (C) baculum from a juvenile fisher trapped in late February or early March, which shows deposition of bone at the basal end; (D) baculum from an adult fisher, which show the characteristic oblique ridge near the basal end and the more massive appearance. (*Redrawn by C. B. Powell from Wright and Coulter 1967*)

A   B   C   D

have an elevated ridge near the proximal end that completely circles the bone in a diagonal fashion when viewed from the side (Figure 18). Bacula of juvenile fishers weigh considerably less than those of adults and do not show the circular ridge. When male fishers approach one year of age, however, their bacula may weigh as much as 2.00 grams and their circular ridges begin to form clearly. At this time, the testes of one-year old males become active. Wright and Coulter (1967) were able to conclude that bacula could be used to age dead fishers at least to juvenile and adult age classes. It may be possible that bacula can be used to separate still older juvenile fishers from mature adults: Douglas and Strickland (1977) did not believe that the bacula of the male fishers in their sample had reached full size by age one year.

Teeth, Skull, and Related Musculature

In all mammals, the shape of the skull is related in many ways to dentition. The shape of the jaws, the shape of the glenoid articulation (jaw joint), the jaw musculature, and the places of origin and insertion of the jaw muscles are all adaptively correlated. Thus, the skull is more than a housing for the brain and sense organs. Since the anterior neck muscles and temporalis muscles originate on the outer surface of the braincase, the size of the brain affects the shape of the skull in more ways than just the size of the housing. If muscles require larger areas for attachment than the braincase provides, bony crests are developed to provide the extra anchoring space. The prominent sagittal and occipital crests of the fisher's skull are examples of this and will be discussed shortly. Fisher skulls are illustrated in Figure 19.

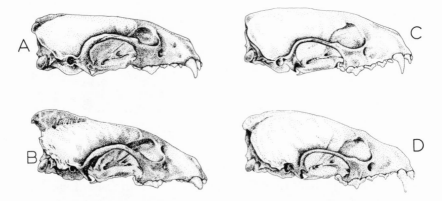

Figure 19. Fisher skulls. (A) A juvenile male fisher; (B) an adult male fisher; (C) a juvenile female fisher; (D) an adult female fisher. (*C. B. Powell*)

The fisher's dentition is highly adapted to a carnivorous way of life. The incisors are used to hold and to tear small items, such as small pieces of flesh from bone. The canines are large and sharp and are used for stabbing and holding prey. The premolars are used for holding and softening flesh and for shearing. The molars are used for shearing and crushing. The fisher's carnassials (the fourth and last upper premolar, P^4, and the first lower molar, M_1, on each side of the jaw), characteristic of the Carnivora, are highly developed and efficient for shearing flesh. The dental formula for the fisher is $I\frac{3}{3}$, $C\frac{1}{1}$, $P\frac{4}{4}$, $M\frac{1}{2}$, making a total of 38 teeth.

Other than being more robust, the fisher's dentition is morphologically similar to that of other martens. There is an exposed external median rootlet on the upper carnassial, which is diagnostic for the fisher, but this is the only major difference (Anderson 1970). The incisors are small and grouped tightly together. There is a small diastema (space) between the third upper incisor and the upper canine into which the lower canine fits when the jaw is closed, allowing the teeth to interlock. The first upper premolar is large and apparently functional (Anderson 1970), which is not the case with many carnivores. The premolars other than P^4 have one major cusp and sometimes small accessory cusps in line in front of and behind the major cusp.

The carnassial teeth are the most specialized teeth in the fisher's jaw. They are specially adapted for cutting and shearing flesh and work with a scissorlike action. According to Ewer (1973, p. 36):

> The posterior two cusps of P^4 and the anterior two of M_1 are laterally flattened and, as the jaws close, the blades shear past each other. The two constituent cusps do not form straight lines but are arranged so that each blade has the shape of a wide open V. This increases efficiency by preventing the meat from slipping out forwards and makes the action really more comparable with that of pruning shears than of ordinary scissors.

This is shown in Figure 20.

A

B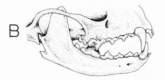

C

Figure 20. Fisher carnassian function. (A) The jaw is partially closed, but the carnassials have not yet met; (B) the jaw is closed farther so that the carnassials have just met; note the shearlike action of the carnassials that guides the material being cut and keeps it from slipping; (C) occlusal views of P^4 and M_1; M_1 is above and P^4 is below and anterior is to the right; the surfaces shown at the bottom of each tooth are the surfaces that shear past each other; the posterior two cusps of P^4 and the anterior two of M_1 show lateral flattening. (C. B. Powell)

The molars behind the carnassials are adapted for crushing. However, the upper molar and the second lower molar are not directly above and below each other but are slightly offset. Therefore, the first lower molar is a dual-purpose tooth: its anterior two cusps are the lower brace of the carnassials and the posterior cusps occlude with M^1 and are part of the crushing apparatus. M_2 occludes with the posterior of M^1. Fishers and other mustelines have fewer molars than most other canoids because of their mostly carnivorous diet. In particular, they are more carnivorous than ursids and procyonids.

When a fisher kills and eats a snowshoe hare, for example, all of the different tooth types with their different functions are used. The canines are used for killing and holding the hare until it is dead. The carnassials are used to open the skin and cut off pieces of flesh and skin. The fisher will turn its head sideways to the dead hare so that it can use the carnassials (Figure 21). Incisors are used to pull off or to loosen pieces of flesh or organs and to help manipulate the hare. Premolars and molars, excluding the carnassials, are used to soften and pulverize flesh so that it can be more easily cut by the carnassials and swallowed.

The jaw of the fisher is relatively short compared to that of most other carnivores, though not as short as those of smaller mustelines. The braincase is long and relatively low and extends far behind the glenoid. There are three sets of muscles responsible for jaw closure, two of which (temporalis and masseter) insert primarily on the outer surface of the mandible (the lower jaw) and one of which (pterygoideus) inserts primarily on the inner surface. The masseter muscle fibers originate along the lower edge of the zygomatic arch and insert on the angle of the lower jaw and on the masseteric fossa (Figure 22). Their action is basically for simple closure when the jaw is not wide open. The zygomatic arch of mustelines is less robust than in other carnivores; this indicates that the masseter muscles are less important in fishers than in other carnivores.

The temporalis arises from the lateral surface of the braincase and the sagittal crest and inserts on the coronoid process. When the jaw is wide open, the anterior part of the temporalis pulls upward on the coronoid process to close the jaw. As the jaw closes, more work is done by the posterior part of the temporalis, which pulls the coronoid process backward. Consequently, when a fisher is using its carnassials or exerting strong force when holding and killing prey, the

Figure 21. Adult female fisher turning her head sideways to use carnassials to cut into a snowshoe hare.

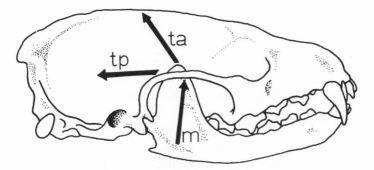

Figure 22. Diagram of a fisher skull showing the direction of the action of the muscles that close the jaw. The arrows show the areas of origin and insertion of muscles and the direction of pull. The *m* stands for masseter, the *tp* for posterior temporalis, and the *ta* for anterior temporalis. (*C. B. Powell*)

posterior part of the temporalis is being used. In other carnivores, the masseter is used for this function. This means that much more torque is exerted on the glenoid by fishers and other mustelids than by other carnivores. The glenoid of most mustelids is very elongate and the preglenoid and postglenoid processes are enlarged almost to encircle the condyle, forming an unusually strong, hingelike jaw joint. This joint is so extreme in some mustelids, such as the mink and the Canadian otter, that it is difficult to extract the lower jaw from the skull without breaking the process.

The large temporalis, which takes over much of the function performed by the masseter in most carnivores, explains the large sagittal crests found in mustelids. Normally, small carnivores with their relatively large braincases have ample space for muscle attachment and therefore have no large crests. The development of the temporalis in mustelids is so great, however, that prominent sagittal crests are even found on skulls of the small members of the genus *Mustela*. The sagittal crest on a large male fisher is extremely well developed because its braincase is relatively small compared to that of a smaller musteline. Fishers also have well-developed occipital crests, which function to increase the surface area for the origins of the anterior neck muscles.

Several investigators have attempted to use skulls as a means of aging fishers (Boise 1975; Coulter 1966; deVos 1952; Eadie and Hamilton 1958; Wright and Coulter 1967). A number of changes take place in a fisher's skull as a fisher ages (Anderson 1970); the sagittal crest forms and increases in size, zygomatic breadth increases, and postorbital breadth decreases. However, no single measurement clearly distinguishes juvenile from adult skulls in either sex. Sex can be quite accurately determined from the size and development of the sagittal crest, which is much greater in males (Figure 19); sexual dimorphism in skulls is greater in fishers than in any other American mustelid (Wright and Coulter 1967).

By using development of the sagittal crest and fusion of skull sutures as criteria, fishers can be accurately aged from skulls (Eadie and Hamilton 1958; Wright and Coulter 1967). In female fishers, the sagittal crest is not developed in juveniles, and distinct temporal lines can be seen on each side of the skull. The crest first develops near the back of the skull by fusion of the temporal lines around the time of first breeding, or one year of age, and grows progressively forward during the succeeding months and years. At one year of age, the sagittal crest is at most just beginning to develop and naso-maxillary, maxillary-frontal, and maxillary-palatine sutures have not fused. In male fishers, the sagittal crest begins to develop during the first winter, and as soon as it is formed it runs its entire ultimate length along the top of the skull. However, the sagittal crest is much better developed in adults and extends over 6 millimeters beyond the posterior margin of the skull. In juvenile male fishers, as in females, the naso-maxillary, maxillary-frontal, and maxillary-palatine sutures have not fused.

The best way to age a fisher is to count teeth cementum annuli. Cementum is added to the outside of the roots of teeth of many mammals on what may be a continuous basis. The rate at which cementum is added appears to differ during different seasons, giving the cementum of tooth roots a pattern that looks similar to tree rings when the teeth are properly decalcified, sectioned, and dyed. These rings are called annuli. This method has been successfully used to age several species of mammals, including fishers (Kelly 1977, Strickland et al., in press). A distinct advantage of this method is that it can be used with live animals.

Stickland and co-workers (in press) have looked at the canines (C_1), first premolars (P_1 and P^1) and second premolars (P_2) of several fishers with known ages ranging from seven months to five years. They and Kelly (1977) have also looked at teeth from fishers of unknown ages caught by trappers. Kelly (1977) removed the lower right premolar (P_1) from the carcasses of 202 trapped fishers and 11 live fishers. The first premolar is a small tooth whose removal causes little or no functional problem for a live fisher, unlike the removal of a canine (Crowe 1975; Crowe and Strickland 1975; Nellis, Wetmore, and Keith 1978) or a molar (Fogl and Mosby 1978), teeth that have been used to age carcasses of other mammals. Clarity and width of annuli vary with the tooth used and with the position on the tooth. Strickland and co-workers (in press) found annuli to be clearest on canines, which should not be removed from live animals. Kelly (1977) found annuli to be most easily observed near the root apex in a premolar sagittal (lengthwise) section.

From the teeth of fishers of known ages, Strickland and co-workers (in press) found that fishers less than 13 months old have no cementum annuli (Table 2). A fisher almost 16 months old had one annulus that was just barely visible, indicating that annuli appear sometime during late spring and early summer. All fishers over one year old had one annulus for each spring after the spring of parturition. From fisher carcasses whose reproductive tracts, skulls, and bacula showed them to be less than one year old, Kelly (1977) found that no annuli were visible. All fishers whose reproductive tracts showed them to be over one year old had annuli, and Kelly also found that annuli appear during the late spring. Thus, a fisher's age is accurately estimated by the number of cementum annuli shown on its canines, first premolars, and second premolars; and live fishers can be aged by removing only a single premolar, which causes the fisher no harm. Kelly (1977) also discussed some technical problems with this method.

It is possible to sex fishers by using only a measurement of the maximum width of the root of fresh lower canine teeth (Parsons, Brown, and Will 1978). No overlap in this measurement was found between 149 female fishers and 98 male fishers captured in northern New York. The measurements are summarized in Table 3. The divid-

Table 2. Tooth Cementum Annuli in Fishers of Known Ages.

Age (Months)	Fisher Identification Number	Tooth Examined	Date Extracted	Number of Annuli
7	1	C_1	November	0
13	2	P_1	May	0
16	3	P_2	19 July 1975	1
31	4	P_1	30 November 1976	2
31	5	P_1	30 November 1976	2
44	6	P_1	28 December 1977	3
44	4	P_1	28 December 1977	3
44	5	P_1	28 December 1977	3
53	6	P_1	7 September 1978	4
53	6	P_1	7 September 1978	4
53	6	C_1	7 September 1978	4
65	5	P^1	17 September 1979	5

Source: M. A. Strickland, C. W. Douglas, M. K. Brown and G. R. Parsons. In press. Age determination of fisher by cementum annuli. N. Y. Fish & Game J. Reproduced by permission of the New York State Department of Environmental Conservation.

ing point for lower canine maximum root width between male and female fishers is at 5.64 to 5.65 millimeters. This width is 2.6 times the standard deviation from the means for males and females and gives a 99.5% probability of correctly sexing a fisher from one tooth measurement.

Table 3. Maximum Root Width Statistics for Lower Canines of Fishers from New York.

	Female	Male
Number	149	98
Mean width root	4.85mm	6.44 mm
Standard deviation	0.298 mm	0.300 mm
Range	3.4-5.7 mm	5.9-7.0 mm

Source: G. R. Parsons, M. K. Brown, and G. W. Will, 1978. Determining the sex of fisher from lower canine teeth. N.Y. Fish & Game J. 25: 42-44. A contribution of New York Federal Aid in Fish and Wildlife Restoration Projects W-130-D, W-135-D, and W-136-D. Reproduced by permission of the New York State Department of Environmental Conservation.

Note: Using 5.645 mm as the dividing point between the sexes gives a 99.5% probability of correct sex identification.

Brain

A lateral view of a fisher's brain is shown in Figure 23; the drawing is taken from an endocast of a fisher's brain. Radinsky (1968a, 1968b, 1971) has shown that such endocasts accurately show external brain morphology. The fisher's external brain morphology differs little from that of other martens, except in its size. The lateral and postlateral sulci are continuous in the fisher, whereas they are not in the American pine marten. It is not known whether this fact has any significance.

Work done by Welker and his co-workers (Welker and Compos 1963; Welker and Seidenstein 1959; and references cited in these reports) has shown that sulci may result from differential growth and elaboration of adjacent cortical regions of the brain. There is also a fairly accurate mapping of primary somatic sensory cortex and primary motor cortex to particular areas of the body. The approximate areas of somatic sensory cortex mapping to different parts of the

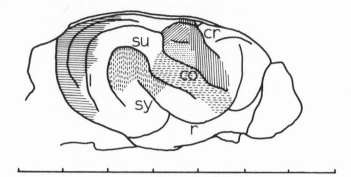

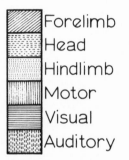

Forelimb
Head
Hindlimb
Motor
Visual
Auditory

Figure 23. Lateral view of the fisher's brain. The areas indicated control the somatic sensory abilities of the forelimb, head, and hindlimb and control motor, visual, and auditory abilities. The *r* stands for rhinal fissure, the *sy* for sylvan sulcus, the *su* for suprasylvan sulcus, the *co* for coronal sulcus, and the *cr* for cruciate sulcus. Sulci appear as grooves on the brain's surface and externally divide it into the areas labeled. (*Drawn by C. B. Powell from a latex endocast of a fisher's brain*)

body and of primary motor cortex for the fisher are shown in Figure 23. Fishers show fairly typical development of these areas and other parts of the brain. This indicates that fishers are similar to most contemporary carnivores and have less dependence on olfaction and more dependence on vision that fossil mustelids or "primitive" contemporary mustelids such as skunks and stink badgers. Brain morphology reinforces conclusions drawn from skeletal morphology that fishers have no major locomotory adaptations. There are no outstanding characteristics of fisher brains like those found in some otters (expanded coronal gyrus corresponding to increased sensitivity on the head [vibrissae] in *Lutra* and *Pteroneura*; expanded lateral portion of the posterior sigmoid gyrus corresponding to increased fore-limb sensitivity in other genera [Radinsky 1968b]), coatimundis (expanded coronal gyrus [Welker and Compos 1963]), and raccoons (expanded lateral portion of the sigmoid gyrus [Welker and Seiden-stein 1959]).

Fishers do possess anal sacs or glands as do all other members of the subfamily Mustelinae and most members of the family Muste-lidae. The odor of the substances emitted from these sacs is neither strong nor offensive in comparison to that of skunks and of the smaller mustelines in the genus *Mustela*. The precise function of these sacs has not been determined. An odor and probably some se-cretion is discharged when wild fishers are frightened, such as when they are handled by humans. It is highly probably that marking with anal-sac secretions may be related to sexual or territorial behavior.

Little else is known about the fisher's anatomy. It can be assumed that, since the fisher is mainly carnivorous, it has a digestive tract that is relatively short and that it does not have even moderate adap-tations for digesting vegetation. Such is the case for most carnivores (Ewer 1973). The fisher's digestive efficiency has been investigated and will be discussed in Chapter 9 (on ecological energetics). No other systems have been studied, nor have the fisher's special senses been tested.

Chapter 3

Life History
and Early Development

Most of the oldest information on the fisher's reproduction and life history came from fur farms. This information established that parturition and the breeding season occur in late winter and early spring and that gestation lasts almost a full year. Laboratory work done on fishers killed by trappers showed that the long gestation resulted from delayed implantation.

Delayed implantation is the interruption of normal development before implantation with a period of embryonic dormancy during the blastocyst stage. Mammals that are characterized by delayed implantation fall into two categories (Daniel 1970): those with *obligate* delayed implantation and those with *facultative* delayed implantation. In the former, delayed implantation is a regular event in the reproductive pattern; in the latter, delayed implantation only occurs when a female breeds before she has ceased lactating for the previous litter. Fishers have obligate delayed implantation.

Breeding Season

Twelve reported matings on an Ontario fur farm occurred between 26 March and 23 April. Female fishers on this farm came into estrus approximately 3 to 9 days after parturition (Hodgson 1937). Laberee

(1941) stated that the female fishers on his ranch near Ottawa, Canada, bred in May. His females were in estrus only about 2 days, starting 3 days after parturition. Twenty-six reported matings on British Columbia fur farms took place between 5 and 17 April, with the average date 12 April (Hall 1942). The British Columbia females were in estrus for 6 to 8 days, and 13 females came into estrus 4 to 9 days after parturition (average 7.5 days). Hodgson (1937) also reported that females occasionally mate during a second "estrus" that follows the first matings by about 10 days. A similar condition has been observed in mink (Enders and Enders 1963).

Coulter (1966) and Wright and Coulter (1967) presented the first reports on the breeding season of wild fishers. Coulter (1966) obtained from trappers 11 reproductive tracts of females in active pregnancy. Using estimated parturition dates in conjunction with Hall's (1942) parturition and breeding dates, Coulter (1966) calculated that the breeding season in Maine ranged from late February to mid-April. Wright and Coulter (1967) obtained two female fisher reproductive tracts with tubal embryos in late March and early April. They calculated that these females must have bred in mid- to late March. In addition, seven male fishers trapped in Maine during March and April all showed signs of sexual activity (Coulter 1966; Wright and Coulter 1967). Male fishers captured before March showed no signs of sexual activity.

Coulter (1966) noticed a marked change in fisher track patterns during March. Fisher tracks indicated that there was a considerable increase in activity during March. Fishers did more back tracking and circling during their daily activities in March than at other times of the winter. Coulter interpreted this to mean that March was the height of the breeding season for his Maine fishers. Laberee (1941) noted that male fishers from fur farms marked (with urine) extensively in their pens during the beginning of the mating season. Thus, it may be that the March peak in fisher activity found by Coulter in Maine corresponds with the beginning of the breeding season.

The breeding season for fishers has been dated from March (Coulter 1966) through April (Hall 1942; Hodgson 1937) to May (Laberee 1941). This variation may correspond to the length of winter in different parts of the fisher's range. If such a correspondence does exist, it should show a north-south change in breeding season, with variation according to local climates.

Table 4. Condition of Reproductive Tracts of Male Fishers Taken in Late Winter and Early Spring.

Date (1957)	Weight of Combined Testes and Epididymides	Paired Testis Weight	Paired Epididymides Weight	Status of Sperm in Testes	Status of Sperm in Epididymides	Baculum Weight	Estimated Age of Animal	Body Weight
January 5	2.7 g	1.8 g	0.4 g	None	None	1262 mg	Juvenile	7 lb 3 oz
February 26	7.4 g	5.6 g	1.4 g	Active spermatogenesis	None	?	?	?
February or early March	6.3 g	4.8 g	1.1 g	None	None	1725 mg	Juvenile	10 lb 7 oz
March 1	6.3 g	4.8 g	1.0 g	Active spermatogenesis	Few	1252 mg	Juvenile	8 lb 5 oz
March 1	8.6 g	6.9 g	1.3 g	Abundant	Abundant	1550 mg	Juvenile	9 lb 12 oz
March 1-15	10.3 g	7.6 g	1.9 g	Abundant	Abundant	1562 mg	Adult	—
March 17	11.3 g	8.6 g	1.9 g	Abundant	Abundant	1522 mg	Adult	11 lb 5 oz
March 27	7.4 g	5.8 g	1.2 g	Abundant	Abundant	1921 mg	Adult	8 lb 3 oz
March 27	13.0 g	9.8 g	2.2 g	Abundant	Abundant	2053 mg	Adult	14 lb 6 oz
April 4	9.0 g	7.0 g	1.7 g	Abundant	Abundant	1800 mg	Adult	9 lb 5 oz

Source: P. L. Wright and M. W. Coulter. 1967. Reproduction and growth in Maine fishers. J. Wildl. Mgt. 31: 70-87, Table 3. Reproduced by permission of the Wildlife Society.

Male Reproductive Biology

In his book, published in 1937, Hodgson mentioned that the testicles of male fishers are enlarged during the breeding season. This was the only information available until the mid-1960s, when Coulter and Wright (Coulter 1966; Wright and Coulter 1967) presented data on the reproductive tracts of 10 male fishers given them by Maine trappers. The dates of capture ranged from 5 January through 4 April. The results of the study are shown in Table 4.

The weights of combined testes and epididymides and the weights of paired testes were greater for those males that had abundant sperm in the testes and epididymides. Unfortunately, no known adult males taken before the breeding season are represented in the sample. However, since one juvenile taken on 1 March was in breeding condition and since Hodgson (1937) noted an increase in testicular size during the breeding season, it may be that adults show a similar increase in testicular weight. Wright and Coulter (1967) stated that the males taken early during the trapping season in Maine generally had inactive testes.

The juvenile male taken in early January was aspermatic. Of four juveniles taken in late February and early March, one showed no signs of reproductive activity and three showed somewhat enlarged testes, but only one of these three was in breeding condition. From early March through April, all adults taken were fully sexually active and had abundant sperm in the epididymides. Wright and Coulter (1967, p. 78) concluded that "the results indicate . . . that adult males are fully sexually active during the breeding season; and the young males, now just 1 year old, are also apparently in breeding condition." The weight and development of the bacula of yearling males in their sample supported this conclusion. (See Chapter 2.)

More recent findings are not in complete agreement with those of Coulter and Wright (Coulter 1966; Wright and Coulter 1967). Douglas and Strickland (1977) became concerned about the fisher's reproductive biology because of a decrease in trapping returns in the Algonquin region of Ontario. In order to obtain the data about fishers required for adjusting trapping quotas, they began a study of carcasses of fishers caught by trappers in 1972. From an unspecified number of male fisher carcasses, Douglas and Strickland concluded that they were unable to state when male fishers become completely mature. They found that "while males at one year of age are producing sperm, their testes and baculum [sic] have not reached full adult size" (1977; p. 2). They then hypothesized that this may make yearling male fishers inefficient breeders. Douglas and Strickland believed that a lack of mature males may have caused the high level of barrenness found in their sample of reproductive tracts from females.

It is certain that two-year-old male fishers are fully sexually mature, but it is not certain whether one-year-old males are fully sexually mature. It is possible that the age of first reproduction varies among regions and/or among individuals. Such a variation could produce the conflicting results on the age of first reproduction in male fishers.

Female Reproductive Biology

The reproductive biology of female fishers is similar to that of other mustelines in general. There are minor differences, most of which are due to size differences between species. Most of the work on the female fisher's reproductive system has used reproductive tracts from fishers caught by trappers.

Female fishers are sexually mature and breed for the first time at one year of age (Douglas and Strickland 1977; Eadie and Hamilton 1958; Hall 1942; Wright and Coulter 1967). Most females of the genus *Mustela* breed for the first time during their first summer. Female American pine martens do not reach sexual maturity until they are two years of age (Wright 1963).

Female Reproductive Tracts and Embryos

The reproductive tract of a female fisher is similar to that of most other female mustelids (Wright and Coulter 1967). The ovaries are completely encapsulated, with only a small ostium through which a small portion of the fimbria extends, and the ovaries are encircled by the oviducts. The average combined weights of the ovaries of 44 adult female fishers in inactive pregnancy (embryos not implanted) studied by Wright and Coulter (1967) was 134.4 milligrams, and the average combined weights of the ovaries of 33 immature female fishers was 76.5 milligrams. Fishers were judged immature when they lacked corpora lutea; all immature female fishers were captured during the fall or early winter of their first years. The ovaries of female fishers with implanted embryos are much larger than those of females in inactive pregnancy. Wright and Coulter found an average combined weight of 231.9 milligrams for the ovaries of 9 actively pregnant females. The corpora lutea are markedly enlarged during active pregnancy, as is the case in other mustelids with a long delayed implantation (Wright 1963), but the increased size of ovaries is not due only to the increase in the size of the corpora lutea (Wright and Coulter 1967).

The corpora lutea of actively pregnant female fishers can be readily identified (Wright and Coulter 1967). The cells of these corpora lutea are highly vacuolated (Eadie and Hamilton 1958; Wright and Coulter 1967), a condition probably correlated with the secretion of progesterone (Wright and Coulter 1967). The diameters of corpora lutea of fishers in inactive pregnancy average approximately 1.25 millimeters (Eadie and Hamilton 1958; Wright and Coulter 1967), and that of fishers in active pregnancy averages approximately 2.8 millimeters (Wright and Coulter 1967). Ovaries containing these corpora lutea have much interstitial tissue and numerous small- and medium-size follicles.

The uterus of a female fisher has a common corpus uteri; the uterine horns are 40 to 60 millimeters long and 2.5 to 4.0 millimeters in diameter in adult fishers. The uterine horns of immature females are smaller, about 30 to 40 millimeters long and 1.5 to 2.5 millimeters in diameter (Wright and Coulter 1967).

Cleavage of the embryo to the blastocyst stage is probably slow. Wright (1948) found that cleavage in the long-tailed weasel embryo is slow; at day 11 the embryo is in the morula stage, and not until day 15 is the blastocyst stage reached. Using the cleavage rate for long-tailed weasels, Wright and Coulter (1967) calculated that two female fishers whose reproductive tracts had tubal embryos in the morula stage must have bred approximately 8 to 10 days before capture. The condition of the ovaries of these fishers indicated that ovulation had also occurred about 8 to 10 days before capture. This supports slow cleavage in the fisher embryo.

The two fisher reproductive tracts with tubal embryos had a total of five morulae. One fisher had three embryos, one of which had about 228 nuclei. The two morulae in the other fisher had 12 and 20 nuclei. Embryos become dormant in the blastocyst stage before implantation (Enders and Pearson 1943). Dormancy is probably related to the proteins in the uterine environment (Daniel 1970). Dormant blastocysts found in the uterus during fall and winter measure from 0.25 to 1.50 millimeters in diameter and are clear, transparent spheres with an inner cell mass plainly visible at one side (Eadie and Hamilton 1958). Enders and Pearson (1943) were able to count 798, 807, and 844 nuclei in three dormant blastocysts taken from two fishers trapped in January and February. However, none of these observations were of well-preserved, well-fixed blastocysts. Well-fixed fisher blastocysts have probably never been seen (P. L. Wright, personal communication).

Implantation, Gestation, and Parturition

Frequently, some time before implantation there is a transuterine migration of blastocysts. In a sample of 12 female fishers' reproductive tracts in inactive pregnancy, Kelly (1977) found 3 tracts that had more blastocysts in one uterine horn than corpora lutea in the respective ovary. Wright and Coulter (1967) found only 1 tract showing transuterine migration in a sample of 11 tracts in inactive pregnancy. However, 5 of 8 tracts in active pregnancy showed transuterine migration. Wright and Coulter believed that transuterine migration may act to space out embryos just prior to implantation when they were asymmetrically derived from the two ovaries.

The implantation of the blastocyst of American pine martens is dependent on day length (Pearson and Enders 1944). Recently, implantation in the mink has been shown to be correlated with prolactin secretion; prolactin secretion is influenced by photoperiod in other mammals (Papke et al. 1980). It is assumed that the same is true for fishers. The postimplantation period for American pine martens is less than 28 days (Jonkel and Weckwerth 1963) and that for long-tailed weasels is about 23 to 24 days (Wright 1948). Therefore, Wright and Coulter (1967) calculated that the expected postimplantation period for female fishers should be about 30 days. From calculations from the known parturition dates given by Coulter (1966), Hall (1942), Hodgson (1937), Laberee (1941), Powell (1977a), and Wright and Coulter (1967), it can be shown that implantation can occur as early as January and as late as early April.

Parturition dates as early as February and as late as May have been recorded. Twenty-two parturition dates reported for fishers on fur farms in British Columbia ranged from 23 March to 7 April, with a mean date of 31 March (Hall 1942). Parturition on two fur farms in eastern Canada occurred in March and April (Hodgson 1937) and late April and May (1941). Douglas (1943) stated that parturition takes place from the middle of March to the middle of April. Hamilton and Cook (1955) reported that a trapper brought home litters of two and three fisher kits in February and mid-March, respectively. Leonard (1980b) observed a wild female fisher with kits calculated to have been born in early April.

Coulter (1966) and Wright and Coulter (1967) reported on 12 female carcasses of fishers that had embryos and fetuses in different stages of development. Estimated parturition dates ranged from mid-February through mid-April. Coulter (1966) listed two known parturition dates as 3 and 20 April. I recorded one parturition date of 29 or 30 March (Powell 1977a).

Litter Size

The average numbers of corpora lutea, unimplanted blastocysts, implanted embryos, placental scars, and kits in a litter recorded by different investigators are listed in Table 5. The average number of corpora lutea reported per female ranges from 2.73 to 3.89. Wright and Coulter (1967) stated that the average number of 3.28 corpora lutea found in the 44 female fishers from Maine was significantly greater than the 2.73 corpora lutea found by Eadie and Hamilton (1958) for fishers in New York. Wright and Coulter (1967) and Kelly (1977) found a decrease from the number of corpora lutea to the number of unimplanted blastocysts. Wright and Coulter examined a special subsample of 11 female fishers' reproductive tracts that were especially well preserved. In these tracts, there were 35 corpora lutea and 33 unimplanted blastocysts; 2 tracts showed a loss of 1 blastocyst each. This is a loss of approximately 6% of the potential embryos. Wright and Coulter also found that the number of corpora lutea in the ovaries of 8 females with implanted embryos was the same as the number of embryos. Consequently, they felt that the actual loss of potential embryos was probably more like 3%. Kelly (1977) found a much greater loss of potential embryos. However, because several of his tracts were very poorly preserved, Kelly be-

Table 5. Average Numbers per Female of Corpora Lutea, Blastocysts, Implanted Embryos, and Placental Scars and Average Litter Sizes for Fishers in Several Studies.

Corpora Lutea				Blastocysts				Implanted Embryos				Placental Scars				Litter Sizes				Source
Average	SD	Range	N	Average	SD	Range	N	Average	SD	Range	N	Average	SD	Range	N	Average	SD	Range	N	
2.73	0.70	2-4	22	2.71	0.95	1-4	7									2.71	0.72	1-6	21	1
																2.50		1-4	2	2
																		2-3		3
												2.93	0.78	2-4	27					4
3.39	0.60	2-5	54					3.45	0.52	3-4	11					3.00		3	2	5
3.28[a]			44																	6
3.38	0.52	3-4	8					3.33	0.50	3-4	9									6
3.18[a]			11	3.00			11													6
													9		9					6
3.67	0.26		12																	7
3.89[b]			9	2.89[b]			9													7
																2.00			1	8
								3.1												9

Sources: (1) Hodgson 1937; (2) Hall 1942; (3) Hamilton and Cook 1955; (4) Eadie and Hamilton 1958; (5) Coulter 1966; (6) Wright and Coulter 1967; (7) Kelly 1967; (8) Powell 1977a; (9) Douglas and Strickland 1977.

[a] Subsample of total sample of 54 reproductive tracts.

[b] Subsample of total sample of 12 reproductive tracts; the deterioration of the carcasses caused the low number of blastocysts in comparison to the number of corpora lutea.

lieved that his number of lost embryos was inflated from the actual value.

The average number of unimplanted blastocysts shown in Table 5 ranges from 2.71 to 3.00. The average number of implanted embryos ranges from 3.10 to 3.45. Only one study (Coulter 1966) recorded the number of placental scars: an average of 2.93 per female.

The only study with a good sample of actual litter sizes comes from fur-farm fishers. Hall (1942) reported an average litter size of 2.71 kits per female for fishers from fur farms in British Columbia. The other litter sizes in Table 5 agree with this average number with reasonable closeness.

It is obvious from the entries in Table 5 that small sample sizes and possible geographic variation have influenced the actual numbers obtained. For example, it is impossible for the average number of unimplanted embryos to be smaller than the average number of implanted embryos in any one fisher, for any one population, or over the entire continent. Nonetheless, it appears that the average litter size for a female fisher is between two and three kits, with a range from one to four or possibly even five or six (one fisher, according to Wright and Coulter [1967], had five corpora lutea; Hodgson [1937] reported one litter of six!).

Reproductive Schedule

With the information already given, a general reproductive schedule for female fishers can be diagrammed (Figure 24). Female fishers are shown to breed around the middle of April. The rate of cleavage of the embryos is probably slow, and the embryos most likely reach the blastocyst stage about 15 days after fertilization. Embryos become dormant during the blastocyst stage and remain so for approximately 10 months. Implantation is induced by the increasing day length during early March, and an approximate 30-day normal gestation ensues. Parturition probably occurs on the average in early April, and females probably breed again within 10 days. Thus, an adult female fisher is pregnant almost all the time, except for a brief period following parturition. Healthy females breed for the first time when they are one year old, produce their first litters when they are two years old, and breed every year thereafter. For fishers in areas with parturition and breeding dates before or after those dates diagrammed in Figure 24, the whole schedule is shifted appropriately.

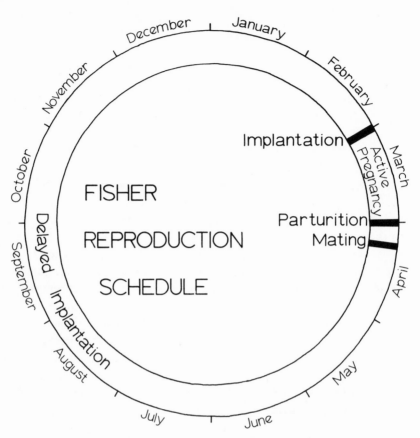

Figure 24. Fisher reproduction schedule. (*C. B. Powell*)

Courtship and Mating

For an animal like the fisher, it is difficult to prove whether matings in the wild are monogamous, polygynous, or polyandrous. Fishers raised on fur farms have been mated monogamously and polygynously (Douglas 1943; Hodgson 1937; Laberee 1941). It is probable that polygamous mating does occur in the wild. Coulter (1966) listed six points that support this conjecture. (1) Fishers' home ranges overlap. (2) Fishers are strongly solitary throughout the winter months preceding the mating season. (3) Field observations commonly find two individuals traveling together beginning in March, and yet the association of individuals does not occur with all fishers, or even with a majority of them, at the same time. Furthermore, there is no evidence that males stay with females for very long. (4) Since fishers are solitary, males probably follow females in estrus by scent. Once a female is out of estrus, she is probably no longer attractive to a male.

(5) The spread of parturition dates indicates a spread of mating dates over approximately six weeks; there would be some females attractive to males over this spread of dates. (6) Considering the other five points, it is probable that males begin to follow the first female in estrus they encounter. Since the sexes do not remain together long, a male probably follows other females coming into estrus at later dates. It is not known whether females mate with more than one male.

The only matings that have been observed have taken place on fur farms. Hodgson (1937) and Laberee (1941) both observed a number of matings and reported that the female appears to dominate the male during the activities. Laberee (1941, p. 102) stated that, when a female "wants to mate, you better provide the necessary facilities and do it promptly." If a female is not receptive, she may act aggressively toward a male; the male's response will not be aggressive, however (Hodgson 1937). Hodgson's (1937, pp. 36-37) most complete description of mating is as follows:

> From the fifth to the ninth day following date of arrival of the litter [the female] shows up for the first time. She runs up and down her pen often stopping at the chute leading in to the male. On being let through, if the male is out, there will be a mating in a very short time, but very often he will be in his nest box. In this case she will investigate the pen, finally landing at the opening leading into his nest box. Then she will make a peculiar crooning noise, as if calling to him. He will soon make his appearance and a mating takes place with little delay.

Laberee related (1941, p. 103) one mating this way:

> Soon the love-making began. And if there was anyone within a mile of us who did not think some large animal was being tortured to death, that person must have been deaf. Such noise! Such yowls! Such howling! No thousand cats caterwauling on a backyard fence at midnight ever could make such noise.
>
> But that was before copulation began. Once the pair mated there was not a sound. And the moment the mating was over, the female insisted on getting back to her pen immediately. As soon as we had removed the heating pad from the young pekans' nest we let her in — and all was serene. The mating lasted from 10:17 AM until 4:27 PM, six hours and ten minutes. The next day she mated again for four hours and twenty-five minutes.

Unfortunately, neither of these descriptions is very precise. It appears that courtship can be brief or prolonged, depending on the receptiveness of the female, perhaps. Elsewhere, both Hodgson (1937) and Laberee (1941) stated that the male grasps the female by the back of the neck during mating. This may cause a noticeable irritation on the neck of the female (Hodgson 1937). The actual mating is similar to that of minks (Hodgson 1937), which is known for being prolonged and very vigorous (Enders and Enders 1963). Matings between fishers on Hodgson's and Laberee's fur farms commonly lasted from one to seven hours, averaging somewhere around four hours. From these rough descriptions, it appears that the courtship of fishers is similar to that of other mustelines (Heidt, Petersen, and Kirkland 1968; Hodgson 1937).

Denning

All known fisher dens used to raise young have been high up in hollow trees. A New York trapper found two litters of fishers in holes in hollow trees during February and March; the hole found in March was between 6 and 9 meters above the ground in a hard maple (Hamilton and Cook 1955). A litter was also found in a hollow tree in Maine (Soutiere, personal communication), and Leondard (1980b) made several observations of a litter being raised in a hollow aspen in Manitoba. Two other possible maternal dens that were not in hollow trees have been found. In California, a female fisher with three kits around three months old used a den in a rockfall. Scats, fur, and other remains of prey were scattered around the rockfall and the area "smelled strongly of fisher" (Grinnell, Dixon, and Linsdale 1937; p. 226). A possible maternity den was found in Upper Michigan by R. B. Brander, who showed it to me on 18 March. The den was a hole with a small entrance under a large yellow birch. The surrounding area had an abundance of fisher tracks of various ages leading to and from the hole, indicating that the den had been used for a longer period than a normal sleeping den would have been used.

The only published description of a fisher's maternal nest is that by Leonard (1980b). The nest was approximately 7 meters up in a hollow, living quaking aspen. There were two entrances: a small entrance too small for the female to use at the bottom of the hollow and a larger hole approximately 10 meters up the tree trunk through which the female entered and descended through the inside of the tree to the kits at the bottom of the hollow. The nest area was on flat, rough wood, and there was no nesting material at all. The nest was extremely neat after the kits left, with no sign that fisher kits had been raised there: no excrement, no regurgitated food, and no food remains.

There are a few descriptions of captive fishers' maternal nests. Hodgson (1937) provided hay as nesting material in his fishers' nest boxes. The female fishers made round nests in the hay, and Hodgson made no mention of them lining the nests with either their own fur or with the fur of prey animals. I observed the nest of one captive female fisher with young. Again, the nest was a round cavity in the hay with no lining of fur.

Except during mating, female fishers raised on fur farms spend little time outside maternal nest boxes after parturition (Hodgson 1937; Laberee 1941). Although mating may keep a female away from her young for several hours when the young are only a few days old, she returns quickly to her young when she has finished mating. Fur farmers have sometimes artificially warmed nests with young in them during the female's absence (Hodgson 1937; Laberee 1941), but it is not known whether this increased the survivorship of the young.

The female fisher with young observed and radiotracked by Leonard (1980a) spent very little time away from her kits at first. Leonard calculated that he established continuous radio contact starting when the kits were less than a week old. At that time, the female spent no more than 2 or 3 hours of 24 away from the kits. During the following 8 weeks, she spent more and more time away from the kits, so that just before the kits left the maternal den the female was spending only about an hour in the early morning with them. As the kits grew, the female was under increasing pressure to hunt in order to meet the energy and nutritional demands of lactation. This undoubtedly explains the increased time spent away from the kits longer and longer after parturition. This need may not affect fishers on fur farms because adequate food is provided by the farmers; this fact would explain why such behavior is not mentioned in the accounts of Hodgson and Laberee.

Evidence suggests that female fishers raise their young with no help from the males. Some male fishers in fur farms have been observed to enter nest boxes with kits and do no harm (Hodgson 1937; Laberee 1941), but other males have seriously injured the young (Hodgson 1937). Coulter's (1966) arguments supporting polygamous matings also suggest that males do not assist females in raising the young. A further argument to support this contention is that the young a female raises were conceived a year earlier and may have been fathered by more than one male. There is no reason to believe that male fishers can remember with which females they mated the previous year. Therefore, a male who helped raise young could be helping raise the offspring of another male, while his own offspring were being raised by another female without assistance. This should lead to less care of the young by males (Grafen 1980).

During the time that the female fisher radiotracked by Leonard (1980b) had kits in her maternal den, her activities and hunting periods were oriented toward parts of her home range distant from the maternal den. This female would travel rapidly in roughly a straight line from her maternal den to the outer edges of her home range each day. She would then stay at long distances from the den until returning, again roughly in a straight line. This female bred on at least one of these active periods away from the den (her reproductive tract, collected during the trapping season the following winter, showed corpora lutea [Leonard 1980b]). Breeding took place far from the maternal den, and her activity patterns may also have oriented the male fisher's activities away from her maternal den (Leonard 1980b).

The use of the maternal/parturition den by the female fisher and her young observed by Leonard (1980b) ceased when the young were approximately eight weeks old. It is not known whether the female took the young to another den, but this is probably the case. Grinnell, Dixon, and Linsdale (1937) reported the den-oriented activities of three-month-old fishers.

Delayed Implantation

There are no convincing explanations for the origin of delayed implantation. General agreement is developing that delayed implantation has evolved independently several times (Heidt 1970; Wright 1963). Table 6 lists many of the placental mammals that exhibit delayed implantation. This table is not complete because there are many placental mammals that have not been studied but may display delayed implantation, such as unstudied *Mustela* species, *Martes* species, and pinnipeds (seals and sea lions). Delayed implantation also occurs in several marsupials.

Six basic theories have been developed to explain the origin of delayed implantation. Fries (1880, 1902) suggested that delayed implantation in the roe deer and the European badger is an adaptation that benefits the young. With only these two species as examples, he argued that the young needed to be born as early in the spring as possible in order to be able to survive the next winter. Without delayed implantation, mating would have to occur during the winter,

Table 6. Placental Mammals That Display
Delayed Implantation

Order and Species	Delay (Months)
Chiroptera	
equatorial fruit bat	3+
big-eared bat	?
Jamaican fruit bat	2½
long-winged bat	?
Edentata	
nine-banded armadillo	3½ - 4½
Carnivora	
Ursidae	
black bear	5 - 6+
brown/grizzly bear	6+
polar bear	8+
Mustelidae	
short-tailed weasel	8½ - 9
long-tailed weasel	7
mink	1/3 - 1 2/3
American pine marten	8
sable	8
fisher	10 - 11
wolverine	6
European badger	6 - 10
American badger	6
river otter	9 - 11
western spotted skunk	5
Otariidae	
northern fur seal	3½ - 4
southern fur seal	4
Phocidae	
harbor seal	2 - 3
gray seal	5 - 6
elephant seal	3½ - 4
Odobenidae	
walrus	3 - 4
Artiodactyla	
roe deer	4 - 5

Source: Data from Daniel 1970 and Wright 1963.

which he presumed would be unfavorable to adults. Thus, delayed implantation uncoupled the normal temporal relation between mating and parturition so that both events could occur at the most favorable times. Although this theory fits the two species Fries used as examples, it falls short with other species, such as the fisher.

Prell (1927, 1930) argued that discontinuous development (delayed implantation and delayed fertilization) developed in "old" genera that were exposed to glaciation; that is, he argued that harsh climatic conditions forced a modification in embryonic development. Prell was not consistent in his aging of "old" and "new" genera, however, and the occurrence of delayed implantation and delayed fertilization in tropical species nullifies his theory (Murr 1929, 1931).

Murr (1929, 1931) believed that delayed implantation may have arisen as a direct effect of environmental temperature on embryonic development. For example, he thought that the delay could be caused by the alleged drop in body temperature of bears and badgers and the chilling of organs and glands in martens and roe deer. The obvious argument nullifying this theory is that delay in most species begins or occurs during the summer.

Hamlett (1935) reviewed these three theories and concluded that Fries's was the only one that held any merit. He further concluded, however, that delayed implantation is a "useless character" that has no value for a species's survival. There is little question today that delayed implantation is not a "useless character" and that it does have survival value in those species that exhibit it (Ealey 1963; Heidt 1970; Wright 1963).

Ealey (1963) presented a good argument for the evolution of delayed implantation in the euro. In summarizing his presentation, he stated (p. 46):

> A seasonal variation in the nutritional state of the euro population has been demonstrated. An increase in reproductive activity occurs at such a time that the young are becoming large when the parents are best able to supply adequate milk. However, this reproductive activity occurs before the main rain has fallen, and there is considerable mortality among the young. Many of the young that die can be replaced by others from quiescent blastocytes. Time is saved, and the replacing young have a better chance of obtaining enough milk for survival when they are larger than if they had been born about a month later, as they would have been if the mothers had gone through another estrous cycle and been fertilized.

When there is a prolonged good season, the mechanism of delayed implantation insures that the maximum number of pouch young are produced in the shortest time.

Although this theory nicely fits delayed implantation for many marsupials, especially those in unpredictable environments, it cannot be applied to fishers or other placentals. Fishers are unable to regulate implantation so that some blastocyts implant while others remain unimplanted for a longer dormancy.

Heidt (1970) believed that Fries's theory for the origin of delayed implantation should apply to mustelids that live in northern climates. In addition, Heidt suggested that species at high trophic levels need no more than one litter per year (which is often necessitated by delayed implantation) and that delayed implantation may be a factor designed to limit populations. There are many problems with Heidt's suggestions. First, the three species of North American weasels are at trophic levels lower than Heidt assumed (Errington 1943, 1967; Powell 1975, 1978b). Thus, Heidt's suggestion could only apply to larger mustelids. Second, minks do have delayed implantation, but this in itself does not limit litters to one per year because the delay is very short (as little as 10 days). And, third, there are no adequate explanations for the evolution of population self-limitation.

Wright (1963, p. 91) has presented what is probably the best explanation to date for delayed implantation in some mustelids.

Apparently not previously mentioned is the possibility that the female heat period during lactation, as occurs in three of these species, might result in a temporary family relationship at the time the young are being weaned. The young of these mustelids may be weaned at about five or six weeks of age and reach full growth at three months, a considerably shorter period than in the case for many carnivores. They require a relative large volume of food, and if the male actively co-operated in bringing food to the young this would be distinctly advantageous to their survival. Generally we think of these animals as largely solitary and unsocial at times other than the breeding season. However, a number of authors (Grigoriev 1938, Hamilton 1933, Seton 1929) have mentioned males of *M. erminea* in attendance at the nest and carrying food to the young. Since females of this species have been found to be pregnant when only two months old, it may be that they are also bred by the same adult male before breakup of this family relationship. In none of these mustelids do the juvenile males reach sexual maturity during their first summer.

Although fishers are not at weaning age when their mother is in estrus, they are at an age when extended attendance by their mother is important. Thus, a male bringing food would reduce the amount of time the mother must be away from her kits. One unsolved problem is that such a male would be bringing food to offspring that are not his own. Of what possible advantage would it be to a male to bring food to a female who is raising another male's offspring? The young a female raises were conceived a year earlier, and there is no reason to believe that a male fisher can remember over the course of a year with which females he bred the previous year. There are two possible solutions to this problem for some mustelids, and these solutions may complement each other. First, for the short-tailed weasel there is the obvious advantage to the male of possibly inseminating more than one female during the period of one family relationship. It would be to his advantage to feed the young to ensure the good health at weaning of the young females he inseminates. Second, for the short-tailed weasel and the other species, by helping to feed the young a male increases the chances of survival for the female with which he wishes to breed. This means that a male fisher would be investing in a female's good health at the time of mating and projecting that good health a year into the future; this is perhaps as dubious as assuming that a male can remember with whom he bred a year after the fact. In any case, bringing food to the female may easily have been built into a male's courtship ritual.

Finally, although Wright's (1963) theory does apply to fishers, it does not apply to the many mustelids that do not have mating seasons before the families break up, such as long-tailed weasels and American pine martens. I believe that the best explanation for the origin of delayed implantation is still to come, though I also believe that this explanation will deal with advantages of uncoupling normal temporal relations between mating and parturition so that each can occur at an optimal time. For the fisher, mating can occur in late winter because at this time males range widely for food and are most likely to be in olfactory contact with females. Delayed implantation probably has a common origin among the Mustelidae—if not in a common ancestor, then at least in a common selective agent. Given that all the extant mustelids acquired delayed implantation for the same reason, I believe that each species has "finely tuned" the evolution of delayed implantation to its own specific requirements. Therefore, to understand the evolution of delayed implantation we must look deeper. We shall have to look at similarities within the Mustelidae, which may be more important than each species's individual use of delayed implantation.

Neonates and Early Development

Some of the observations I made on my two hand-raised fisher kits have not been previously reported. In this section, information about my kits that is not followed by a citation to previously published work has been taken directly from my journal notes.

Neonates

Newborn fishers are completely helpless (Coulter 1966; Hodgson 1937), and their eyes and ears are tightly closed (Coulter 1966). Coulter (1966) observed the development of a litter of fishers born in captivity and consisting of two females and one male. Although he did not handle the young until they were 37 days old, he was able to observe them almost from their birth. His description (1966, pp. 81-82) of 1 to 4-day-old fisher kits can be paraphrased as follows:

> Fishers are altricial. Neonates are blind, helpless, and only partially covered with a sparse growth of fine, light gray hair over the mid-dorsal area. From the first day, they utter short, high-pitched cries somewhat similar to those of domestic kittens.
>
> Growth and development is rapid during the first few days. By the third and fourth days, almost the entire body has a growth of fine, fawn-gray hair up to 6 millimeters long along the mid-dorsal line and extending partway down the tail. Even at this early stage, young fishers show several characteristics typical of adults, long and slender bodies, rounded heads and rather flat faces, dark feet, curved claws, and relatively long, tapering tails. The male and female 3-day-old kits from a litter I did not observe closely weighed 39.0 grams and 41.2 grams, respectively.

Similar observations have been made on fur farms (Hodgson 1937).

Leonard (1980b) has suggested that being so altricial may be adaptive in fishers because little developmental or physiological damage would be done to neonates if their temperatures were to drop during their mother's absence for hunting or mating shortly after their birth.

Other mustelines are born in a similar condition. Newborn least weasels are naked and acquire only fine, white hair during their first day of life (Heidt 1970; Heidt, Petersen, and Kirkland 1968). At one day of age, short-tailed weasels and long-tailed weasels are covered with only fine, white hair (East and Lockie 1965; Hamilton 1933). In all three species, the hair is most profuse along the back. Newborn least weasels weigh about 1.4 grams (Heidt 1970), and newborn short-tailed weasels weigh about 1.7 grams (Hamilton 1933).

Pelage

My two kits were completely covered with downy, gray hair at 18 days of age. By the time they were 25 days old, they were still gray in color, but a small, light-colored mark was detectable on the chest of the female. That mark later developed into a white chest patch. At 3 weeks of age, the litter Coulter (1966) observed had changed to a chocolate-brown color over the back, with sparse, light straw-colored hair on the flanks and sparse, fawn-gray hair 2 to 4 millimeters long on the chest and stomach. In both litters, hair around the mammae in both sexes and around the penis of the males was distinctly light gray colored.

Coulter (1966) was first able to detect a white patch in the genital region of a kit at 7 weeks; the white patch was completely developed by the time the kit was 10 weeks old. At about 10 to 12 weeks my kits changed to the chocolate-brown color Coulter's had acquired when several weeks younger. From this age on, the tricolored guard hairs characteristically found on the head, neck, and shoulders of adults could be seen (with a restricted distribution) on the kits. Thus, through the summer and the early autumn, young fishers are the same general color as adults but are more uniform in color.

The white hair on least weasels, short-tailed weasels, and long-tailed weasels persists until they are about 2½ to 3 weeks old. By this time, some darker pigmentation can be found leading down from the back and some brown hairs have appeared on the back. By shortly after 3 weeks of age, least weasels have acquired adult pelage. The black tail tip on long-tailed weasels can be distinguished by 3 weeks of age, and by 5 weeks long-tailed weasels have acquired pelage closely resembling that of adults. Short-tailed weasels do not acquire adult pelage until they are approximately 6 to 7 weeks old (East and Lockie 1965; Hamilton 1933; Heidt 1970; Heidt, Petersen, and Kirkland 1968). Thus, it appears that fishers retain distinguishable juvenile pelage to an older age than the three species of weasels.

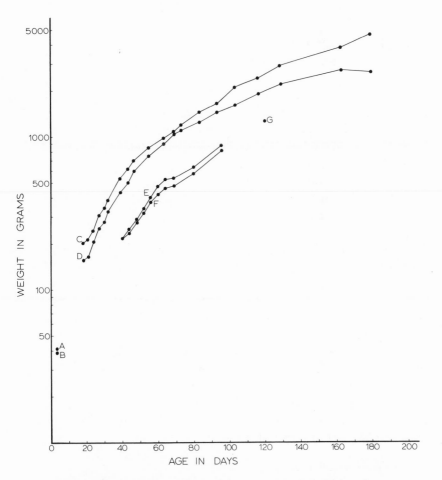

Figure 25. Weights of fisher kits at different ages. (A and B) Weights of two
dead kits weighed by Coulter (1966); (C and D) weights of my two kits; C was
the male and D was the female; (E and F) weights of Coulter's two kits (Coulter 1966); both were females; (G) weight of a male kit approximately four
months old weighed by Coulter (1966). (*C. B. Powell*)

Weight

Coulter (1966) obtained the weights of two dead 3-day-old fisher
kits, the weights of two female kits as they grew from 40 through 96
days of age, the weight of one male kit 44 days old, and the weight
of a wild kit aged approximately 4 months. I was able to follow the
weight gain of my two kits from 18 through 177 days of age. These
weights are shown in Figure 25. My kits weighed more than Coulter's,

probably because my kits were fed almost as much food as they wished while they were growing.

Sexual dimorphism in weight is pronounced by late autumn (Coulter 1966; Hodgson 1937). Although the male kit in my litter was heavier than his sister from the time they were first weighed, the male in the litter observed by Coulter (1966) weighed less than his sisters at 44 days of age. Unfortunately, that male kit died at 44 days of age, so a comparison of the male's weight to the females' weights at later ages could not be made. Noticeable differences in weight may not be apparent until fishers are around 4 months old. At that age the female in my litter weighed slightly more than 75% as much as the male. The captured wild kit weighed by Coulter (1966) weighed approximately the same as the kits in his litter at 4 months of age.

Sexual dimorphism develops much faster in the smaller mustelines. American pine martens reach full size at about 3 months of age and, therefore, have shown sexual dimorphism for some time before reaching maturity (Markley and Bassett 1942). Sexual dimorphism in body size begins to become pronounced sometime after the fourth week of age in least weasels (East and Lockie 1965; Heidt 1970) and after the eighth week in minks (Travis and Schaible 1961). At these ages, these species have reached 50% to 75% of their full size. Sexual dimorphism in weight of European fitch ferrets of laboratory stock may be apparent at birth (Hahn and Wester 1969).

Other Physical Development

As I have already pointed out, newborn fishers are completely helpless (Coulter 1966; Hodgson 1937). By 18 days of age, my kits were able to grasp with their claws. By 21 days, they were able to crawl around on the wool rags in their box and crawl up the sides (approximately 15 centimeters high) well enough to put their heads over the edge. At 21 days of age, the male stood up to defecate, but he was very unstable. My kits did not make consistent attempts to hold themselves up until they were about 7 weeks old. By 7½ weeks, they were walking clumsily. At about 8 weeks, they began uncoordinated climbing on the branches propped up in their enclosure. Even though by 10 weeks both of them could run with the typical fisher gait, they still crawled frequently, too. At 12 weeks of age, the female kit climbed 3 meters up a tree.

In contrast, the kits Coulter (1966) observed did not begin their awkward crawling until they were 8 weeks old, and they did not walk until they were over 9 weeks old. Grinnell, Dixon, and Linsdale (1937, pp. 226-27) mentioned that fisher kits about 3 months old could "scamper about as young squirrels do" on the rocks surrounding their den.

One of my kits began to open one eye on day 45, and both kits had both eyes open by day 49. Coulter (1966) noted that his kits had their eyes open when they were 53 days old. These ages are consistent with Hodgson's (1937, p. 41) description of fishers raised on fur farms: "They are about seven weeks old before their eyes open."

My kits' teeth began to break through when they were about 40 days old. The deciduous premolars came first. The canines had completely broken through at 7 weeks. In Coulter's kits, the canines did not completely erupt until 9 weeks of age.

Fisher kits are completely dependent on milk until they are 8 to 10 weeks old. Starting at 8 weeks, my kits became fussy about taking formula from a bottle, and by 10 weeks they were completely weaned. Coulter (1966) first noticed his mother fisher taking meat to the kits when they were 62 days old. "During the following few days the kits ate small portions of meat, but were unable to tear pieces from larger chunks. By the 83rd day they were eating much meat regularly, although the only visible teeth were the canines and first premolars" (Coulter 1966, p. 91). Weaning of Coulter's kits took place at around 4 months, but the kits still occasionally nursed up to 114 days of age.

As with fishers, least weasels, short-tailed weasels, and long-tailed weasels are all born with their eyes and ears closed. Eyes open at 26 to 30 days in least weasels and at around 35 days of age in the other two species. Sound can probably first be heard between 3 and 4 weeks of age, depending on the species. The deciduous canines and premolars erupt at about 10 to 14 days of age in least weasels, but not until 21 to 25 days of age in short-tailed weasels and long-tailed weasels. The young of all three species begin ingesting solid food at around 3 weeks of age, and weaning occurs when they are between 5 and 8 weeks old (East and Lockie 1965; Hamilton 1933; Heidt 1970; Heidt, Petersen, and Kirkland 1968). American pine martens are weaned at about 6 to 7 weeks of age (Markley and Bassett 1942).

It appears that fishers may be relatively older than these other mustelines when they begin to take solid food; for example, the weasels
take solid food before their eyes are open.

Behavioral Development

Most observations of the behavioral development of fishers have
been made on behaviors related to prey catching and feeding. At
about 53 days old, my hand-raised female fisher kit began grabbing
and shaking pieces of bedding material in play. She did this frequently by day 55; the male did it occasionally. After being fed puree on
day 55, the female kit rubbed her chin back and forth on the towel
in my lap. I have observed adult fishers, American pine martens,
long-tailed weasels, short-tailed weasels, and European polecats rub
their chins back and forth on the ground after eating and during
play. Glands have been found on the skin of the necks of infant
sables (Petskoi and Kolpovskii 1970), and it is likely that other neck
and chin glands will be found in other species of the Mustelinae.

Coulter (1966, p. 92) described the development of killing behavior in growing fisher kits as follows:

> Beginning at age 90 days, dead Coturnix quail were placed in the pen. At
> the first trial the kits sniffed the strange object and began to play with it.
> In a few minutes they dragged it into the nest box where the adult began
> to tear it up. The young became increasingly excited on the second and
> third trials at intervals of three days. On the third trial they pounced upon
> the dead bird and began to eat it. After the fifth trial with dead birds a
> live one was introduced. The larger, dominant kit immediately seized it,
> carried it to shelter, and both young began to eat from it, but without
> killing it. It was obvious that they did not know how to kill at age 106
> days. In later trials the kits attacked live birds, crippled mice and red
> squirrels. They were about 125 days old before the dominant kit began to
> attack the head and neck region of small prey as is typically done by
> adults.

I presented my fisher kits with their first live prey—a wild baby
snowshoe hare—when they were 93 days old. They generally ignored
it. The male did chase the hare some in what appeared to be play. At
this same age, he began to play pounce on objects within his enclosure.

When they were 121 days old, I again presented my hand-raised
kits with a young snowshoe hare. The male cautiously nipped at the

hare's rump and neck while both he and the hare were confined in a small cage. The hare then escaped into the kits' enclosure and was chased by the male kit. When the hare was again confined, the male kit made a directed bite to the back of the hare's neck. He was surprised by an accidental disturbance in the enclosure, however, and released his grip on the hare. After this age, both kits killed hares in the same manner as adults.

Young American pine martens are able to kill proficiently by 2½ months of age (Remington 1952), a considerably younger age than fishers. This is probably related to their rapid attainment of full adult weight.

Young least weasels show aggressive behavior toward live mice as early as 32 days of age, but until about their 38th day they will only play with dead mice (Heidt 1970). When a litter of least weasels was 40 days old, Heidt and his co-workers (Heidt 1970; Heidt, Petersen, and Kirkland 1968) observed their mother presenting them with one dead mouse and one immobilized live mouse. The young played with the immobilized mouse. Gillingham (1978) made a similar observation on a family of short-tailed weasels when the kits were 51 days old. Heidt (1970) and Heidt, Petersen, and Kirkland (1968) interpreted this behavior to be parental instruction of the kits on how to kill. Young least weasels are adept at killing by 42 to 45 days of age (Heidt 1970; Heidt, Petersen, and Kirkland 1968). Short-tailed weasels begin to show interest in live mice at around 9 weeks of age and may kill as early as at 10 weeks of age (Gillingham 1978), but killing may not begin until 11 or 12 weeks of age (East and Lockie 1965; Gillingham 1978). By 12 weeks of age, short-tailed weasels can kill proficiently (Gillingham 1978). Gillingham also found that young short-tailed weasels will not kill mice until they have become proficient at seizing and securing mice. The weasels did this by wrapping themselves around the mice and holding them with all four paws.

Fishers do not require parental instruction in order to learn proper killing techniques (Powell 1977a; Kelly 1977). My hand-raised kits killed snowshoe hares, red squirrels, and porcupines with the proper techniques even though a live porcupine was first presented to the female when she was 2 years old (Powell 1977a). Kelly gave live red squirrels to two hand-raised female fishers who were several years old (they were believed to be littermates). According to him (1977, p.

164), "both fishers killed squirrels quickly by biting the base of the head." To Kelly's knowledge, neither of these fishers had been given live prey before that time.

Intraspecific aggression in fishers begins to appear when the kits are around 3 months old. Coulter (1966) and I had to take special care to see that both kits in our respective litters obtained enough food when the kits reached that age. I had to separate my kits at age 5½ months because of their aggressive behavior over food (Powell 1977a). Coulter (1966) observed that his fisher mother became increasingly hostile toward her kits beginning late in their fourth month. The kits began sleeping in a nest box separate from their mother at that time and shortly thereafter began sleeping in individual nest boxes. At age 5½ months, one kit was killed and the other injured by the mother. Hodgson (1937, p. 42) said of fishers raised on fur farms:

> They should be separated from their mother when about ten weeks of age up to twelve weeks. By this time they have learned to eat well and like some children have learned to scrap as well. It is necessary to feed them in separate pens. They are best placed two in a pen at three months of age and it may be necessary in a short time to place them in individual pens.

Coulter (1966, p. 85) speculated that a delay in the development of the pronounced sexual dimorphism in body size may be "an adaptation of definite advantage to the growth and survival of females." Because of aggression between littermates, differences in weight could place small littermates at a distinct disadvantage when food is not provided regularly and in good quantity. This is a kin selection argument.

One final behavior of interest has been noted. Up until they were about 5 months old, my hand-raised kits readily accepted the presence of strange people in their enclosures. After 6 or 7 months, however, both acted very aggressively toward strangers in their enclosures and attacked people who entered. Laberee (1941) also made this observation, but he stated that adult fishers could be tamed to accept new people when properly handled. Similar behavior has been identified in other solitary carnivores (Fox 1978).

Longevity, Disease, Parasites, and Mortality

Fishers have been known to live longer than 10 years in zoos (unpublished records, Bronx Zoo, New York Zoological Society), but their longevity in the wild is not known. Weckwerth and Wright (1968) provided data on seven fishers released in Montana in 1959 and 1960 and subsequently trapped in sets for other furbearers. One female fisher was recovered in February 1966, at least 6 years after her release. Other tagged fishers were recaptured at earlier dates. Because all the fishers were at least yearlings when they were released, a minimum of 7 years is the maximum wild longevity. By counting cementum annuli, Kelly (1977) calculated that of 202 fishers caught by trappers in New Hampshire, one female and two males were 6 years old and four males were 7 years old. Data on the recovery of tagged fishers from Wisconsin and Michigan releases is even less extensive than that from Montana and New Hampshire (Irvine and Brander 1971). However, I captured no tagged fishers during intensive trapping near one of the Michigan release sites between 1973 and 1976. Thus approximately 10 years may be an upper limit to the life expectancy of wild fishers.

Sarcoptic mange, a contagious skin disease caused by the mite *Sarcoptes scabei,* is the only disease reported to affect the fisher (Coulter 1966; O'Meara, Payne, and Witter 1960). Two individuals have been found to be infested with the mite.

Incidence of parasites in fishers is lower than in many other mustelids (Hamilton and Cook 1955). Even in those studies of animals in which infestation has been common, individual fishers had few parasites (Coulter 1966). There have been no reports of fishers showing any signs of suffering from parasitism (Coulter 1966; deVos 1952; Hamilton and Cook 1955; Powell 1977a).

Twelve genera of nematodes, two genera of cestodes, two genera of trematodes, and a protosoan have been found in fishers (Table 7). In addition, two ectoparasites have been reported: one tick and one flea.

Natural causes of fisher mortality are not known. Mange or any of the parasites listed in Table 7 could adversely affect a fisher's health if the infestation were extremely advanced. Death could then result from the parasitism or the effects of the parasitism (such as susceptibility to disease and reduced hunting ability and the animal's consequent starvation or predation). There is no evidence that healthy adult fishers are subject to predation. However, it is likely that any predator would kill and eat a fisher that was unable to defend itself.

Table 7. Parasites and Incidence of Parasitism in Fishers.

Organism	Incidence (%)	Source
Nematodes		
Arthrodephalus lotoris	11	Hamilton and Cook 1955
Baylisascaris devosi	5	deVos 1952
	32	Dick and Leonard 1979
Ascaris mustelarum	25	Meyer and Chitwood 1951
	—	Coulter 1966
Capillaria mustelorum	35	Hamilton and Cook 1955
Capillaria spp.	5	Coulter 1966
Crenosoma spp.	15	Coulter 1966
	3	Meyer and Chitwood 1951
Dioctophyma renale *	—	Coulter 1966
Dracunculus insignis	13	Hamilton and Cook 1955
Dracunculus spp.	—	Coulter 1966
Molineus spp.	5	Hamilton and Cook 1955
	1	Dick and Leonard 1979
Physaloptera maxillaris *	11	Hamilton and Cook 1955
Physaloptera spp.	5	deVos 1952
	6	Dick and Leonard 1979
Soboliphyme baturini	—	Erickson 1946
	—	Morgan 1942
Trichinella spiralis	1	Dick and Leonard 1979
Uncinaria stenocephala	2	Hamilton and Cook 1955
	—	Chitwood 1932
Cestodes		
Mesocestoides variabilis	7	Coulter 1966
	5	deVos 1952
	6	Hamilton and Cook 1955
	50	Meyer and Chitwood 1951
Taenia spp.	9	Coulter 1966
	15	Dick and Leonard 1979
Trematodes		
Alaria spp.	6	Coulter 1966
	1	Dick and Leonard 1979
Metorchis conjunctus	1	Dick and Leonard 1979
Protozoa		
Isopara *	—	deVos 1952
Ticks		
Ixodes cookei *	—	deVos 1952
Fleas		
Oropsylla arctomys	—	Holland 1950

Note: A dash indicates the presence of a parasite whose incidence was not reported. An asterisk means that the identification was tentative at the time the source was published.

Chapter 4

Past and Present Distribution and Population Density

The genus *Martes* is Holarctic in distribution, but fishers are found only in North America. Their present range is reduced from their range before the settlement of the continent by Europeans (Hagmeier 1956), but most of this reduction has occurred in the United States (Figure 26). The northern limit to the fisher's range during historical times has always been around 60° north latitude in the west and somewhat south of the southern tip of James Bay in the east. Habitat preference has probably determined this northern limit. The tree line, and probably the northern limit to fisher's habitat, is farther north west of Hudson Bay than east of it (Drew and Shagg 1965; Larsen 1965; Marr 1948). Once fishers ranged from what is now northern British Columbia into central California in the Pacific coastal mountains and south into Idaho and Montana in the Rocky Mountains. In what is now the central United States, fishers ranged as far south as southern Illinois (Hagmeier 1956). In the eastern part of the continent, Hagmeier reported that fishers once ranged as far south as what is now North Carolina and Tennessee in the Appalachian Mountains, Pringle (1964a) stated they once ranged into Georgia, and Barkalow (1961) found remains of fishers in Alabama. It is possible, however, that this latter account is an artifact created by American Indians trading hides. The fisher's former range is very similar to the combined distributions of northern hemlock-

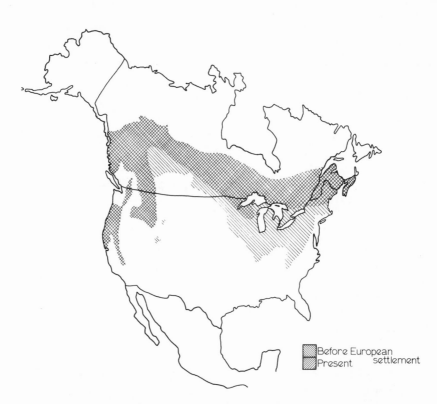

Figure 26. Map of fisher species range before settlement of North America by Europeans and at present. (*Drawn by C. B. Powell; based on Banville 1980, Earle 1978, Hagmeier 1956, Petersen, Martin, and Pils 1977, and Powell 1977a*)

hardwood, western mountain, and boreal forests (forest ranges taken from Cronquist 1961).

Population Decline

During the last part of the nineteenth century and the early part of this century, the number of fishers decreased strikingly, and they were exterminated over much of their former range in the United States (Brander and Books 1973; Coulter 1966; deVos 1951, 1952). The decline in population was significant in almost all areas populated by humans, and it was precipitous in some places. Fishers were exterminated in the East, the Midwest, and much of the West in the United States and from much of eastern Canada (Bensen 1959; Coulter 1966; deVos 1952; Dodds and Martell 1971; Dodge 1977; Hall 1942; Ingram 1973; Rand 1944; Schorger 1942; Weckwerth and Wright 1968).

There were two reasons for the decline in fisher populations: trapping and logging. Fishers are known by fur trappers as one of the easiest animals to trap (Young 1975). Before the 1920s, there were no trapping regulations for fishers, and the prices paid for fisher pelts were high enough to provide trappers with much incentive to trap fishers. Prices paid for fisher pelts, especially the silkier, glossier pelts of females, have always been high. Between 1900 and 1930 an excellent fisher pelt could bring up to $150 (Balser 1960; Hamilton and Cook 1955; Irvine, Magnus, and Bradle 1964; Petersen, Martin, and Pils 1977), and around 1920 one pelt went for $345 (Seton 1929). Except for prices in recent years, the peak prices paid for fisher pelts came in 1920; the average price paid that year was around $85 (Brander and Books 1973). In 1916 and 1921 the average prices in New York were around $16 and $65, respectively (Balser 1960; Hamilton and Cook 1955). By 1924 the average price in New York had dropped to around $38; then it picked up to around $50 during the late 1920s and finally dropped again during the early 1930s to around $20 (Hamilton and Cook 1955). Prices were not the same all over the United States at that time, however. For example, California prices were slightly lower than New York prices during this period (Grinnell, Dixon, and Linsdale 1937). For the 10-year period from 1930 to 1940, fisher prices in Ontario averaged nearly $49, with the yearly averages ranging from around $40 to around $53 (Rand 1944). The highest prices paid for excellent pelts were in the $75-to-$100 range (Rand 1944). In 1940 the average price paid in Ontario for fishers ($53) exceeded that paid for lynxes ($36), American pine martens ($30), beavers ($18), and silver foxes ($15) (Rand 1944), so it seems there was still considerable incentive for trappers to trap fishers. Fashions changed during the 1940s and the demand for fisher fur dropped. Consequently, by 1951 fisher pelts brought only $20 to $25; and by the late 1950s and 1960s less than $15 (Balser 1960; Brander and Books 1973; Hamilton and Cook 1955).

However, the demand for fisher fur has recently increased again, and prices during the late 1970s have set records. In 1979 the Hudson's Bay Company paid $410 for an excellent, pale-colored female fisher pelt! The average price paid that year was around $100, with the pelts of females averaging about $15 to $20 more than those of males (Anon. 1977a). Prices in 1978 were somewhat less (Max Bass, [a fur buyer], personal communication). The total numbers of fishers trapped and the average pelt values in Canada from the 1948-1949 through 1976-1977 trapping seasons are shown in Table 8.

Fishers have seldom been considered to be common animals anywhere. Nonetheless, changes in fisher populations have been noticed. The decrease in fisher populations began earlier in the eastern than in the midwestern and western states, undoubtedly because of the higher human population densities in the East. New York fisher populations had already begun to decrease by 1850 (Hamilton and Cook 1955), but the decrease in Wisconsin was not great before the first part of this century. In Wisconsin, 559 fishers were trapped during

Table 8. Numbers of Fishers Trapped and Average Pelt Values in Canada from the 1948-1949 through 1976-1977 Trapping Seasons.

Season	Number	Average Value ($C)
1948-1949	4407	27.42
1949-1950	2710	28.95
1950-1951	3707	24.80
1951-1952	5274	23.03
1952-1953	5533	20.30
1953-1954	5794	17.63
1954-1955	6790	22.75
1955-1956	6324	22.04
1956-1957	5076	19.20
1957-1958	5720	17.08
1958-1959	4850	17.33
1959-1960	6462	18.24
1960-1961	6206	11.05
1961-1962	5863	11.57
1962-1963	6254	10.84
1963-1964	8364	10.62
1964-1965	7950	8.33
1965-1966	8216	14.29
1966-1967	6856	10.97
1967-1968	5535	11.76
1968-1969	7627	17.69
1969-1970	8146	19.91
1970-1971	6637	26.59
1971-1972	8278	29.35
1972-1973	13,798	36.86
1973-1974	12,566	48.81
1974-1975	10,163	45.63
1975-1976	8698	80.82
1976-1977	9664	95.38

Source: Can. Min. Indus., Trade & Comm. Ottawa. 1978. Fur Production, Season 1976-1977, Table 4. Reproduced by permission of the Minister of Supply Services Canada.

the 1917-1918 trapping season; the following year, only 17 fishers; the next year, 5; and in the 1920-1921 trapping season, only 3 (Scott 1939). (Schorger [1942] noted that the 559 figure may be inflated since otters were sometimes reported as fishers.) Wisconsin closed its fisher season in 1921. There were scattered reports of fishers in Wisconsin for the following few years (Scott 1939), but by 1932 the fisher was believed to be extinct in Wisconsin (Hine 1975). A similar history is known for the fisher in Michigan. The last native fishers reported from Michigan were trapped during the 1931-1932 trapping season in the Upper Peninsula (Schorger 1942), although a few still may have existed as late as 1936 (Manville 1948).

Fishers were probably never completely exterminated from a few of the inaccessible mountain regions in the northwestern and Pacific coastal regions of the United States. Extremely small fisher populations were able to hold on in California, Oregon, and, perhaps, Washington (Schempf and White 1977; Yocum and McCollum 1973). However, the last reliable reports of native fishers in Montana and Idaho came from no later than the 1920s (Dodge 1977; Weckwerth and Wright 1968).

Because of warnings from biologists, other states followed the example set by Wisconsin and closed their fisher-trapping seasons. Minnesota closed its season in 1929; New Hampshire, in 1934; Maine, in 1935; New York and Wyoming, in 1936; and Oregon, in 1937 (Brander and Books 1973; Coulter 1966; Kelly 1977). Montana also closed its season sometime in the 1930s (Weckwerth and Wright 1968). However, despite warnings as early as 1925, California delayed closing its fisher-trapping season (Hall 1942). The number of fishers trapped in California dropped from 102 in 1920 to 34 during 1924 and did not rise above 20 after 1926 nor above 10 following 1933 (Hall 1942). By the time California finally closed its fisher season in 1946, no other states had open fisher-trapping seasons (Brander and Books 1973).

The decrease in the fisher population in Canada was more confusing than in the United States, but it was still obvious. Because of the large numbers of fishers trapped in Canada, the cyclic nature of changes in the fisher population over time showed up in the trappers' returns. This confused some people attempting to analyze the fisher-trapping returns. However, between 1920 and 1950 the number of fishers trapped, adjusted to the phases of the 10-year population cycle, declined by 75% in Ontario (deVos 1952; Rand 1944). Populations over all of Canada showed significant declines; the fisher-trapping returns for the entire country declined by approximately 40% between 1920 and 1940 (deVos 1952; Rand 1944). Fishers were completely exterminated from Nova Scotia (Bensen 1959; Dodds and Martell 1971; Rand 1944). However, along with the increase in pelt prices during recent years, recent fisher-trapping returns have nearly doubled those of the 1940s (Anon. 1978) (See Table 8).

At the same time the pressures from trapping increased, the fisher's habitat was destroyed. In New Hampshire, the forested area of the state was reduced to approximately 50% in the mid-nineteenth century from 95% 200 years earlier (Silver 1957). A similar reduction in forested area occurred over much of the northeastern United States at about the same time (Brander and Books 1973; Hamilton and Cook 1955; Wood 1977). Forests were cleared by loggers and farmers and in frequent forest fires (Hamilton and Cook 1955; Silver 1957). Land clearing in the Midwest occurred during the early twentieth century (Brander and Books 1973; Irvine, Bradle, and Magnus 1962; Irvine, Magnus, and Bradle 1964). "The forests of [Wisconsin and Upper Michigan] were cut over by the early 1900's and much of the area was burned over during and after the logging era" (Irvine, Bradle, and Magnus 1962; p. 2). Because of the fisher's preference for extensive forests with continuous canopy, there is no question that logging and the associated fires had an adverse effect on fisher populations. In some places, the loss of habitat may have been more devastating than the overtrapping (Hamilton and Cook 1955).

Either trapping or habitat destruction by itself could have dramatically reduced fisher populations. Together, their effect was extreme. During the 1930s, the remnants of the fisher populations in the United States could only be found on the Moosehead Plateau of Maine, in the White and Adirondack Mountains in New Hampshire and New York, in the "Big Bog" area of Minnesota, and in scattered regions of the Pacific coastal mountains (Brander and Books 1973; Coulter 1966; Ingram 1973; Schorger 1942). Canada's only remnant population in the East was on the Cumberland Plateau in New Brunswick (Coulter 1966).

Reintroduction and Recovery

With the closure of trapping seasons during the 1930s and the end of the big logging boom, fisher populations in those states with remnant populations began to recover (Balser and Longley 1966; Brander and Books 1973; Coulter 1966; Hamilton 1957; Hamilton and Cook 1955; Kelly 1977; Yocum and McCollum 1973). At the same time, there was an increase in forested area when some farmland in the Northeast was abandoned. New York felt that its fisher population had recovered enough to reopen its fisher-trapping season in 1949. Trapping seasons were reinitiated in Maine in 1950, New Hampshire and West Virginia in 1969, Massachusetts in 1972, Vermont in 1974, and Minnesota in 1977. Unfortunately, the populations have not remained stable. Maine reclosed its season from 1951 through 1954 and limited the harvest in 1977; New Hampshire reclosed its season in 1977; and New York limited its season in 1977.

Following the reduction in fisher populations, porcupine populations climbed to extremely high densities in much of the forested lands in the United States (Cook and Hamilton 1957; Earle 1978). Porcupines were blamed for much timber damage (Brander and Books 1973; Cook and Hamilton 1957; Earle 1978; Irvine 1960a, 1960b, 1961; Irvine, Bradle, and Magnus 1962; Irvine, Magnus, and Bradle 1964), though the damage was often exaggerated (Earle 1978). Earle (p. 7) summarized the damage as follows:

> The porcupine conflicts with human interests in its choice of winter foods. Consumption of the phloem disrupts the downward flow of sugars in a tree (Baldwin 1934). The resulting wound also provides an avenue for the entry of disease and insects (Frothingham 1915). Some species of trees respond to porcupine damage by impregnating the xylem beneath the surface of the scar with resin. An over-rolling of tissue from the perimeter of the scar is another method of responding to this damage, separately or in conjunction with xylem impregnation.

Many biologists have attempted to quantify economically the amount of damage that porcupines inflict on timber stands (Curtis 1944; Curtis and Wilson 1953; Krefting et al. 1962; Taylor 1935). This is difficult because porcupines also beneficially prune trees (Curtis

1941). However, damage does occur in areas with very high porcupine populations. Krefting and co-workers (1962) reported that porcupines damaged 9.4% of the trees sampled in an area where porcupine population density had reached 81.1 porcupines per square kilometer in 1948-1949. This is an exceptionally high porcupine population density, however, and the most common densities found during the 1940s and 1950s ranged from 7.7 to 22.4 porcupines per square kilometer (Brander 1973; Curtis 1944; Irvine 1960a).

During the 1950s, interest in reestablishing fisher populations in some of the fisher's former range began to increase. Blaser (1960), Coulter (1966), and Hamilton and Cook (1955) noted concurrent declines in the porcupine populations in those areas of Minnesota, Maine, and New York where the fisher populations were increasing. Cook and Hamilton (1957) suggested using fishers as a biological control for extremely high porcupine populations. They found during their study of fishers in the Adirondacks that high porcupine populations were never found in areas with fisher populations. Anecdotal evidence from trappers and loggers indicated that predation on porcupines by fishers was the reason for the low porcupine populations in areas with fisher populations (Cook and Hamilton 1957). Coulter (1966) warned, however, that there was no evidence that fishers could limit porcupine populations for long periods of time.

Nonetheless, during the late 1950s and early 1960s, many states whose fisher populations had been eliminated or dramatically reduced reintroduced fishers. The purpose of these reintroductions was twofold: to reestablish a native mammal and to reduce high porcupine population densities, which were believed to be causing damage to the timber crop (Irvine, Bradle, and Magnus 1962; Irvine, Magnus, and Bradle 1964). The latter reason was given the most emphasis. Most introductions involved the cooperation of state wildlife officials from recipient and donor states, U. S. Forest Service officials, and, in some cases, wildlife officials in Canadian provinces. The first release of fishers actually took place in 1947-1948 in Nova Scotia, where 12 fishers raised on fur farms were released (Bensen 1959; Dodds and Martell 1971). The release appears to have been successful since there were scattered observations of fishers in the area during the 1950s and early 1960s. Between 1963 and 1966, Nova Scotia released 80 more fishers that had been caught wild in Maine. The fisher now appears to have been reestablished in Nova Scotia (Dodds and Martell 1971), and in

1977 the first limited fisher-trapping season since the 1947 reintroduction was allowed in the province (van Nostrand 1977).

With the apparent success of the reintroduction of fishers in Nova Scotia and the suggestion that the fisher could be used as a biological control for the porcupine, many states in the United States initiated reintroduction programs. Between 1956 and 1963, Wisconsin released 18 fishers from the New York Adirondacks and 42 fishers from Minnesota into the Nicolet National Forest. Then, during 1966 and 1967, 60 more fishers from Minnesota were released into Wisconsin's Chequamegon National Forest. Both releases were successful, and the fisher is now well established in northern Wisconsin (Irvine, Bradle, and Magnus 1962; Irvine, Magnus, and Bradle 1964; Olson 1966; Petersen, Martin, and Pils 1977; U.S. Forest Service, unpublished files; Wisconsin Department of Natural Resources, unpublished files). During the same period (1961 to 1963), Michigan released 61 fishers from Minnesota into the Ottawa National Forest in the western Upper Peninsula, just across the border from the Nicolet National Forest in Wisconsin (Irvine 1961, 1962; Irvine, Bradle, and Magnus 1962; Irvine, Magnus, and Bradle 1964; Olson 1966). The Michigan release has also been successful (Brander and Books 1973; Irvine and Brander 1971; Powell 1976, 1977a, 1977b; Michigan Department of Natural Resources, unpublished files; U.S. Forest Service, unpublished files).

Montana, Oregon, and Idaho all cooperated with British Columbia to obtain fishers for release during the late 1950s and early 1960s. In 1959 and 1960, Montana released 36 fishers (Morse 1961; Weckwerth and Wright 1968), Oregon released 24 in 1961 (Kebbe 1961; Morse 1961), and Idaho released 39 in 1962 and 1963 (Dodge 1977; Morse 1961; Williams 1962). The Montana and Idaho releases appear to have been successful (Dodge 1977; Weckwerth and Wright 1968), but the reports of fisher sightings from Oregon are sparse and are mainly from the areas near the release sites (Yocum and McCollum 1973). Ingram (1973) believed that the transplanted fishers barely supplemented the existing population.

In 1969, West Virginia released 23 fishers from New Hampshire (Dodge 1977; Wood 1977). Unfortunately, due to a gross misunderstanding of the fisher by the citizens of that state, the 1971 West Virginia state legislature passed a law forbidding further releases of fishers into that state.

Fishers were probably never exterminated in Vermont. However, the population density was so low and emigration from established populations in nearby states so slow that wildlife officials decided to release 124 fishers from Maine in the state between 1959 and 1967 (Dodge 1977; Wood 1977). The population in Vermont appeared to be well established by 1974 (Dodge 1977).

Similarly, New York never lost its fisher population, and the population seems to have expanded its range during the 1970s. In 1975, state hunters agreed to an increase in license fees to cover the expenses of reestablishing fishers in the Catskill Mountains. By 1977, at least 24 of the planned 40 fishers had been transferred from the Adirondack Mountains to the Catskill Mountains (Kelsey 1977; Wood 1977).

The other eastern state that has a reestablished fisher population is Massachusetts. The highest fisher densities are in north-central Massachusetts, probably due to fishers that emigrated from Maine and New Hampshire (Dodge 1977). By 1977, there were scattered sightings along the coast north of Boston (Wood 1977), an area that has never supported a high fisher population (Dodge 1977).

There have been scattered sightings of fishers in Washington, and the fisher population in the far-northern counties of California appears to be growing (Schempf and White 1977; Yocum and McCollum 1973). Populations farther south in California, however, are either low and stable or low and decreasing, depending on how far south they are (Schempf and White 1977).

During the last decade or so, fishers have also occasionally been sighted in a few other states. Two fishers were taken in Wyoming during the 1960s and 1970s (Brown 1965; Dodge 1977). A fisher was trapped in far-northeastern North Dakota in December 1976 (Anon. 1977b), and a fisher was shot in Rhode Island in 1966 (Dodge 1977). Tracks were seen in Maryland in 1974 and 1975, and a fisher was trapped in Maryland in 1977; these all probably resulted from the West Virginia release (Cottrell 1978).

Thus, by the late 1970s, the range of the fisher had recovered much of the area lost during the first part of this century. There are areas to which the fisher will never return unless there are major changes in the habitat. Such midwestern states as Illinois, Indiana, and Ohio may never again have forested areas extensive enough to support a fisher population. But the fisher is again living in areas from northern British Columbia to northern California, Idaho, and Montana in the West, from northeastern Minnesota to Upper Michigan and northern Wisconsin in the Midwest, and in the Appalachian Mountains of New York and throughout most of the forested regions of the far Northeast (Balser 1960; Bradle 1957; Coulter 1966; Earle 1978; Irvine, Bradle, and Magnus 1962; Irvine, Magnus, and Bradle 1964; Kebbe 1961; Kelly 1977; Kelsey 1977; Morse 1961; Penrod 1976; Petersen, Martin, and Pils 1977; Powell 1976, 1977a; Weckwerth and Wright 1968; Williams 1962; Wood 1977).

Population Densities

Fisher population densities vary with habitat and prey. Most of the first estimates of fisher population density were obtained from trapping records and from tracking fishers in the snow (deVos 1951, 1952; Grinnell, Dixon, and Linsdale 1937; Hamilton and Cook 1955; Quick 1953a; Rand 1944), which are at best only indexes of actual densities. deVos (1952) interpreted fisher tracks to arrive at an estimate of 1 fisher per 2.6 square kilometers in his study area in Ontario. In contrast, Quick (1953a) estimated a density of approximately 1 fisher per 208 square kilometers from 20 fishers trapped along 1335 kilometers of registered traplines in British Columbia. Many other estimates have ranged from one extreme to the other. (See Coulter 1966.)

From the first long-term study involving both extensive trapping returns and extensive snow tracking, Coulter (1966) arrived at estimated fisher densities ranging from 1 fisher per 2.6 square kilometers to 1 fisher per 11.7 square kilometers of suitable habitat in Maine. The higher density figure was found in an area from which fishers had never been extirpated, and Coulter doubted that such a high density could be sustained. Kelly (1977) used live-trapping and radiotelemetry to arrive at figures of 1 fisher per 8.9 to 9.2 square kilometers in the White Mountains of New Hampshire. Adjusting this estimate to fisher density with respect to suitable habitat, he arrived at figures of 1 fisher per 3.9 to 7.5 square kilometers of suitable habitat. He also believed that such high densities could not be maintained, and he reported a decrease in the number of fishers in both New Hampshire and Maine since 1972.

Information on fisher densities outside the Northeast is limited.

Petersen, Martin, and Pils (1977), Earle (1978), and I (Powell 1977a) all estimated fisher population densities in northern Wisconsin and Upper Michigan to be at most 1 fisher per 13 square kilometers. These estimates were based on responses to questionnaires printed in magazines and sent to trappers, wardens, and county officials (Petersen, Martin, and Pils 1977); on state and federal records (Earle 1978; Petersen, Martin, and Pils 1977); and on findings from tracking and live-trapping (Powell 1977a).

The reasons for the varying densities reported are many. In areas of recent reintroduction (Michigan and Wisconsin), low population densities are probably related to a lack of time to build up large populations. In areas where fisher populations were reduced but not eliminated (California and Washington), a similar situation may exist. Population fluctuations in the Northeast probably stem from two causes. Fisher populations are known to exhibit 10-year cycles in densities (Bulmer 1974, 1975; deVos 1952; Rand 1944) in response to 10-year cycles in snowshoe hare population densities (Bulmer 1974, 1975). However, trapping in New England has at times been intense even during recent times (Young 1975), and overtrapping may again be reducing populations in some areas (Kelly 1977; Wood 1977; Young 1975).

Chapter 5

General Habits, Home Range, and Movements

The word *solitary* is subject to various interpretations. Animals are seldom completely out of contact with other members of their species, and, therefore, in the strict sense of the word they are never solitary. But, in general, *solitary* applies to an animal that goes about its daily activities by itself and is not in close physical proximity with one or more members of its species, except for reproductive purposes. Under this generally accepted interpretation of the word, fishers are quite solitary (Coulter 1966; deVos 1952; Powell 1977a; Quick 1953a). Occasionally, trappers have claimed that two or three adult fishers traveled together, but their reports are subject to question (deVos 1952; Quick 1953a). Outside the breeding season, a fisher may sometimes follow the trail of another fisher for short distances, but there is little evidence that fishers ever travel together (Coulter 1966; Powell 1977a; Quick 1953a). During the winter, their tracks are generally spaced out, and fishers appear to avoid close proximity to other fishers (Powell 1977a). Directed agonistic behavior has been observed between a captive adult female fisher and her young, among the young within captive litters five months old and older, and between two captive adult female fishers (Coulter 1966; Kelly 1977; Powell 1977a); these observations support the interpretation that fishers are solitary. Most fur farms have found it best to house fishers singly, but a few reports indicate that a single adult male and a single adult female have been housed in adjacent, connected pens for an extended period of time (Hall 1942; Hodgson 1937). Zoos have also been able to house two fishers of opposite sexes together for extended periods of time (Lincoln Park Zoo, Chicago Zoological Society, unpublished files; Bronx Zoo, New York Zoological Society, unpublished files), but this behavior may be an artifact of captivity.

The limited information available on American martens suggests more strongly that they are solitary animals (Hawley and Newby 1957). Wild American pine martens show social tolerance toward other martens only during the breeding season, and martens in the wild have been observed to show unsocial behavior toward other martens. When two martens meet, there may be growling from a distance, but the two individuals tend to avoid close approaches to each other (Hawley and Newby 1957). Because of the close evolutionary relationship between the American pine marten and the fisher, the pine marten's behavior supports the evidence that the fisher is solitary.

Home Range

Early estimates of fishers' home ranges from tracking data were substantiatially larger than those based on more recent data gathered by radiotelemetry. deVos (1952) and Quick (1953a) reported that fishers' home ranges were approximately 12 to 30 kilometers in diameter and so were approximately 100 to 800 square kilometers in area. These figures were obtained from tracks of what appeared to be the same fisher for several days and from trappers' reports of distances fishers were followed. Using similar data-collecting techniques, Hamilton and Cook (1955) estimated that fishers' home ranges were approximately 25 square kilometers.

During the winters of 1974-1975 and 1975-1976, I obtained sufficient radiotelemetric data to use the convex polygon method to estimate the home ranges of four fishers: one female and three males (Powell, unpublished data). My estimates of the sizes of the fishers' home ranges varied from 15 to 35 square kilometers, with the female having the smallest estimated home range. However, the female and one male with home ranges of similar sizes were only radio-tracked for approximately three weeks each and may not have been utilizing their entire home ranges during the time they were tracked.

The best data available on fishers' home ranges have been collect-ed by Kelly (1977). He was able to estimate home ranges by using the convex polygon method for six fishers from November 1973 to September 1974 and for five fishers from December 1974 to June 1975. Yearly sizes of home ranges varied from 6.6 square kilometers to 39.6 square kilometers, with an overall average of 19.2 plus or minus 12.1 square kilometers (the standard deviation). Adult and subadult females had similarly sized home ranges (average 15 square kilometers), which tended to be smaller than those of males, especially subadult males (the average subadult male's home range was 26 square kilometers; adult male's average home range was 20 square kilometers). Because of the small sample sizes and significant individual variability, these differences are not statistically significant.

Kelly (1977) was also able to estimate 24 monthly home ranges. Monthly home ranges were significantly smaller than mean yearly home ranges, but there were no significant differences in monthly home ranges by month, season, or sex or age of fishers. Nonethe-less, the monthly home ranges did appear to show a cycle with two peaks. Monthly home ranges tended to be small in midwinter, ris-ing to a peak during April, May, and June; decreasing during the rest of the summer and early autumn; and rising to the second peak during early winter. Kelly was unable to collect sufficient data to estimate the average sizes of monthly home ranges during March, October, and November. It would have been interesting to have data on the home-range sizes of females during the month of par-turition (presumably March). The increase in the mean size of monthly home ranges in April coincided with the breeding season.

Despite the fisher's apparent solitary nature, fishers' home ranges appear to overlap extensively. Coulter (1966), deVos (1952), Kelly (1977), and I (Powell 1977a) have observed that fishers' home ranges frequently overlap extensively, and none of us were able to determine any clear organization among the home ranges of individuals. There is evidence, however, that the apparent lack of a specific pattern among fishers' home ranges is due to the limited nature of the data and to inappropriate analyses (Powell 1979b).

Clark and Campbell (no date), Erlinge (1974, 1977), Hawley and Newby (1957), King (1975), Lockie (1966), and Moors (1974) have all found the same spacing pattern for American pine martens, least weasels, and short-tailed weasels. The males of these species behave

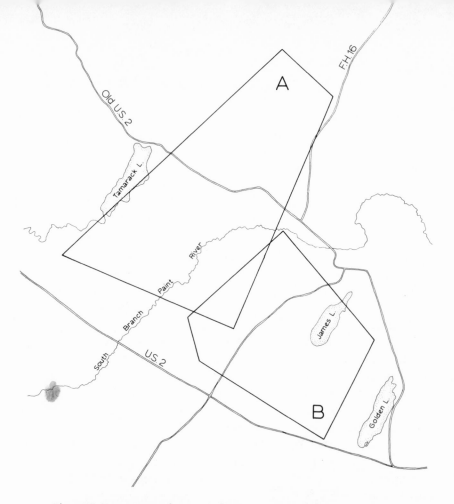

Figure 27. Home ranges of two male fishers (A and B) during the winter of 1975-1976 in the Ottawa National Forest, Upper Michigan. Note that the home ranges are almost completely nonoverlapping. The small overlap was created by a single location of fisher A inside fisher B's home range. (*C. B. Powell*)

territorially against other males and the females against other females, but there is extensive territorial overlap among members of opposite sexes. This pattern is called intrasexual territoriality (Powell 1979b). In these species, the males tend to have larger home ranges and the home ranges of the females are often located within those of the males. Evidence in the literature suggests that mink (Gerell 1970), black-footed ferrets (Henderson, Springer, and Adrian 1969; Hillman 1968), beech marten (Jensen and Jensen 1972), and wolverines (Krott 1959; Rausch and Pearson 1972) have the same type of social organization.

In most studies of fishers, it has not been possible to analyze the data on home ranges by sex. In tracking studies (Coulter 1966;

deVos 1951, 1952), the sex of individuals is unknown. Kelly (1977) did provide data on fishers by sex. Analysis of his data by sex for periods outside the breeding season indicates that fishers may have intrasexual territories similar to those found for American pine martens, least weasels, and short-tailed weasels. Least weasels' and short-tailed weasels' territories tend to break down during the breeding season (Erlinge 1974, 1977; Lockie 1966; Moors 1974). The failure to analyze data by sex, the failure to separate fishers' movements during the breeding season from the rest of the year, and the failure to allow for shifts in home ranges may explain why Kelly (1977) did not feel that there was a pattern to fishers' home ranges in his data. Buck, Mullis, and Mossman (1979) have preliminary data also suggesting the intrasexual territoriality of fishers in California.

Figure 27 illustrates the home ranges of the two male fishers for which I have over two months' worth of radiotelemetric data from the winter of 1975-1976. The period over which the data was collected was not as extensive as that for some of Kelly's (1977) fishers, but there was almost no overlap of the two home ranges. One of the home ranges overlapped extensively with the home range of a third male fisher that had been radiotracked during the winter of 1974-1975 and was no longer in the study area. It appeared that the two fishers whose home ranges are mapped in Figure 27 were the only male fishers living in the area during the winter of 1975-1976.

Fishers may communicate with other fishers by scent marking. Lockie (1964) found evidence of chemical communication among European pine martens. During the winter, fishers sometimes walk over and apparently drag their bellies on small stumps or mounds of snow that protrude from the surface of the snow (Figure 28). They usually urinate on the stump or the snow mound. Fishers also frequently walk along the tops of fallen logs or climb up on stumps. To date, no one has collected data on whether fishers react to marks left by other fishers. I did follow two sets of fisher's tracks, both of which walked over and showed signs of urinating on the same stump within the space of four days. I do not know whether the tracks were made by the same fisher or by two different fishers; in either case, this particular stump apparently was recognized by the animal or animals.

If fishers have developed some sort of chemical communication, they could be expected to mark prominent places (Ewer 1973). Marks on such places would be noticeable by olfaction and vision.

Figure 28. Small stump on which a fisher urinated. The fisher approached the stump from the right of the photo, apparently dragged its belly over the stump while urinating, and left going to the left.

If fishers do leave a scent mark from the glands on the central pads of their hind paws, the mark could be smelled from a longer distance when it is placed on top of logs and stumps than it could be when only placed on the forest floor. Answers to some of the questions about marking and chemical communication among fishers will shed light on the fisher's social organization as well.

Habitat

The preferred habitat for the fisher is continuous forest (Clem 1977; Coulter 1966; deVos 1952; Kelly 1977; Powell 1977a). Fishers have been found in extensive conifer forests (Cook and Hamilton 1957; Coulter 1966; Hamilton and Cook 1955; Kelly 1977), in mixed conifer and hardwood forests (Clem 1977; Coulter 1966; Kelly 1977; Powell 1977a, 1978a), and in open hardwood forests (Clem 1977; Coulter 1966; Powell 1977a, 1978a). They are always found in areas of continuous overhead cover. Though there have been infrequent reports of observations of fishers in bogs, on frozen lakes, and in burned-over forests (deVos 1952), fishers have an unexplained aversion to open areas (Coulter 1966; Kelly 1977; Powell 1977a, 1978a; Quick 1953a). This aversion may be responsible for the strange character of local distributions in some states. It appears that the Penobscot River limited the distribution of the fisher population in Maine (Figure 29) and delayed the geographic expansion of the population to the east side of the river by almost a decade (Coulter 1966). In Upper Michigan, the 1977 distribution of the fisher pop-

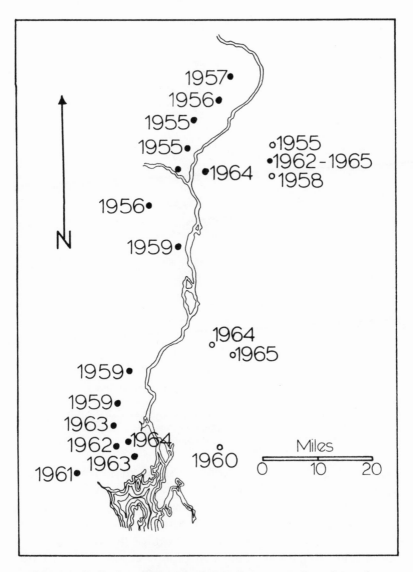

Figure 29. Distribution of fishers detected along the west and east shores of the Penobscot River, 1955 to 1965. The solid circles represent fishers trapped or collected, and the open circles represent track sightings only. Track sightings were not recorded for the east side of the river. By 1965, fishers had been trapped in 12 of the 18 townships on the east side of the river but in only from 1 of the 15 townships on the west side. (*Redrawn by C. B. Powell with the permission from M. W. Coulter, 1966, Ecology and management of fishers in Maine, Ph.D. thesis, by permission of the author*)

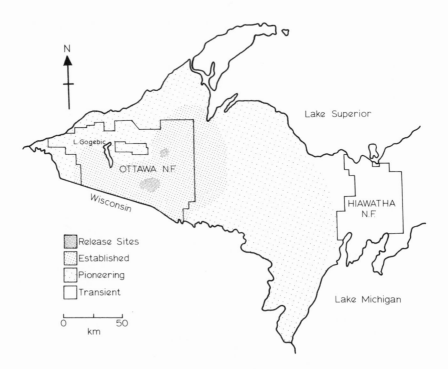

Figure 30. Distribution and abundance of fishers in Upper Michigan in 1978. Note the concave shape of the area of established population, which bends around Lake Gogebic and around the area of private lands in the middle of the national forest (this area is open farmland). (*Redrawn by C. B. Powell from R. D. Earle, 1978, The fisher-porcupine relationship in Upper Michigan, M.S. thesis, by permission of the author*)

ulation (Figure 30) had a concave shape that bent around a large area of open farmland and Lake Gogebic (Earle 1978).

The habitat preferences of animals are limited by the habitats available. The one clear characteristic of all habitats preferred by fishers is overhead cover, and, according to Kelly (1977), fishers selectively use habitats with high canopy closure (80% to 100% closure) and avoid areas with low canopy closure (less than 50%). High canopy closure is characteristic of dense lowland forests, and these are often the preferred habitat of fishers (Coulter 1966; Kelly 1977; Powell 1977a, 1978a). Fishers also appear to use areas with low canopies selectively (Kelly 1977), but this behavior correlates with the availability of lowland habitat with dense canopy cover and low height (Kelly 1977). In Maine, the percentage of fisher tracks found in spruce-fir forest types is greater than the percentage of forest cover that is of the spruce-fir type (Coulter 1966). Fishers also show strong selection for dense wetland forest types that are characterized by alder, with some cover by spruce, fir, cedar, and hardwoods. Wetland forest types also tend to be dense and have high canopy closure.

When selecting for areas with overhead cover, fishers select against habitats with less overhead cover. Open hardwood forest types are frequently avoided (Clem 1977; Kelly 1977), and, depending on the other available habitats, mixed hardwood-conifer forest types may be avoided when they are less dense than other habitats available (Coulter 1966). Nonforested areas are always avoided (Coulter 1966; Kelly 1977; Powell 1977a, 1978a), though areas that have been subjected to clear-cutting are only avoided during the winter (Kelly 1977). The reason for this is that during the summer clear-cuts have dense ground cover that fishers apparently perceive as giving adequate overhead cover (Kelly 1977).

The habitat preferences outlined above are found during all seasons for both male and female fishers, although female fishers may be less selective during the summer (Kelly 1977). There may be differences between the use of forest types for sleeping and for hunting, however (Kelly 1977). In New Hampshire, fishers tend to sleep in lowland, wetland, and conifer-hardwood forest types more than they use these types for hunting. deVos (1952), Coulter (1966), Kelly (1977), and Brander and I (Powell 1977a, 1978a; Powell and Brander 1977) have all found that hunting fishers will use both open hardwood and dense conifer forest types, though foraging strategies appear to be different in different habitats (Clem 1977; Powell 1977a, 1978a; Powell and Brander 1977). Fishers hunting in open hardwood forests during the winter often alter their direction of travel in order to travel through small conifer stands (Coulter 1966; Powell 1977a). This reflects their preference for conifer forest types. It is not known whether the directional change is connected with the availability of prey in different forest types, preference for overhead cover, or some combination of these and other factors.

Kelly (1977) investigated the relationship between the type of forest selected by fishers and the availability of small mammals (shrews, mice, and squirrels). He sampled small mammal populations with snap traps and pit traps in the major forest types in his study area during the autumns of 1974 and 1975. His trapping results were partially biased because slugs removed some of the bait in low wetland forests but this does not appear to have affected the qualitative results of the study. There were no significant differences in the number of small mammals trapped in the different forest types, but there were significant differences in the diversity of small mammals in the different forest types. Kelly measured diversity with the Shannon-Wiener information measure:

$$H_S = - \sum_{i=1}^{s} p_i \log p_i,$$

where H_S is a symbol of the diversity in a group of s species and p_i is the proportion or relative abundance scaled from 0 to 1 of the ith species. The measure H_S increases as the number of species increases and as the relative abundance of each species approaches the average relative abundance of all species. Those habitats with the highest diversity of small mammals were those habitats with many small mammal species all of similar abundance. Habitats with high small mammal diversity—wetland and mixed conifer-hardwood forest types—were preferred by fishers in Kelly's study area. The hardwood forests in his study area had less-than-average small mammal species diversity and were avoided by fishers. However, the clear-cut forest type had above-average small mammal diversity and was still avoided by fishers during the winter. Kelly believed that this was because of the lack of overhead cover in the clear-cut during the winter and the greater snow depth there that made small mammals less accessible.

Grinnell, Dixon, and Linsdale (1937) and Schempf and White (1977) reported that fishers in California are most commonly found in forests between 610 and 2440 meters in elevation. Forests at these elevations are commonly Douglas-fir and mixed conifer types. At least through the early part of this century, fishers were also found in areas as low as sea level in the northwestern counties in California (Grinnell, Dixon, and Linsdale 1937). The highest elevation recorded for an observation of a fisher in California was 3475 meters (Schempf and White 1977). Kelly (1977) found fisher activity predominantly between 300 and 900 meters in New Hampshire. Activity in New Hampshire did not correlate with forest type as it did in California because of the less dramatic vegetational changes with altitude in New Hampshire. Fishers in New Hampshire significantly selected for elevations below 600 meters and against elevations above 600 meters. There was no correlation between the elevation selected and the season, but there was between the elevation selected and the sex of the fishers. The mean elevation selected by males was 505 meters, and that of females was 556 meters. Kelly also recorded a significant difference in the elevation selected for a male and a female occupying mostly overlapping home ranges. He hypothesized that the selection of elevation within overlapping home ranges may be a means of maintaining exclusive home ranges in mountainous areas.

Activity and Movements

Fishers have been found to be active predominantly during the day, the night, and both day and night (Coulter 1966; deVos 1952; Grinnell, Dixon, and Linsdale 1937; Hamilton and Cook 1955; Pittaway 1978). Sightings of fishers during the day have been the most common evidence of the fisher's daytime activity. Nighttime activity has been deduced from the appearance of fresh tracks during the night and from observations at feeders. Coulter (1966) based his conclusion that fishers are predominantly active at night in part on observations of animals in captivity.

I was unable to find any readily apparent patterns in activity with respect to the time of day (Powell 1977a). Figure 31 shows the periods of activity of three fishers during five periods of extensive and continuous radiotelemetric monitoring. The fishers monitored

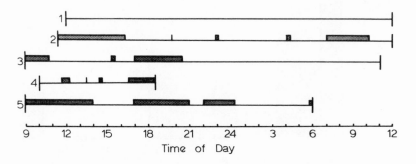

Figure 31. Fishers' activity patterns during five periods of extensive, continuous monitoring by radio. The broad blocks denote activity. Abscissa is time of day. Fishers were active both day and night and showed a small number of active periods that lasted for two to five hours each. The numbers preceding each bar are the same as the watch numbers in Table 13. (*C. B. Powell*)

were active both day and night and had a small number of activity periods (one to three) that lasted for 2 to 5 hours during each period of monitoring. These activity patterns are similar to those found for short-tailed weasels in Sweden (Erlinge and Widen 1975). I also noted the activity on 176 radiotelemetric locations of six fishers taken between 07:30 and 22:30 hours (Figure 32). The fishers were active on 56 locations (32%) and inactive on 120 (68%); activity during any one hour ranged from 0% to 100% of the time active. My hand-raised fishers were active at all times of the day and night, but my captive wild fishers in general only came out of their nest boxes during the night. This activity pattern of captive fishers and the fisher's general avoidance of humans has led me to question the conclusion made by Coulter (1966) and Pittaway (1978) that fishers may be predominantly nocturnal.

Leonard (1980b) obtained good data on the times a female fisher was at or away from her maternal den before her kits were weaned (Figure 33). Again, no readily apparent pattern of absence from the den and, hence, activity can be seen. However, the only possible pattern of activity that can be constructed from the data is that the female may have had a tendency to be in the maternal den during the early morning hours, some time between 24:00 to 06:00 hours.

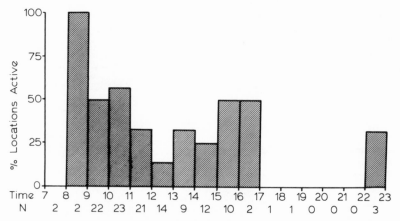

Figure 32. Percentage of 122 radiotelemetric locations that showed that six fishers were active. The locations are grouped in one-hour time blocks from 07:00 hours to 23:00 hours. The bottom row of numbers is the number of locations active during each one-hour block. Fishers' activity or inactivity was noted for 54 additional radiotelemetric locations for which the time of location was imprecise. (*C. B. Powell*)

During these hours, the ambient temperature would be at its lowest and the kits would presumably be in the greatest need of warmth from their mother. It was also during these early morning hours that the fishers I monitored showed the lowest amount of activity. (See Figure 31.)

Kelly (1977) was able to identify activity patterns during the day and different amounts of activity with changing seasons for his radiotracked fishers in New Hampshire. Those fishers showed activity peaks around sunrise and sunset during all seasons; they had a period of least activity between 08:00 and 12:00 hours. The fishers Kelly followed were much more active during all daylight hours during the summer than they were during the winter. During the summer the fishers were often active over 75% of the day, but during the winter they were seldom active more than 50% of the time. In general, there was little difference in activity between the sexes, although males tended to be more active during the morning and

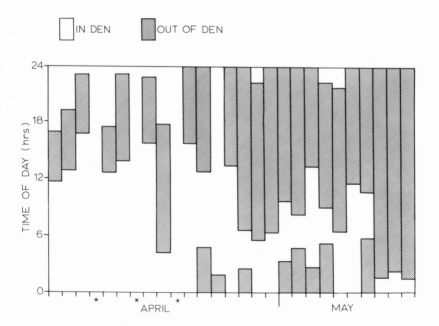

Figure 33. Times that a female fisher with kits spent in and out of her maternal den in Manitoba. On days marked with an asterisk, the female did not leave the den because she was disturbed by an observer. *(From R. D. Leonard, 1980, Winter activity and movements, winter diet and breeding biology of the fisher in southeast Manitoba, M.S. thesis, used by permission of the author)*

females during the evening peaks. These activity patterns are illustrated in Figure 34.

Fishers may travel long distances during short periods of time. deVos (1952) reported that a trapper followed a fisher approximately 97 kilometers during the course of three days. Hamilton and Cook (1955) reported that another trapper had followed a fisher for 48 kilometers during two days and that one fisher was known to have

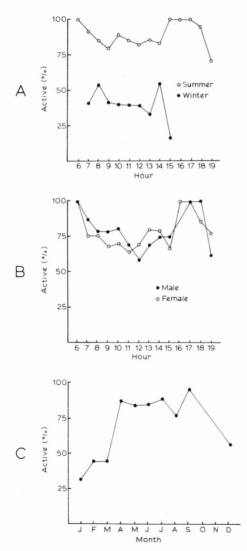

Figure 34. Fishers' activity patterns in New Hampshire, recorded by Kelly (1977). (A) Percentage of radiotelemetric locations that found fishers active, recorded by time of day and by summer or winter (summer is May through November; winter is December through April). Fishers were more active during daylight hours in the summer than in the winter. (B) Percentage of radiotelemetric locations that found fishers active, recorded by time of day and by sex. There was little difference in male and female activity patterns. (C) Percentage of radiotelemetric locations that found fishers active, recorded by month. (*From G. M. Kelley, 1977, Fisher* (Martes pennanti) *biology in the White Mountain National Forest and adjacent areas, Ph.D. thesis, used by permission of the author*)

traveled 10 to 11 kilometers in only a few hours. These long distances were undoubtedly caused partially by the fact that the fisher was being followed; less extensive daily travel is more common. Kelly (1977) found that straight-line distances between radiotelemetric locations for a fisher on two consecutive days averaged between 1.5 and 3.0 kilometers. Though the fishers may have traveled considerably farther than these distances, it is unlikely that any of them traveled 50 kilometers. Looking at averages for the entire year, Kelly found that there was a significant difference in activity by sex and by sex-age class. Adult males were the most mobile; and adult females, the least mobile. Subadults of each sex were intermediate. Kelly felt that sexual dimorphism in body size was largely responsible for the differences in movement. There was also a significant difference in mobility by month and a significant interaction of mobility with sex and season. Distances covered were greater during the winter months (when the average distance between locations was greater than 1.5 kilometers) than during the summer months (when the average distance between locations was less than 1.5 kilometers). Also, males moved significantly greater distances during the summer than did the females, and females moved significantly greater distances during the winter than they did during the summer. Kelly concluded that both of these latter patterns resulted from a female fisher's restricted mobility during the summer when she has young. The female's restricted mobility probably also influences yearly mobility and may explain why subadult females are more mobile than adult females. Daily distances covered peaked during May and then declined through the autumn months.

Kelly (1977) recorded minimum distances traveled between two consecutive radiotelemetric locations of the same fisher during the same diurnal period. Movements during a daylight period closely paralleled those during whole-day periods, except daylight movements averaged shorter distances and peaked during the summer rather than during May.

I tracked fishers to sleeping sites 32 times on 33 tracks; 18 tracks included no sleeping sites (Powell 1977a). Counting the tracks with no sleeping sites as one active period and the tracks with sleeping sites as being divided into the appropriate number of active periods, I obtained a minimum estimate of the distance traveled per active period of 2.5 kilometers. Figure 31 shows that the fishers I followed tended to have a small number of active periods each day. Assuming two active periods each day and 2.5 kilometers traveled per active period yields a rough estimate of approximately 5 kilometers traveled per day. This estimate agrees closely with Kelly's (1977) minimum estimate from straight-line distances.

Although Kelly's (1977) movement data do not show any special movements during March and April, his home-range-size data do show a seasonal peak during those two months. Coulter (1966) and deVos (1952) concluded that the fisher's activity is at its peak during that period. Coulter found that fisher tracks in Maine during these two months frequently showed much circling and backtracking, which made the track patterns so confusing that he was unable to discern exact temporal movement patterns. I found similar track patterns in Michigan (Powell, unpublished data). The highly circuitous patterns prevalent at this time of year might explain why Kelly (1977) did not record increased movement: a fisher's activity may be very concentrated in small areas, where it moves many kilometers in total distance but only a few kilometers in straight-line distance. Such track patterns are shown in Figure 35.

I was able to discern one activity pattern in two radiotracked fishers during the autumn and early winter. Their activity appeared to be centered around lowland conifer forest habitats. Each fisher spent several consecutive days in an area of this habitat type, moving only about 0.5 kilometers in straight-line distance between radio locations on consecutive days. After several days in a particular patch of lowland conifer habitat, the fisher moved up to 5 kilometers through upland hardwood forest to another patch of lowland conifer forest in which it spent another several days. This pattern was repeated many times with only minor changes (the number of days spent in each lowland conifer habitat varied, the distance through upland hardwood to another lowland conifer patch varied, et cetera).

deVos (1951, 1952) noted from trappers' reports that the fisher's movements appeared circuital. Depending on food and habitat, fishers visited a particular area at fairly regular intervals of time and appeared to make a circuit around their home ranges during these regular time intervals. Each circuit was from 65 to 160 kilometers long. Brander and I (Powell and Brander 1977) suspected that the fishers in our study area traveled circuits that brought them by porcupine dens at regular intervals, but we could not present any data

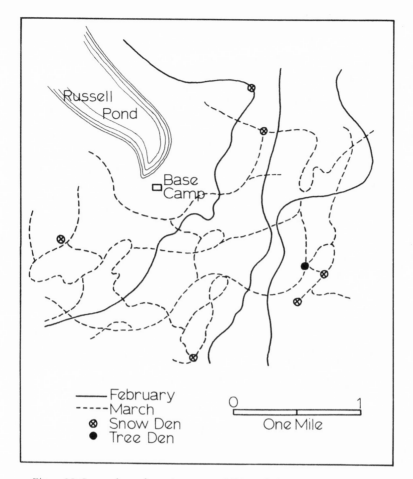

Figure 35. Comparison of travel patterns of fishers during three-day periods, February and March 1953. Note the circuitous track patterns for March compared to those for February. (*From M. W. Coulter, 1966, Ecology and management of fisher in Maine, Ph.D. thesis, used by permission of the author*)

to support that suspicion. Coulter (1966) did not mention such circuital movements for Maine fishers, although his data should have shown such patterns had they been present. Therefore, fishers in Maine probably do not travel in circuital patterns. Kelly's (1977) radiotelemetric data clearly show that fishers in New Hampshire do not travel in regular circuits.

Winter movements have been well documented by investigators who followed fisher tracks in the snow. deVos (1952, pp. 5-7) described one day's time spent in the field following a fisher track this way:

March 11th, 1949. The fresh tracks of a fisher, which crossed an old beaver house . . . in a creek, were followed. The animal covered about

1/3 mile running up a hill. After about 1/4 of a mile a fox track was noticed to approach the fisher track and to follow it for about 30 feet. The
fisher crossed several snowshoe hare, red squirrel and grouse tracks, without changing its course. Before it travelled another 1/3 mile its trail ran
into the track of a smaller fisher. The larger animal made a few jumps in
the direction in which the other was going, but subsequently proceeded in
the opposite direction. After following the track for another 1/5 mile,
urine was found on a little heap of snow along the trail. Farther on I came
upon four beds made in the snow close to each other. In one of these
several porcupine quills were found. The track subsequently turned in a
southeasterly direction and crossed the creek close to where it was first
picked up. The animal first crossed the creek about one and a half hours
after I passed there. It walked about 300 yards in the open part of the
creek valley and then dispppeared in a fringe of white cedar along the
opposite shore. This shore was followed partly under the cover of the
cedar and partly in the open. Track evidence indicated that snowshoe
hares were common under the cedars. The fisher followed their tracks in
several places, possibly in pursuit. At the mouth of the creek the tracking
work was given up for the day. The fisher was noticed to walk on top of
three logs during the entire tracking period.

deVos was able to follow fisher tracks along lakeshores during the
summer. The movement patterns he found did not appear to differ
between the summer and the winter. deVos (1952, p. 12) was able to
conclude from his tracking that:

> although the travelling may appear to be more or less random, it be-
> comes clear by following the tracks repeatedly that the animals have a de-
> tailed knowledge of the area covered. Short cuts across points in the lake
> and crossing of creeks are made at definite places, where frequently used
> trails can be seen. Occasionally an animal will back-track.

One of my more interesting days of fisher tracking went like the
following (Powell, unpublished field journal). (The pipeline mentioned in the journal is a 25-meter-wide, cleared right-of-way for a buried
gas pipeline that runs northwest-southeast.) The track is mapped in
Figure 36.

10 December 1974. I found a fisher track going south or southeast across
[Forest Road] 345 ca. 100 m south of the pipeline. The tracks looked no
older than night before last. The fisher was walking except for crossing
345. About 25 m east of 345 the fisher went up a hemlock and then
jumped off. There was lots of red squirrel sign in this area. 25 m further

east to northeast the tracks led into a large, fallen, hollow yellow birch and back out. Some 20 m more, the fisher dug about a 15 X 20 cm hole in the snow under a fallen tree. Another 10 m further easterly the fisher crossed a coyote track; the fisher went about 1 m beyond the track and then came back to sniff it (a spot in the snow looked like a nose print) and then took off easterly at a slightly faster pace.

The fisher reached an alder stand and headed south parallel to and ca. 10 m out of the alders in hemlocks. There was lots of squirrel sign here, too. The fisher suddenly turned 90° to the west, went some 5 m and appeared to have scavenged a grouse. There was very little blood and only a few breast feathers.

The fisher retraced its steps to the 90° turn and then continued south again for some 25 m. It turned into the alders (hare tracks all over) going southeast, turned south and came out of the south end of the alders not too far from where it had entered. Not too much further the fisher came to the north end of an open space with few standing trees. It went southeast through this area into a spruce bog with lots of hare sign.

Well into the bog the fisher ate part of a hare. There was very little blood so it seems as though the fisher found another old kill (scavenge) and finished off what was left. Skin may have been all that had been left.

The fisher continued southeast quite a ways through the bog to the southeast edge. In the bog near the edge it climbed on a big stump; I could not tell if it urinated. About 15 m further southeast it went into a large, hol-

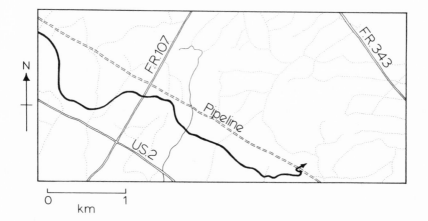

Figure 36. Map of fisher track described in the text. The dotted lines represent overgrown logging roads. The track was initially found where it intersected the old logging road just off the upper-left edge of the figure. (*C. B. Powell*)

low, fallen, very old white cedar. Then it headed out of the bog going southeast still.

The fisher went into an area with lots of [downed tree-tops from a logging operation]. Here it went over, around and through the tops, zig-zagging a lot. After one good sized zig-zag it dug a small hole but I could not see anything [in the hole, e.g., blood, mouse fur, etc.]. After going fairly straight for about 50 m beyond the tops, the fisher made a sharp turn back west, dug in the snow and deposited a scat. The scat contained seeds resembling apple seeds and smelled only faintly of the characteristic fisher scat smell. It urinated on a mossy rock at the same spot. It left the spot going southeast again.

After another 100 m the fisher turned abruptly north-northeast. At one spot it looked as though the fisher stopped and snuzzled [sniffed] after a mouse. There were small mammal tracks around a seedling and the fisher seemed to have sniffed the area thoroughly and dug a very little bit. A little further northeast the fisher came close to and ran parallel with [Forest Road] 107 in a northeasterly direction for some 50 m. Then it turned and crossed 107 about 50 m south of the pipeline. The tracks crossing 107 were fresh since when I drove down 107 in the morning of 9/12/74, so I may have picked up a day on the fisher.

The fisher headed almost due east from 107 into a spruce-fir stand. The fisher got pretty close to the pipeline. Here it defecated again. The urine was maybe 5 cm from the scat—male? The fisher ran on through the spruce-fir stand and then south down the east side. Shortly after this it came to 3 trees (8-15 cm dbh) with a similarly sized tree fallen against them at a height of about 1 1/2 m. The fisher climbed one of the trees at least to the fallen one and then walked down the fallen one.

Continuing southeast and east, the fisher climbed up on several stumps, all ca. 1 m in diameter. Then it crossed a creek. There was hare sign in the creek bed and in the alders and squirrel sign on the east side of the creek. The fisher ran some 25 m in a deer trail. Then it climbed onto more big stumps. Was it looking around? Was it looking for a specific stump? Some stumps were hollow, others not. Soon after this, the fisher caught a small mammal. The fisher was going east, then zigged back west-southwest. There was a little spot of blood and a small packed down area. The fisher made a tail swish in the snow.

About 50 m further east the fisher crossed [Forest Road] 504 about 150 m south of the pipeline, heading southeast. It dug at another spot and then 10 m further defecated again—this time urine was about 7 cm from the scat—probably a male. Shortly after this last scat the fisher defecated a 4th time, this one filled with what appeared to be vegetable matter. 25 m further southeast the fisher dug a 5 X 7 cm hole. Another 25 m and the fisher turned northeast, ran through an alder stand and out going east-southeast. There were a lot of Collembola in the snow and the weather was getting warm (ca. 5° C). The fisher defecated for a 5th time and then pulled its first real trick of the day. Two sets of tracks came together from opposite directions and one set of double tracks left going north. I followed the double tracks. They headed north and northeast to about 20 m from the pipeline then turned back west parallel to the pipeline. They went right to the pipeline, even walked to the very edge, then went back further west and into a spruce-fir type. Finally the double track crossed the pipeline in a narrow spot with spruce-fir types on both sides.

I stopped tracking at this point. During 6 hours and 15 minutes, I had tracked the fisher for approximately 8.5 kilometers.

Sleeping Sites

Fishers use a variety of sleeping sites. Most sleeping sites are temporary (Coulter 1966; deVos 1952; Powell 1977a), but some may be used more than once by the same fisher (deVos 1952). Hollow trees, logs, and stumps; brush piles; rockfalls; holes in the ground; and even abandoned beaver lodges are commonly used as temporary sleeping sites during all times of the year (Coulter 1966; deVos 1952; Grinnell, Dixon, and Linsdale 1937; Hamilton and Cook 1955; Powell 1977a; Pringle 1964a). Fishers sometimes make a very direct approach to a temporary sleeping site; this indicates that the location of the site may be known to the fisher (deVos 1952; Powell, unpublished data). During the winter, fishers often use snow dens (Coulter 1966; deVos 1952; Powell 1977a). Snow dens are burrows under the snow consisting of one or more tunnels leading 0.5 to 2.0 meters to a larger, hollowed space under the surface of the snow. During three years of fieldwork, I found 31 winter sleeping sites, all of them temporary and used for not more than a day. Of these, 10 were snow dens, 9 were hollow logs, 8 were holes in the ground, 2 were holes in trees, 1 was a hollow stump, and 1 was in a rockfall (Powell 1977a). Coulter (1966) and deVos (1952) found similar distributions of winter sleeping sites.

A den is used for various lengths of time, depending on the availability of food, the weather, and the condition of the fisher (deVos 1952). Fishers often den close to the carcass of a large food item (a dead deer or moose, for example) for many days until the food supply dwindles. deVos (1952) reported that some trappers believed that fishers even den up inside frozen carcasses, but there is no supporting evidence for this claim from other sources. Fishers den up for shorter periods of time by smaller carcasses (porcupines). I once found a fisher that had pulled a porcupine carcass into the hollow log it was using for a sleeping site. Fishers may den up for several days during a bad storm. deVos (1952) believed that fishers entered the closest available den when a storm began.

deVos (1952) interpreted his field results to suggest that fishers used a system of dens. He interpreted tracks to indicate that particular dens were used repeatedly by the same animal. He found that fishers used one den for several days and then switched to another permanent den. Coulter (1966) and I (Powell 1977a) were unable to find such a pattern in our field studies.

Arboreality

All martens (members of the genus *Martes*) have clear adaptations for arboreality (Leach 1977a, 1977b; Sokolov and Sokolov 1971), but this may be partially due to their relatively unspecialized limb anatomy (Leach 1977a, 1977b). (See also Chapter 2.) Early reports about fishers often emphasized their arboreal habits. Fishers can and do climb high into trees to reach holes and possibly to reach prey (Coulter 1966; Grinnell, Dixon, and Linsdale 1937; Leonard 1980a; Powell 1977a). Lewis and Clark stated in their journal that the fisher is marvelously adept at climbing (Haley 1975, p. 40) and chases prey from tree to tree (deVos 1952, p. 16). Ernest Thompson Seton (1926, p. 472) quoted Bachman, who recorded the killing of an Ontario fisher in this way: "A fisher was shot by a hunter named March, near Port Hope, who said it was up a tree, in close pursuit of a Pine Marten, which he also brought with it." Fishers in California have been observed to travel from tree to tree to avoid dogs and hunters, sometimes leaping great distances from the branches of one tree to the branches of the next (Grinnell, Dixon, and Linsdale 1937, pp. 224-25):

> The fisher was near a fir, up which it soon climbed about fifty feet.
> . . . From there on for one-fourth mile we were treated to a rare spectacle. The fisher traveled through the tree tops nearly as fast as we could

run. It leaped from a branch of one tree to a branch of another with the ease and assurance of a bird. It finally reached an extra large red fir with a heavy crown into which it ascended to within a dozen feet of the top.

Because of stories like these, to this day the popular literature describes fishers leaping through the treetops. The fisher has gained the reputation of being the fastest North American mammal and North America's most active arboreal mammal. For example, a photograph of a treed male fisher is shown in *Sleek & Savage* (Haley 1975, p. 53) and accompanied by this caption: "The fleet-footed fisher is the fastest tree-travelling animal." Morse (1961, p. 26) repeated the idea: "Fisher[s] are as much at home in the trees as on the ground; in fact, they have a reputation as the fastest tree-travelling animal, and will make long leaps from tree to tree in pursuit of prey."

Recent work, however, indicates that fishers may be less arboreal than the popular literature claims (Coulter 1966; deVos 1952; Powell 1977a, 1980b). During the winter in Maine, "most of the fisher's activity is terrestrial, but the animals do climb trees readily and sometimes often. Arboreal activity [is] variable between animals and perhaps with individuals at different times" (Coulter 1966, p. 62). The same holds true for fishers in Michigan (Powell 1977a). There is no recent evidence that fishers regularly climb from tree to tree through the branches (Coulter 1966; Powell 1977a, 1980b; Pringle 1964a). It is probable that the fishers in the early reports traveled through the trees only as a method of fleeing pursuers (who were on the ground, could catch them on the ground, but could not climb trees). If this is the case, it is probable that fishers seldom travel in this manner even though they are able to do so.

Fishers do frequently climb under and about in brush piles and downed treetops while they are hunting; and they do often jump or climb up on large stumps, fallen logs, and leaning logs. It is not uncommon for fishers to climb up a leaning log and jump to the ground from 1 to 2 meters.

It is likely that there is a sexual difference in the arboreal abilities of fishers (Leach, personal communication; Pittaway 1978; Powell 1977a). When fishers approach six months of age, the sexual dimorphism in body size has begun to develop and males become less adept at climbing (Powell 1977a). On the few tracks I followed for which I knew the sex of the fisher, a male fisher climbed a tree once out of six tracks, whereas females climbed trees on both of two tracks. Pittaway (1978, p. 488) observed a wild male fisher and a wild female fisher climbing the same tree: "The larger male climbed slowly and carefully and it was awkward on branches less than 6 cm in diameter. The smaller female climbed the same tree with much less difficulty and was a much more agile climber."

Swimming

Fishers are not known for their swimming, but there are scattered reports that indicate that fishers may swim at times. deVos (1952) recorded two observations of fisher tracks along a lakeshore that indicated that the fishers making the tracks had at least walked in the water. One of the tracks led directly from the water into the forest. Cahalane (1947), Hamilton (1943), and Seton (1926) all mentioned that the fisher is known to swim in lakes and rivers. More recently, some of the fisher home ranges plotted by Kelly (1977) had a river flowing through them. However, though the fishers crossed the river where it was narrow, farther downstream its size appeared to be a barrier the fishers could not cross. Coulter (1966) also observed that a river could act as a barrier to fishers' movements.

Chapter 6

Food Habits

The diet of any predator varies with the prey available to it. The availability of prey, however, depends on more than the simple abundance of prey (Charnov, Orians, and Hyatt 1976; Ewer 1973). Some prey are less easily found than others because of their coloration, hiding places, and other characteristics. Other prey are harder to kill once they are found because of their running ability or other defenses. And, once the prey have become alerted to a predator, they are less easily caught by surprise. Prey are also more or less palatable to various predators; therefore, predators may prefer to kill one type of prey over another. Predators learn techniques to catch particular types of prey and so catch some types more often than their relative abundance (compared to other prey animals) would otherwise indicate. All of these factors (the abundance, catchability, and palatability of prey and the predator's experience) undoubtedly determine the fisher's diet in different parts of the fisher's range.

Characteristics of the Fisher's Diet

Fishers are generalized predators. They eat any animal they can catch and overpower, and they readily eat carrion. All the fishers in a population eat the same prey species, and there do not appear to be fishers that cannot kill particular prey species. Because fishers are solitary hunters, the size of the prey they can catch is determined by their own size. Mammals that hunt in groups or packs can kill prey much larger than they are. Large mammals, such as adult deer and moose, obviously are too large for a fisher to kill; a fisher weighs only a small percentage of the weight of such mammals. Therefore, fishers are limited to hunting animals of approximately their own size and smaller (Rosenzweig 1966): prey that they can catch and handle without the help of other fishers. Fishers actively hunt only small- to medium-size animals.

All the predominant prey species fishers hunt are herbivores. Herbivores are generally adapted to escaping predation by fleeing rather than fighting. So, when a fisher is able to overtake a prey animal, the fisher has only to overpower it and does not have to be careful of the animal's fighting back. Other predators are only eaten by fishers as carrion, except, perhaps, the small weasels.

One species that is an obvious exception to the rule of fleeing herbivores is the porcupine. Porcupines are well armored with quills and do not depend on flight alone for escape from predators. Fishers use different techniques to kill porcupines than they use to kill other prey.

Early reports listed medium- to small-size rodents (such as mice and squirrels), hares and rabbits, birds (especially ruffed grouse), and porcupines as common food items for fishers (Coues 1877; Grinnell, Dixon, and Linsdale 1937; Hardy 1899; Quick 1953a; Schoonmaker 1938; Seton 1937). Recently, more specific data have supported the early reports (Table 9). These data have been collected from fishers' gastrointestinal tracts (G-I tracts) (primarily those obtained from trappers) and feces (scats) collected along fisher tracts.

deVos (1952) was the first to perform quantitative analyses of the fisher's food habits. Between 1939 and 1951, he obtained 50 fishers' stomachs from Ontario trappers and from the Royal Ontario Museum of Zoology. These were augmented by 32 intestinal tracts deVos collected between 1948 and 1951. Two of the stomachs were completely empty. In the rest of the G-I tracts, deVos found that snowshoe hares and porcupines were by far the most common food items. deVos suspected that trap bait was the source of the beaver and fish remains in his G-I tracts.

Hamilton and Cook (1955) made the next report on the fisher's food habits. During five trapping seasons (October through January) from 1949 through 1953, they obtained 65 G-I tracts from trappers in the Adirondack Mountains of New York. Of these tracts, 60 contained recognizable food items. In contrast to deVos's (1952) results, Hamilton and Cook (1955) found relatively few remains of snowshoe hares and porcupines. The most common food items in their fishers' tracts were mice, squirrels, deer, and a considerable amount of vegetation.

Coulter (1966) made the most extensive diet analysis to date. From 1950 through 1964, he was able to obtain 334 G-I tracts of fishers. These fishers had been trapped during the regular trapping season in Maine or were submitted to Coulter by Maine game wardens. The fishers were collected from almost all parts of the state, except the extreme southwestern corner. Of the 334 G-I tracts, 242 contained recognizable food items. Coulter also collected 135 fisher scats while tracking fishers in the eight areas where most of his fieldwork was done. Of these scats, 127 contained recognizable food items. The results of the G-I tract and scat analyses obtained by Coulter appear at first to be quite different. However, the relative amounts of non-scavenged prey (such as snowshoe hares, procupines, mice, squirrels, and birds) are similar in both the G-I tracts and the scats. It appears that a bias was introduced through the large number of scats retrieved from tracks located near deer and moose carcasses (Coulter 1966).

Stevens (1968) examined 174 fisher stomachs and 337 fisher scats for the New Hampshire Fish and Game Department. Twenty-one of the stomachs were empty. The stomachs were arranged by sex, and the scats were separated by calender season of the year. Stevens's diet analysis is one of the only two to find domestic animals (cats and chickens were the most prevalent). Stevens also found the highest incidence of vegetation, especially fruits and nuts, but this is because his is the only good sample of a summer diet. Fruit and nuts were found in 30% of the scats from the summer months.

Clem (1977) obtained 472 fishers' G-I tracts turned into the Ontario Ministry of Natural Rescources by local trappers during the 1973 and 1974 trapping seasons. The tracts came from the Algonquin region of Ontario. Clem separated them by sex and as being from one or the other of two study areas. Of the 472 G-I tracts, 270 contained recognizable food items. Snowshoe hares, porcupines, and birds were common foods for both male and female fishers in

Table 9. Food Habits of Fishers.

Food Item	Calif.[a]	Maine[b]	Maine[c]	Mich.[d]	N.H.[e]	N.H.[f]	N.H.[g]	N.Y.[h]	N.Y.[i]	Ont.[j]	Ont.[k]	Ont.[l]
Snowshoe hare	25 (2)	28 (67)	9 (12)	31 (11)	5 (7)	17 (58)	3 (3)	13 (8)	12 (40)	44 (25)	21 (25)	14 (21)
Porcupine	(3)[s]	26 (62)	9 (12)	20 (7)	3 (5)	(1)		8 (5)	6 (21)	35 (20)	32 (38)	20 (31)
White-tailed/ black-tailed deer	25 (2)	24 (59)	50 (63)	20 (7)	7 (11)	11 (37)	2 (1)	18 (11)	19 (61)	22 (8)	3 (3)	8 (12)
Mice		23 (55)	6 (8)	20 (7)	24 (37)	36 (121)	50 (20)	23 (14)	(66)[s]	9 (5)	11 (13)	16 (25)
white-footed	25 (2)	7 (14)	2 (2)		14 (21)	16 (53)	17 (7)	7 (4)	5 (17)		6 (7)	12 (18)
red-backed		6 (16)			5 (8)	15 (50)	30 (12)	17 (10)	3 (11)	9 (5)		
meadow		5 (11)	4 (5)						9 (30)		5 (6)	5 (7)
misc. & unident.	12 (1)	5 (11)	1 (1)		5 (8)	8 (28)	2 (1)		(8)[s]			
Shrews/moles		24 (58)	6 (8)	8 (3)	12 (18)	52 (176)	12 (5)	13 (8)	(22)[s]	7 (4)	8 (9)	8 (12)
short-tailed shrew		12 (29)			5 (7)	50 (168)	2 (1)	13 (8)	2 (8)	4 (2)	5 (6)	4 (6)
masked shrew		2 (4)			1 (1)	2 (8)	10 (4)		1 (4)	4 (2)	3 (3)	4 (6)
misc. & unident.	12 (1)				7 (10)				(10)[s]	10 (25)		
Squirrels	12 (1)	19 (45)	9 (11)	14 (5)	16 (25)	21 (70)	20 (8)	18 (11)	(73)[s]	4 (2)	3 (4)	3 (5)
red		10 (23)	1 (1)		7 (10)	11 (36)	12 (5)	17 (10)	20 (63)	2 (1)	2 (2)	1 (1)
flying		8 (19)	6 (8)		2 (3)	6 (20)	5 (2)	2 (1)	(1)	2 (1)	1 (1)	1 (1)
eastern chipmunk		(1)	2 (2)			4 (14)			1 (4)		1 (1)	2 (3)
gray and fox	12 (1)	1 (2)			8 (12)		2 (1)		2 (5)			
Muskrat[m]		(1)			4 (6)	1 (3)	7 (3)	2 (1)	5 (17)			
Raccoon[m]		1 (3)	4 (5)		4 (6)	(1)	5 (2)		1 (3)		3 (4)	
Beaver[m]		1 (2)	6 (7)				5 (2)		2 (6)	2 (1)		
Moose		2 (5)								2 (1)		
Misc. & unident. mammals[o]	(8)[s]	7 (18)	6 (8)	14 (5)	25 (37)	(1)	7 (3)	2 (1)	(148)[s]	9 (5)	23 (27)	22 (34)
Birds		24 (58)	8 (10)		30 (47)	18 (61)	15 (6)	12 (7)	(27)[s]	11 (6)	16 (17)	8 (13)
blue & gray jays		7 (17)					2 (1)	5 (3)	(1)			
ruffed grouse		2 (5)	2 (3)		12 (18)		2 (1)	5 (3)	3 (11)	4 (2)	9 (10)	14 (21)
misc. & unident.[p]		15 (36)	6 (7)		19 (29)		19 (4)	2 (1)	(15)[s]	7 (4)		

Table 9—*Continued*

Food Item	Calif.[a]	Maine[b]	Maine[c]	Mich.[d]	N.H.[e]	N.H.[f]	N.H.[g]	N.Y.[h]	N.Y.[i]	Ont.[j]	Ont.[k]	Ont.[l]
Misc. & unident. vertebrates[q]	(7)[s]	2 (4)			4 (6)	3 (11)		2 (1)	(10)[s]	12 (7)	13 (15)	12 (18)
Arthropods	(3)[s]	3 (7)			5 (8)	4 (15)		3 (2)	(9)[s]	21 (12)		
Plant material[r]	(8)[s]	3 (7)	15 (19)	6 (2)	33 (51)	24 (82)	12 (5)	32 (19)	(204)[s]			

Note: For each entry, the first number is the percentage occurrence of remains of that prey type in gastrointestinal tracts or scats for that study, and the second number (in parenthesis) is the actual number of G-I tracts or scats containing remains of that prey type.

[a] Grenfell and Fasenfest 1979, 8 stomachs collected, 1977-1978.
[b] Coulter 1966, 242 G-I tracts collected, 1950-1964.
[c] Coulter 1966, 127 scats collected, 1950-1964.
[d] Powell 1977a, 35 scats collected, 1974-1976.
[e] Stevens 1968, 153 stomachs collected in 1968.
[f] Stevens 1968, 337 scats collected in 1968.
[g] Kelly 1977, 40 G-I collected, 1973-1974.
[h] Hamilton and Cook 1955, 60 G-I tracts collected, 1949-1953.
[i] Brown and Will 1979, 332 G-I tracts collected, 1975-1977.
[j] deVos 1952, 57 G-I tracts collected, 1939-1951.
[k] Clem 1977, 117 male G-I tracts collected, 1973-1974, in Algonquin region.
[l] Clem 1977, 153 female G-I tracts collected, 1973-1974, in Algonquin region.
[m] Includes bait.
[n] Miscellaneous and unidentified mice: southern bog lemming, woodland jumping mouse, meadow jumping mouse, house mouse, western harvest mouse, unidentified.
[o] Miscellaneous and unidentified mammals: moles, cottontail rabbit, mink, red fox, American pine marten, weasels, otter, caribou, fisher, skunk, woodchuck, domestic mammals, unidentified.
[p] Miscellaneous and unidentified birds: red-breasted nuthatch, thrushes, owls, black-capped chickadee, downy woodpecker, yellowshafted flicker, sparrows, dark-eyed junco, red-winged blackbird, starling, crow, ducks, domestic chicken, unidentified.
[q] Miscellaneous and unidentified vertebrates: snakes, toads, fish, unidentified.
[r] Plant material: apples, winterberries, mountain ash berries, blackberries, raspberries, strawberries, cherries, beechnuts, acorns, swamp holly berries, miscellaneous needles and leaves, mosses, club mosses, ferns, unidentified.
[s] Estimated from tables in sources.

Clem's sample. The high occurrence of muskrat in the G-I tracts was probably from trap bait (Clem 1977).

Kelly (1977) analyzed 40 G-I tracts from fishers trapped in New Hampshire. Three-quarters of the tracts came from northern New Hampshire, and all contained food items. Mice and squirrels were the most common foods in his sample.

During the winters of 1973 through 1976, I collected 35 scats along over 150 kilometers of fisher tracks in Upper Michigan (Powell 1977a, 1978a). All of these contained recognizable food items. Remains of snowshoe hares, porcupines, deer, and mice were the most common.

The two most recent fisher diet studies were done in New York (Brown and Will 1979) and California (Grenfell and Fasenfest 1979). Brown and Will obtained 405 fishers' G-I tracts from trappers during 1975 through 1977. Of the 405 tracts, 322 contained recognizable food items. Although their results are qualitatively very similar to the results of Hamilton and Cook (1955), this recent New York study points out clearly the opportunistic nature of the fisher's eating habits. Because of the large number of G-I tracts they used and the detailed analyses they made, Brown and Will were able to find a much wider variety of foods than has been found in any other study.

It is unfortunate that the only study of the food habits of West Coast fishers was limited to the analysis of eight G-I tracts. Grenfell and Fasenfest (1979) found a high frequency of plant material, a large amount of which was mushrooms (false truffles). Black-tailed deer and mice were also common food items; deer and domestic cattle were probably taken as carrion.

Noting the frequency of the occurrence of different foods (the percentages of the total number of G-I tracts or scats that contain a given food type) is one of the most common methods of describing the diets of carnivores. This method is often used in conjunction with the total volume of each type of food found in the tracts or scats or in conjunction with minimum or maximum number of prey individuals estimated present in the samples. Even so, these methods are at best only indexes of foods eaten and are not precise, quantitative measurements of the relative amounts of various foods eaten. These methods *do* give a qualitative measurement of the foods eaten in a particular place at a particular time.

G-I tracts and scats contain those parts of animals that are most resistant to digestion. Therefore, those food items with a relatively large proportion of undigestible parts are overrepresented in tracts and scats. Small mammals and birds have more fur/feathers and bones than large mammals because small mammals and birds have larger surface-to-volume ratios. In addition, small food items are eaten whole, whereas large food items are selectively eaten, reducing still further the amount of recognizable remains to be found in tracts and scats. Floyd, Mech, and Jordan (1978) have shown that in wolf scats the weights of the remains of small mammals are overrepresented and the number of individuals distinguishable are underrepresented compared to large food items. Similar results have been obtained for the remains of prey in red fox scats (Lockie 1959; Scott 1941). A quantitative analysis of scat or G-I tract contents and weight of prey has yet to be performed for fishers.

A list of the foods identified from fecal remains or G-I tract contents gives little information about where foods were obtained, when they were obtained, or how they were obtained. Coulter (1966) gave the example of a hunter looking at Table 9 and concluding that fishers are a major predator on white-tailed deer in Maine. The hunter's conclusions would be strengthened by the popular literature, which exaggerates the predatory habits of fishers. Our data on the fisher's habits and our familiarity with the tracks from which scats were collected led Coulter (1966), deVos (1952), Kelly (1977), and me (Powell 1977a) to conclude that the remains of such large food items as deer and moose in fishers' scats and G-I tracts resulted solely from scavenging.

Almost all of the G-I tracts collected for the studies listed in Table 9 were obtained from trappers during legal trapping seasons. Trap bait is commonly found in G-I tracts of such animals, and this increases the difficulty of distinguishing between kills initiated by fishers and items obtained as carrion. As Kelly (1977, p. 97) pointed out, however, "Trap-bait is a legitimate component of the fisher's diet during the trapping season." That fishers are easy to trap (Young 1975), that they readily take trap bait, and that they habitually scavenge on deer carcasses suggest that fishers have a predilection to consuming carrion. Kelly (1977, p. 97) continued:

Before Europeans populated North America, ungulates were regularly cropped by carnivores capable of killing them and by normal winter mortality; thus carrion was probably more available on a regular basis than it has been in modern times. Man has reduced or eliminated most large carnivores and removes the yearly ungulate crop from the fisher's environment, leaving only incidental hunting losses and, because of management, minimal winter mortality. The fisher must therefore be more dependent on availability of prey species that it can kill than it once was; these prey species may be primarily on a seasonal basis. Unfortunately, seasonal abundance of carrion coincides with the trapping season, when material is most readily obtainable for food-habits analysis.

Trap bait and carrion may not be quite the problem that Kelly implied they are. First, because bait is a legitimate component of the fisher's diet during the trapping season, it must be acknowledged. It would be desirable to obtain an estimate of how much is carrion scavenged from other sources. The two scat analyses listed in Table 9, though more limited in scope than most of the G-I tract analyses, do not differ in a substantial qualitative manner from the G-I tract analyses. In addition, information from the kills and scavenges I gathered along fisher tracks agrees qualitatively with the G-I tract analyses (Powell 1977a, 1979a). All of the evidence suggests that fishers eat those medium- to small-size mammals and birds and the carrion that they can find in their habitat.

Second, fishers do not have a source of carrion that Kelly (1977) did not mention: deer and other animals that are killed along highways. Highway deer kill is a source of carrion that is totally unrelated to the trapping season and has peaks at different times of the year than the peak of trap bait as a source of food. Bashore (1978) showed that the number of highway-killed deer has seasonal spring and autumn peaks all over North America. The spring peak is the higher peak and does not coincide with trapping seasons. Earle (1978) found that spring highway kill of porcupines was substantial enough to be used as an estimate of several populational and demographic parameters. I suspect from the location of the deer carcasses I found during my study that most dead deer found by fishers in my study area were killed on the highway.

The Fisher's Prey

Snowshoe Hares

Remains of snowshoe hares (Figure 37) are the most common

items found in fishers' G-I tracts and scats. The species range of the snowshoe hare is coincident with almost the entire fisher species range (Figure 38), and, therefore, the snowshoe hare should be expected to occur frequently in the diets of fishers. Trappers generally believe that the snowshoe hare is the fisher's most common food (deVos 1952; Hamilton and Cook 1955; Young 1975), and they occasionally use hares for bait. Such use is not common enough to influence the incidence of hare remains in fisher scats and G-I tracts to any significant degree. It is notable that there is a range of occurrence of snowshoe hare remains in fisher scats from 7% to 44%, and there appears to be a correlation between low incidence of snowshoe hare remains and high incidence of bird, deer, mouse, and squirrel remains (Table 9). Snowshoe hare populations are known to have an approximate 10-year cycle in population size. Hare-plant interactions best explain the cycle (Keith and Windberg 1978), but hare-predator interactions and even sunspots and moon cycles have been mentioned in explanations of the cycles (see Archibald 1977; Bulmer 1974, 1975; Keith 1963). Fisher populations follow a cycle approximately 3 years behind the hare cycle. This is the expected timelag for a predator on which a shortage of prey has the greatest effect through increased juvenile and adult mortality and not through depressed reproduction (Bulmer 1975). The alternation of hare remains with other prey species's remains in fishers' G-I tracts and scats may reflect different phases of the hare cycle, or it may simply reflect generally low hare populations in some study areas.

Hares utilize a variety of habitat types (Keith and Windberg 1978), but areas with sparse cover appear to be poor hare habitat (Keith 1966). Hares tend to concentrate in conifer and dense lowland vegetation during the winter (Coulter 1966; Keith 1966; Powell 1977a, 1978a; Powell and Brander 1977; Wolff 1975) and to avoid open hardwood forests (Powell 1977a, 1978a). Fishers often hunt in those forests utilized by hares (Chapter 5; Clem 1977; Coulter 1966; Kelly 1977; Powell 1977a, 1978a; Powell and Brander 1977) and may direct their travel toward those forest areas (Chapter 5; Coulter 1966; Kelly 1977). Hares rest in well-protected hiding places such as under boughs, brush, and fallen logs. They generally remain motionless until approached closely by a predator. Coulter (1966), however, felt that in areas frequented by fishers hares became wary and fled more quickly when they preceived danger.

Figure 37. A snowshoe hare in white, winter pelage.

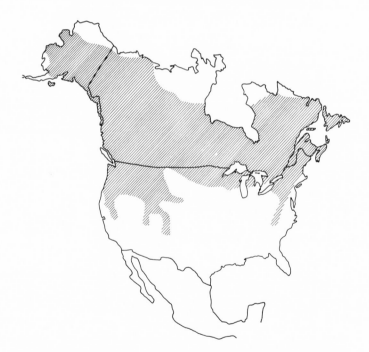

Figure 38. Map of the species range of the snowshoe hare. Note the broad over-lap of this range with that of the fisher (shown in Figure 26). (*From W. H. Burt and B. P. Grossenheider, 1964,* A Field Guide to the Mammals, *2nd ed., Houghton Mifflin Company, New York,* © *1952, 1964, 1976 by William Henry Burt and Richard Phillip Grossenheider, reproduced by permission of the publisher*)

Figure 39. A porcupine leaving its winter den.

Porcupines

The fisher-porcupine relationship is discussed specifically in Chapter 8; therefore, this discussion will be brief.

Porcupines (Figure 39) have received by far the most attention of any of the fisher's prey. Both the popular literature and the early scientific literature emphasize the fisher's ability to kill porcupines. Porcupines are an important food for fishers, and the frequency of their occurrence in the fisher's diet samples is as high as 35% (Table 9). But porcupine remains are seldom as common as hare remains and are even completely absent from one diet sample; this is the never the case with snowshoe hares.

The importance of the porcupine as a prey animal for the fisher is reflected in the evolution of the unique hunting and killing techniques used by fishers on porcupines (Chapter 8). By developing these techniques, fishers have acquired a prey for which they have almost no competition. The importance of this fact cannot be overlooked and should not be underemphasized. Though the popular literature may have overemphasized the porcupine as a fisher food, that overemphasis may not be completely out of line.

Figure 40. Deer carcass used extensively by a fisher. The fisher slept in the vicinity of this carcass for several days and is responsible for much or most of the packed snow, scattered hair, and scattered bones around the carcass.

White-Tailed Deer

Remains of deer (Figure 40) were found in G-I tracts and scats in all the studies listed in Table 9. In those studies in which deer remains were common, however, the total volume of deer remains was small in comparison to its incidence (Clem 1977; Coulter 1966; deVos 1952). Coulter (1966, p. 113) observed that fishers "returned to the remains of deer carcasses long after all edible parts were gone. They dug about the sites, carried tufts of hair and bones for short distances, and hunted intensively in the immediate areas." Coulter and I have both observed that fishers habitually paw in the snow around the places where deer died, picking up small pieces of hide with hair. Some fishers may have deer hair in their digestive tracts and scats almost all winter and still have eaten few meals of venison.

I found that deer carrion is an important component in the diet of fishers in Upper Michigan (Table 9), but I felt that its importance may have been overemphasized in the scat analysis because of the small number of scats I analyzed. Deer remains occurred almost exclusively in the scats of a few fishers that were tracked in the vicinity of deer carcasses (Powell 1977a). Coulter (1966) also felt that deer and moose might have been overestimated in his scat analysis because of the location of the fisher tracks around deer and moose carcasses.

No recent research has been able to substantiate the secondhand reports of Hardy (1899, 1907) that fishers can kill healthy adult deer. Coulter (1966) devoted particular attention to fisher-deer relationships in order to clarify the falseness or reality of such reports. He questioned more than 100 game wardens from the Maine Department of Inland Fisheries and Game and 14 field biologists. None had ever observed a single instance of a deer having been killed by a fisher. Coulter also spent considerable time in deeryards during the periods of deepest snow. During these times, the deer were confined to deep, narrow paths in restricted areas. Fishers did hunt in these areas for other prey, but "they did not hunt deer" (Coulter 1966, p. 114). McCord (1974) found deer remains in almost 80% of the bobcat scats he collected while studying the bobcat's predatory behavior in relation to its habitat. His data showed that the high incidence of deer remains in his bobcat scats *was* due to the bobcats' predation on deer and not from scavenging of deer carrion. Marston (1942) reported similar results in his study of the bobcat's predation on deer. It is likely that, if fishers actively hunted deer, deer remains in fisher G-I tracts and scats would be consistently more common and would be found in greater volumes than those reported.

It should be noted, however, that Pringle (1964b) recorded a secondhand report of a fisher "about the size of a small fox" attacking a white-tailed deer fawn that was "only a few days old." The observers chased the fisher away from the fawn, which died a few days later in captivity. Fishers may occasionally attempt to kill very young fawn when their mothers are absent, but this is the only possible source of active fisher predation on deer.

Mice

As a group, many species of mice appear in fishers' G-I tracts and scats almost as frequently as snowshoe hares. White-footed mice, red-backed voles, and meadow voles are the most common mice found in fishers' diets and are generally the most common mice in the fisher's habitat. Mice are probably not as important to fishers as the frequency of their occurrence in the diet samples indicates. Because they are small, have a relatively large amount of fur and bones, and are eaten whole, mice are overrepresented in the G-I tracts and scats of fishers.

Mice are often active on the surface of the snow during the winter, especially white-footed mice and red-backed voles (Coulter 1966; Powell 1977a, 1978a). Mouse tracks can frequently be seen on the snow's surface between mouse-size holes that descend to the surface of the ground. These holes are usually located around trees, shrubs, and sticks protruding above the surface of the snow. When the snow is deep, meadow voles tend to use runways beneath the surface and in some areas may girdle many shrubs along their runways (Craighead and Craighead 1956). Fishers may catch mice on the snow's surface or dig into the snow after them during the winter. Meadow voles are probably less common in the fisher's diet than the other two species of mice because of their low relative abundance and because they are much less active on the surface of the snow (Table 9).

Shrews

Shrews are found with unexpectedly high frequencies in the G-I tracts and scats of fishers. In general, carnivores are reluctant to attack shrews (Jackson 1961). Lockie (1961) concluded that insectivores are distasteful to carnivores, and many mammalian predators are reluctant to eat shrews even after they have been killed (Lockie 1961; Lund 1962; Jackson 1961). Insectivores only appear consistently in most carnivores' diets when other small mammals are scarce (Lund 1962). Weasels, however, are known to eat shrews more frequently than most other carnivores (Aldous and Manweiler 1942; Glover 1942; Hamilton 1933).

Coulter (1966) found abundant signs of shrews under fallen trees, under accumulations of forest litter, and in ground cover. Such places are often inspected by fishers while they are hunting, and this fact may help to explain the high incidence of shrews in fishers' diets. Shrews are often active during periods of extreme cold (Getz 1961) and, therefore, may sometimes be relatively abundant locally. Thus, though shrews are probably overrepresented in fishers' G-I tracts and scats because of their size, fishers (unlike other carnivores) apparently still catch and eat shrews whenever they can find them.

Squirrels

Squirrels are common mammals throughout the fisher's range but are fed upon less heavily than mice. Red squirrels and flying squirrels are found over more of the fisher's range and are, therefore, fed upon more often than gray squirrels and fox squirrels. Because diet analyses have all been done on winter diets, chipmunks and other hibernating ground squirrels do not show up as frequently in the diet as they might in a summer diet study.

Red squirrels are common residents of northern coniferous forests and so are present in areas hunted heavily by fishers. Coulter (1966) felt that the difference in times of activity for fishers and red squirrels was the primary reason that squirrels were not eaten more often in Maine. Coulter also noted that red squirrels are not particularly vulnerable in the trees. Jackson (1961, p. 174) stated that "natural enemies seldom capture a red squirrel."

Flying squirrels can be very abundant locally, but their nocturnal habits make population sizes difficult to estimate. Fishers may capture flying squirrels in nest holes in trees (Coulter 1966) or on the ground (Powell, unpublished data).

Birds

Although I found no evidence that fishers eat birds in Michigan, all the other diet studies listed in Table 9 show that birds are often eaten by fishers. Jays and ruffed grouse, common winter birds in the fisher's range, are the birds most commonly eaten by fishers. Jays are habitual scavengers, as are fishers, and it is likely that fishers capture some jays around deer carcasses and other carrion on which they are both scavenging. Grouse frequently rest beneath the snow and may be vulnerable to predation at these times. Brander and Books (1973) and Coulter (1966) could find no evidence that fishers hunted for or ever captured grouse in their snow roosts, however.

Plant Materials

Vegetation of some sort has been found in all studies of the fisher's diet. Coues (1877) wrote that fishers sometimes are forced to eat beechnuts when other food is scarce. The popular press has repeated the fact that fishers eats nuts but tends not to mention the scarcity of other foods as a reason of the fisher's behavior (Pringle 1973). Hamilton and Cook (1955) and then Coulter (1966) and Stevens (1968) substantiated Coues's (1877) report that fishers do eat beechnuts but showed that they were not an important part of the fisher's diet. Fishers in captivity generally refuse to eat any kind of fruit or nut (Davison 1975).

It is obvious from the wide varity of fruits listed in a footnote to Table 9 that fishers *will* eat a wide variety of fruits. Goszczynski (1976) and Lockie (1961) both found that European pine martens eat a great deal of fruit especially during the summer. There is no reason to believe that fishers would do otherwise, especially given that they will eat fruits during the winter and fruits are more common during the summer than the winter. However, other evidence suggests that Coues's (1877) statement was correct: fruits and nuts are only eaten when other food is difficult to obtain.

Diet Analysis by Season and Sex

Clem (1977), Coulter (1966), and Stevens (1968) analyzed fishers' diets by season and by sex. Coulter divided his G-I tracts into three groups by season: autumn was represented by 85 tracts collected during late September through November; early winter, by 99 tracts collected during December and January; and late winter, by 48 tracts collected during February through early April. Coulter felt that these periods are real and represent different hunting and prey conditions for fishers in Maine. Autumn is a period of low snow cover, bird migration, and the onset of hibernation for mammals that hibernate; autumn is probably the period when the greatest number of prey species is available to fishers. Early winter is characterized by deep, soft, fluffy snow and by the inactivity of winter mammals that do not hibernate; fishers experience a period of relative unavailability of prey. Late winter is characterized by firmly packed snow, shallow snow depth as the period ends, increased animal activity, and the return of migratory birds; this increases the availability of prey for fishers again. The frequency of occurrence of major food types in the fisher digestive tracts is shown in Figure 41. Coulter used a chi-square test on his raw data to test whether the proportions of each food type were the same for all periods. He found that the probability was between 0.05 and 0.10 that the proportions were the same, and he rejected the null hypothesis that season does not affect diet.

Coulter (1966) also found significant differences in the occurrence of some specific food types during the course of the winter. The change in the frequency of birds in fishers' diets (shown at the right in Figure 41) was significant at the 0.005 level. The decrease in the number of shrews in fishers' diets as the winter progressed was significant only at the 0.10 level. However, considering the large number of prey types in the fisher's diet, a change in the frequency of a few items is to be expected from chance alone.

Clem (1977) had a slightly more extensive sample of G-I tracts, but they were only collected from November through February. Clem was unable to detect any significant change in the fisher's diets by month in his sample (the level of significance was 0.05), nor could he find any significant differences for any individual food types. Stevens (1968) found a significant increase in plant materials, especially fruits and nuts, during the summer.

Clem (1977), Coulter (1966), Kelly (1977), and Stevens (1968) were all unable to find any differences in diet between the sexes. This is of special interest because differences in diet between the sexes have been hypothesized as one mechanism that might explain the substantial sexual dimorphism in the body size of fishers. The hypothesis predicts that substantial sexual dimorphism results in there being different diets for each sex and thus reduces competition for food. Kelly (1977) did find significantly more male than female fishers with porcupine quills in their heads, chests, shoulders, and legs ($p < 0.01$). In contrast, female fishers in one of Clem's study

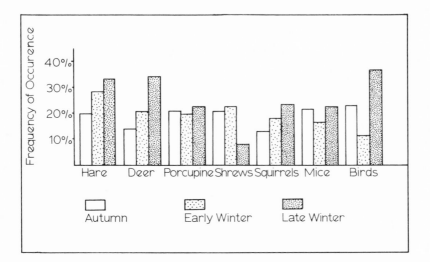

Figure 41. Frequency of occurrence of different prey types in the diet of fishers from Maine during different seasons. *(from M. W. Coulter, 1966, Ecology and management of fishers in Maine, Ph.d. thesis, used by permission of the author)*

areas had more porcupine remains in their G-I tracts than males did ($p < 0.01$), and there was no difference in the number of quills in Stevens's small sample of males and females with quills.

No real, significant differences have been found between the diets of male and female fishers. Male and female fishers are both opportunistic predators that eat anything they can catch. Both sexes can kill porcupines, the largest living prey in their diets. During the winter in northern North America, the next largest active potential prey after the porcupine is the white-tailed deer, and it is known that fishers cannot kill healthy adult deer. It may be that a sexual difference is fishers' diets can only be found in the difference of the maximum size of porcupines that can be killed. (See Chapter 8.) Or there may be no sexual differences in diets because there are no prey in the size range that males can kill but females cannot. Summer diet analyses may uncover a difference between the sexes in predation on mammals around the size of the beaver.

Chapter 7

Hunting and Killing Behavior
of Fishers Hunting Prey
Other Than Porcupines

Fishers have two distinctly different techniques that are used for hunting different prey, at least during the winter. The use of two hunting techniques has been well correlated with habitat by investigators who have followed fisher tracks during the winter to note the animal's foraging patterns (Clem 1977; Powell 1976, 1977a, 1977b, 1978a; Powell and Brander 1977). They found that different prey animals are available to the fisher in different habitats. During the winter, the foraging patterns used by fishers to hunt porcupines are characterized by long-distance, straight-line travel directed toward porcupine dens. This foraging pattern is largely confined to hunting in open, upland hardwood forests, which are good winter porcupine habitat. Because of the many unique aspects of the fisher-porcupine relationship, the fisher's hunting and killing behaviors for porcupines are discussed specifically in the next chapter (Chapter 8). The foraging pattern used by fishers to hunt all other prey animals is characterized by frequent changes in direction and zigzags. This hunting pattern is usually used in lowland and dense coniferous forests where snowshoe hares are found in high densities, but it is also used in other habitats where prey are found in high densities. This hunting pattern is typical of the hunting patterns used by members of the subfamily Mustelinae and may have been used by primitive mustelids and by miacids. This foraging pattern and related killing behaviors are the subjects of this chapter.

Hunting Behavior

Fishers use the zigzag foraging pattern typical of mustelines to hunt snowshoe hares, their most common prey. Fishers do not lie and wait to ambush hares, and they do not often chase hares for long distances. Rather, hunting consists of investigating places where hares are likely to be found (Brander and Books 1973; Coulter 1966; Powell 1976, 1977a, 1978a; Powell and Brander 1977). Brander and Books (1973, p. 54) wrote that the fisher's "hunting pattern is a random investigation of brushy areas, windfalls, hollow trees and other places where hares and smaller mammals are likely to be found." In reality, this foraging pattern is hardly "random" in the strict sense of the word. "Random" is used because of the apparently unpredictable nature of fishers' track patterns. I prefer to use "zigzag foraging." Coulter (1966, p. 117) stated, "In hare cover they dart beneath every low-hanging bough, fallen tree top, log or similar place where a hare might be sitting." Fishers also run along hare runs (Powell 1977a, 1978a; Powell and Brander 1977). Coulter (1966) believed that sometimes, when a fisher enters an area with dense cover and high hare density, the hares scurry in all directions. The fisher then crisscrosses the area and intercepts fleeing hares by chance. No other studies of fishers have found hare or fisher tracks that lead to this interpretation, however.

Hares are killed where they are found resting or, when they have perceived a fisher at the last minute and have been flushed from cover, after a short rushing attack (Powell 1978a). Hares may also be flushed from forms, or hiding places, when a fisher is some distance away. Coulter (1966) interpreted tracks in the snow to show that hares would sometimes be flushed from their forms when a fisher was as far away as 10 meters, even when the fisher was going in another direction. There are a few reports of fishers chasing hares for long distances (Hardy 1899, 1907; Mech, personal communication). None of the long-term fisher studies have reported such behavior, however, which implies that long chases occur only rarely.

The fisher's hunting success is difficult to quantify, because it is difficult to determine temporal relationships between fisher and hare tracks. Temporal relationships between tracks can only be determined when the tracks are on top of each other or when the tracks are made during a light snowfall. Even under these conditions, the temporal relationships between tracks are known only on a crude basis —either before or after. How often hares escape from fishers is usually impossible to calculate. Coulter (1966) believed that a fisher's success after a short rush attack was low. The quantified hunting success of other predators is often low (e.g., for wolves there is a 6% success rate for capturing perceived moose; Mech 1966, 1970). Therefore, fishers can be expected to have low hunting success rates.

When fishers actively hunt prey other than snowshoe hares and porcupines, they use the zigzag method they use when foraging for hares. Coulter (1966) found that fishers in Maine actively hunted for mice. He followed tracks of fishers that investigated hollow logs and piles of forest litter. The fishers sometimes tore apart rotten stumps and scattered mouse nests and seed caches. From Coulter's findings, it is apparent that fishers investigate potential hiding places for mice the same way they investigate potential hiding places for hares. During my field study, I followed one very confusing set of fisher tracks that led to a gray squirrel kill. The tracks could be interpreted to indicate that a fisher was hunting gray squirrels by using the zigzag method in an area of high gray squirrel activity. However, it was the fisher's breeding season and the tracks criss-crossed, backtracked, and doubletracked much more than normal. In addition, there was evidence that the tracks may have been made by more than one fisher. Therefore, another interpretation of the tracks is that one fisher was trying to find another fisher during the breeding season and that one of the fishers happened to catch a squirrel.

Fishers clearly are not mouse, shrew, or squirrel specialists. Though mice, shrews, and squirrels are commonly found in diet studies (Table 9), as the discussion in the preceding chapter suggests, they may all be overrepresented in G-I tracts and scats compared to their importance in fishers' diets. In addition, track patterns indicate that these prey are often taken fortuitously.

Fishers do not hunt in the best mouse-hunting habitats (Powell 1977a). Fishers never hunt in the open habitats that are frequently used by foxes and coyotes hunting mice. Wide, overgrown, unplowed logging roads and the right-of-way to a buried gas pipeline in my study area were frequently utilized by foxes and coyotes hunting mice. I once tracked a fox that killed four mice in less than 1 kilometer along a wide, overgrown logging road. In contrast, I tracked fishers for over 200 kilometers during my study and found only two small mammal kills. Both kills were found in forest habitat; the fishers made small zigzags from their lines of travel and dug down into the snow to get the mice. There is no evidence from track patterns that fishers catch mice with their paws with a pounce like the one used by foxes and coyotes to catch mice. Fishers avoid the habitats that provide the most successful mousing and do not use mousing techniques used by habitual mousers.

Despite stories of fishers chasing red squirrels in the trees (Grinnell, Dixon, and Linsdale 1937; Morse 1961; Seton 1937), there is no evidence that this takes place regularly (Brander and Books 1973; Coulter 1966). Fishers can catch squirrels in trees only when they happen to find the squirrels in holes large enough for a fisher to enter (Coulter 1966). On the ground, squirrels are caught only when a fisher happens upon one that is foraging (Coulter 1966; Powell 1977a) or when a fisher is able to dig one out from a shallow ground den after it has fled from the fisher (Coulter 1966).

The foraging patterns discussed so far fit into a larger pattern. In habitats where prey are found in low densities, fishers travel through the habitat in fairly straight lines with few changes of direction and zigzags. When fishers catch prey or find a carcass in such habitat, their subsequent foraging pattern does not change. However, when fishers find a habitat where prey are present in high densities, they do change their foraging behavior. In high-prey-density habitats, fishers forage by frequently changing directions and zigzagging.

The zigzag foraging method is also used by weasels (Powell 1977a, 1978a; Powell and Brander 1977). It is likely that this foraging behavior may also have been used by the miacids (Anderson 1970; Colbert 1969; Ewer 1973). Miacids had rather generalized limb structure and relatively long, slender bodies without long limbs. Their body structure was similar to that of present-day mustelines, though not so extreme in its slenderness. The most common prey for the miacids were probably small animals that could be captured on the ground. Because some miacids were probably good climbers, some prey may have been captured in the trees. It is likely, therefore, that miacids used foraging patterns much like those used by mustelines today.

I have quantified the foraging patterns of fishers and weasels in order to make a comparison (Powell 1978a). Five tracks of fishers hunting snowshoe hares in lowland coniferous forest were measured to determine the ratio of the actual distance traveled by the fisher to the distance along its general line of travel. The same was done for 18 tracks of fishers foraging for porcupines in upland, hardwood forest and for 20 tracks of weasels hunting mice. For all these tracks, the distances the animals actually traveled were measured by pacing along the track (for fishers) or by measuring the distance with a tape measure (for weasels). Then, the tracks were precisely mapped and the distances along the general line of travel were taken from the map. The results are shown in Table 10. Total distance along the line of travel was 0.3 kilometers for the weasel tracks, 5.0 kilometers for the fishers hunting hares, and 10.4 kilometers for the fishers hunting porcupines. Fishers hunting hares and weasels hunting mice change direction frequently and travel a considerable distance farther than the distance along their line of travel. The ratio of distance traveled to distance along the line of travel is about 1.5 for both animals, though the weasels had a much higher variance.

Weasels not only zigzag on the surface of the ground or snow, they also frequently change directions up and down. Sometimes weasels forage in low trees and shrubs, and during the winter weasels frequently forage beneath the snow (Klimov 1940; Kraft 1966; Nyholm 1959; Powell 1977a, 1978a; Seton 1929; Teplov 1948). Although there are trappers' reports of fishers foraging under the snow for mice (deVos 1952), fishers are too large to forage extensively beneath the snow. They do occasionally forage in trees, however. Con-

Table 10. Mean Ratios (± Standard Deviation) of Distance Run (R) to Distance along the Direction of Travel (T) for Weasels and Fishers Foraging in Michigan.

	$R/T \pm SD$	Range	Number of Observations	Total T's for All Observations (km)
Weasels*	1.48 ± 0.68	1.04-3.52	20	0.3
Fishers in hare habitat†	1.55 ± 0.24	1.26-1.90	5	2.8
Fishers in porcupine habitat*†	1.03 ± 0.03	1.00-1.11	18	10.4

* Difference significant, $p < 0.01$, Student's t test.

† Difference significant, $p \ll 0.01$, Student's t test.

Source: R. A. Powell, 1978. A comparison of fisher and weasel hunting behavior. Carnivore 1 (1): 28-34. Used by permission of the publisher.

sequently, their foraging resembles that of weasels in this way, also. I believe that by frequently changing direction while foraging, weasels decrease their chances of being preyed upon by other predators (Powell 1977a, 1978a, 1978b). Weasels are preyed upon by raptors (Craighead and Craighead 1956; Errington 1967; Mendall 1944; Selwyn 1966), martens (Weckwerth and Hawley 1962), foxes (Latham 1952), and cats (Gaughran 1950). An avian predator unable to predict a weasel's movements may be more likely to miss it when striking.

Predation on fishers is infrequent at most, and it is unlikely that fishers are under any selective pressure to adjust foraging patterns to reduce predation by predators other than humans. However, fishers and weasels have evolved from small, common ancestors (Anderson 1970) that probably had selective pressures for predator avoidance similar to those of present-day weasels. Therefore, the selective pressure for zigzag foraging that reduces predation has been secondarily lost by fishers.

I suggest that the fisher's foraging pattern is correlated with prey density and habitat in the following manner. First, it is assumed that prey are hidden in high density in localized patches of habitat. When a fisher (or any other predator) is in such a patch, it can increase its chances of finding and catching prey when it frequently changes direction. If the fisher foraged along a relatively straight line, inspecting only those likely hiding places for prey that were found along that line, the fisher would soon find itself outside the habitat patch with high prey density. By changing direction frequently, the fisher is able to stay within the patch. In addition, the fisher should minimize in some manner the frequency at which it recrosses its own tracks (Pyke, Pulliam, and Charnov 1977): in areas already searched by the fisher, the prey animals would be alert to the fisher's presence or they would have left. Thus, the foraging pattern cannot be completely random (Pyke, Pulliam, and Charnov 1977).

Fishers should forage in a zigzag manner with frequent directional changes in any habitat that has prey in high density. In general, hare habitat is the most common habitat utilized by fishers in which this is the case. Thus, that is the only habitat in which fishers consistently forage by frequently changing direction and zigzagging. When a fisher is traveling through habitat that is not hare habitat but in which prey are found in high density, the fisher should forage in the zigzag manner. Fishers do occasionally forage in this manner for mice and squirrels (Coulter 1966; Powell 1977a).

At all other times, when a fisher perceives an isolated prey, the fisher should attempt to catch it but not begin foraging in a zigzag manner. Remaining in the area would be of no advantage to the fisher because prey are in low density. This has been found to be the case when fishers find single mice, squirrels, and grouse (Coulter 1966; Powell 1977a).

Pyke (1978) analyzed the theoretically optimal directionality of foraging in a habitat where prey are evenly distributed. He visualized the habitat in which an animal foraged as a grid of points. Food was only found at those points and the foraging animal could only move from the point at which it was located to the four adjacent points (forward, back, left, right). The probabilities of moving in each of the four directions were chosen to be discrete approximations to the truncated normal distribution with different variances; Pyke found support for these choices in the literature. The probabilities of moving to the left and to the right are assumed to be equal. Thus, the directionality of a foraging bout is simply the probability of moving forward minus the probability of moving backward for that bout. This measure of directionality ranges from 1, when there is only forward movement, to 0 when movement is random (forward and backward probabilities are equal). Computer simulation was used to investigate how the number of points in the grid reached during a foraging bout was affected by the directionality of the bout, the size of the grid, the length of the bout, and the behavior of the animal at the edge of the habitat.

Pyke's (1978) analysis can be applied to the fisher's foraging habits. Fishers foraging in snowshoe hare habitat are foraging in large grids: each point on the grid is a potential hiding place for hares and there are extremely large numbers of hares and hiding places in each patch of hare habitat. Foraging bouts are long because a fisher inspects a large number of hiding places during each hunting bout. And fishers run along the edge of a habitat patch (they do not always immediately move back into the interior of a patch when they reach its edge). With these aspects of foraging known, one can predict the optimal foraging directionality for a foraging bout: it is between 0.8 and 1.0.

Equivalent to Pyke's (1978) measure of directionality is the inverse of the ratio of actual distance traveled to distance along the line of travel given in Table 10. The inverse of the value for fishers in hare habitat is 0.64. Because of the large variance for the values in Table 10, this directionality measure for fishers is not significantly different from 0.8. However, since several other vertebrates have similar values for their measures of directionality (Pyke 1978), there may be a real difference between the directionality measure for the fisher and the theoretical optimum. Other factors not considered by Pyke may be affecting the fisher's foraging behavior. A major factor affecting the directionality of foraging not considered by Pyke is memory. Fishers do appear to be able to remember certain aspects of their home ranges (Powell 1977a, 1978a; Powell and Brander 1977), and it is conceivable that they are familiar enough with the patches of hare habitat in their home ranges that they can forage in a pattern that reduces the amount of reinvestigation of areas already searched. Such behavior would decrease the directionality measure by decreasing the probability of moving forward when an area already searched is approached.

Killing Behavior

Fishers kill small prey such as mice and shrews either by applying the capture bite, by shaking them, or by eating them. Small prey are eaten whole, with little or no chewing, and they often show up in fishers' stomachs as identifiable, whole individuals (Kelly 1977). Prey as large as squirrels are killed with a bite to the back of the neck or head (Kelly 1977).

Prey the size of snowshoe hares and rabbits are also killed with a bite to the back of the neck or head (Coulter 1966; Powell 1977a, 1978a), but the fisher may use its feet to assist with the kill (Powell 1977a, 1978a). (See Figure 42.) When a fisher attacks a hare, the fisher first attempts to secure a hold on the animal. The fisher bites any place available but tries to bite the back of the hare's neck or head. When this initial hold is not on the hare's neck or head, the fisher wraps itself around the hare and grasps it with all four feet. The fisher then releases its bite and finds the back of the hare's neck or head. Once the fisher has a firm hold on the hare's neck with its teeth, it releases the hold with its feet and waits for the hare to become immobilized. During this time, the fisher may repeatedly bite and loosen (but not release) its grip on the hare's neck and may relocate the bite a little without releasing its hold. Fishers sometimes shake hares after they are immobilized. Hares may be immobilized in an exceedingly short time; I recorded one killing time of 15 seconds when a fisher did not need to utilize the wrap around assist. However, hares are not always killed immediately by fishers. On three occasions I have observed satiated captive fishers immobilize hares that later attempted escape after about 15 minutes of apparent death.   These hares had faulty equilibriums and impaired running abilities and were killed immediately after the fishers noted their attempted escapes. It is doubtful that free-living fishers are often satiated enough not to eat a hare immediately after it is caught.

Before beginning to eat a squirrel, rabbit, or hare, a fisher often licks the bloody eyes, nose, and mouth of the dead prey. A fisher does not commence eating a rabbit or hare at any particular body

Figure 42. Adult male fisher killing a snowshoe hare with a bite to the back of the neck.

region and is just as likely to start at the head as at the rump. Rabbits, hares, and smaller prey are usually consumed in one meal. After eating, a fisher usually sleeps for several hours in a temporary den (Powell 1977a, 1978a, 1979a).

Fishers that are satiated still kill prey but cache those they cannot eat. Captive fishers cache food in their nest boxes (Powell 1977a, 1978a). Free-living fishers probably seldom encounter situations in which food items the size of a hare or smaller cannot be eaten. On those infrequent occasions, it is likely that a satiated fisher would cache a hare or similar food item in the temporary sleeping den in which it sleeps. Large items such as deer carcasses may be left after the fisher has finished eating, though the fisher usually sleeps in close proximity to the carcass. There was a temporary sleeping den within 25 meters of all the deer carcasses utilized by fishers that I found during my study.

Weasels kill mice by using the same behavior fishers use to kill hares (Powell 1977a, 1978a). Weasels kill or immobilize mice with a neck bite (Allen 1938; Ewer 1973; Gillingham 1978; Glover 1943; Hamilton 1933; Llewellyn 1942; Powell 1977a, 1978a) and use the wrap around assist (Gillingham 1978; Heidt 1970; Miller 1931; Powell 1977a, 1978a). (See Figure 43.) Weasels may curl on their sides or over the prey in their wrap around assists (Gillingham 1978) and may sometimes scrape at the prey with their hindpaws (Ewer 1973). Like fishers, weasels do not always kill mice that are immobil-

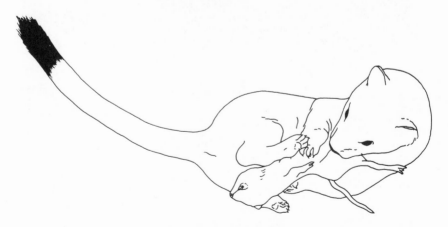

Figure 43. Long-tailed weasel using the wrap around assist to handle a deer mouse. (*C. B. Powell*)

ized. I have observed mice that had been immobilized by a weasel but not eaten recover and run away with no apparent impariment after 5 or 10 minutes. Weasels able to catch more mice than they can eat kill all the mice but cache uneaten ones (Erlinge, Bergsten, and Kristiansson 1974; Ewer 1973; Moors 1974, 1977; Powell 1977a, 1978a).

A neck bite is the most common killing technique used by species in the order Carnivora. Nevertheless, there is considerable variation and diversity in how the method is employed by species within the order. (See the review of carnivores' killing techniques in Ewer 1973.) As Ewer (pp. 225-226) pointed out:

> It is impossible to believe that any carnivore could have evolved a dentition of the miacid type without some corresponding behavioral adaptations, the most obvious of which is not to attack at random but to direct the bite to the anterior region of the prey and aim at head or neck. This has the double advantage of giving a high probability of a quick kill and of making a retaliatory bite difficult. . . . One would not expect any very precise orientation of the bite in the early stages of evolution and the miacids probably increased the efficacy of a somewhat labile orientation in the two ways adopted by living viverrids—by iterant biting and snapping and by shaking.

The neck bite used by members of the Mustelinae, a bite directed to the back of the prey's head or neck, is a moderately developed neck bite. The bite is directed with fair precision, but a bite anywhere along the back of the head or neck usually suffices. The bite is a simple bite or a repeated bite and is not as developed as that of many felids. However, the wrap around assist is an important evolutionary advance over primitive killing methods.

The wrap around assist is not characteristic of canoids other than mustelids. This is probably because of the mustelids' body shapes. The wrap around assist is used by genets (*Genetta* spp. [Ewer 1973, Plate 9b] ; genets are members of the Viverridae and thus are feloids), which are not dissimilar in shape to fishers. The wrap around is not used by mongooses (Ewer 1973), indicating that the behavior is not a direct correlate to body shape.

Movement by prey is an important stimulus for attack in fishers and other mustelines (Powell 1977a, 1978a). The fact that fishers sometimes lose interest in immobilized prey and allow them to recover indicates that movement may be a necessary stimulus for attack. Although hunger may affect a fisher's readiness and quickness of attack, hunger is not a necessary stimulus for attack because satiated fishers attack hares. Separating hunger from other stimuli for attack is important. Wild fishers seldom encounter conditions with overabundant food. Except when a fisher is camping next to a large carcass, its next meal is uncertain. Since hunger is not a necessary stimulus for attack, on those few occasions when several prey are encountered a fisher can kill more prey than its immediate requirements demand and cache uneaten prey. Repeated killing and caching is one method of ensuring the future availability of food (Ewer 1973; Hall 1951; Kruuk 1972; Moors 1974, 1977). A satiated fisher attacks moving prey and thus acquires a future supply of food.

Repeated killing and caching explains the "hen-house syndrome." Many members of the weasel family, fishers included, have been known to raid hen houses and other poultry enclosures. Fishers have been known to raid duck pens on game farms. These raids are usually characterized by lots of feathers and lots of poultry killed and left uneaten. So much poultry is left uneaten that members of the weasel family have gained a reputation for being ruthless, wanton, wasteful, and bloodthirsty killers. But a hen house is essentially a new, super-food-rich environment in which mustelids have not evolved and to which they are not adapted. When they are in new environments, animals act the same as they do in the environments to which they are adapted. So, in a hen house mustelids kill as many chickens as possible, eat what is needed for satiation, and save the rest for *later*. Obviously, there are too many chickens to be carted off to sleeping sites, so a mustelid may take one or two, leave the rest, and return the next time it is hungry. The behavior is completely understandable, though it does not endear mustelids to farmers who have lost chickens. Fortunately for the fisher, its range does not overlap with much agricultural land, and chicken coops are seldom located close enough to forested land to be accessible to fishers.

Chapter 8

The Fisher-Porcupine System

The relationship between the fisher and the porcupine, first noted by early trappers and explorers, has long interested naturalists and everyone else who has heard of it. That any predator could habitually kill an animal so protected with quills is fascinating. Certainly, this aspect of the fisher's biology is the most widely known, though much of what people read and hear about the subject is more myth than reality. Reality, however, is just as interesting as myth in most cases, and the case of the fisher-porcupine relationship is no exception. The predator-prey relationship between fishers and porcupines and the evolution of this relationship do deserve an important place in any discussion of fishers.

The Porcupine

The Canadian porcupine (Figure 39) is the only porcupine native to North America. It is found over much of the United States and Canada in areas where there are extensive forests (Figure 44). Porcupines are large rodents, weighing 4 to 8 kilograms or more, and are well adapted to an arboreal existence. Taylor (1935, pp. 32-33) described the porcupine well:

> The body of the porcupine is short, heavy, and obese in appearance. When at rest, the animal assumes almost the form of a sphere. The head, legs,

and tail are never conspicuous. The neck is short and indistinguishable, the body appearing to swell out from the nose back to the middle, with no intervening constriction. The face is short, the muzzle blunt, the nostrils prominent. The whiskers are long and black. The eyes are small, usually somewhat protuberant and bearing a striking resemblance to shoe buttons. They are usually watery in daylight, probably indicating their imperfect adaptation to strong light. . . . The ears are small, almost hidden by the surrounding hair. The upper incisors, yellowish in color, are usually visible when one catches sight of the lower part of the face.

The legs are short, and conspicuously bowed. The claws are long and prominent, grooved beneath. The soles of the feet are naked and rough. They have been compared to those of a bear, and they are admirably suited to maintain contact with the bark of trees or surface of boulders. The feet are well adapted to either climbing, standing, or walking erect on a horizontal surface . . . . The forefeet are more mobile than the hind feet and especially adapted to grasping and holding. The tail is relatively short, thick and muscular, with a blunt and squarish appearance. It is a most important organ; on the side of a tree it is used as a prop. "The thickly set and rigid bristles covering its lower surface stick to the bark." When the porcupine walks along a branch, the tail is pressed down against the branch to help keep the animal's balance. When the porcupine sits up to eat with its hands, the tail serves as one "leg" of a tripod, the other two being the hind legs. The tail is also an effective weapon of defense.

Porcupines have never been known for the beauty of their pelts, but they have a unique beauty that is easy for the casual observer to overlook. The nose, muzzle, and face almost to the tiny, hidden, round ears are covered with fine, black fur. The muzzle is rounded, the lips are dark, and the eyes are black and liquid. All of these features give a porcupine a most beautiful face.

The porcupine's pelage is characterized by three types of hair: woolly underfur, long and coarse guard hairs, and the well-known quills. The woolly underfur acts as insulation but is not evenly distributed over the entire body (Clarke and Brander 1973). Quills (Figure 45) are found all over the porcupine's body, except its belly and face. The quills are usually creamy white with glossy dark brown tips and are longest and most prominent on the porcupine's rump and tail. The guard hairs are frequently all that can be seen on the upper back, sides, and neck, although there is a prodigious number of quills under the guard hairs. Quills are modified guard hairs filled with a spongy substance that makes them sturdy. There are numer-

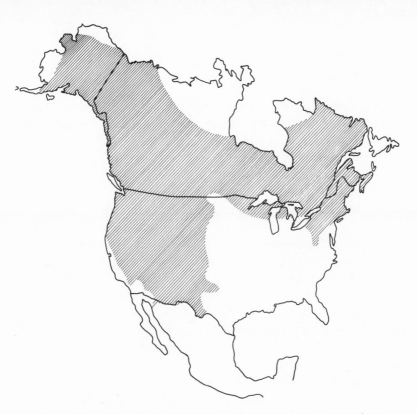

Figure 44. Species range of the Canadian porcupine. Note the overlap of this range with that of the fisher (shown in Figure 26). (*Redrawn by C. B. Powell, from Taylor 1935; and from W. H. Burt and R. P. Grossenheider, 1964, A Field Guide to the Mammals, Houghton Mifflin Company, New York, ©1952, 1964, 1976 by William Henry Burt and Richard Phillip Grossenheider, by permission of the publisher*)

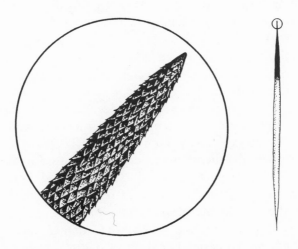

Figure 45. Porcupine quill with enlarged inset of tip showing barbs, which resemble sharp, overlapping scales. (*C. B. Powell*)

ous microscopic barbs at the end of each quill (Figure 45). These barbs are most accurately called scales and do not resemble the barb of a fishhook. They look more like the overlapping shingles on a roof. This arrangement of scales makes it easier for the quills to move into the body of a victim and more difficult for them to be pulled back out. The quills contain no poison or irritant and cannot be thrown. They are only lightly connected to the skin and pull loose easily when the points have entered another object. The rump of the porcupine is covered mostly by quills, and pelage in this area is sparse; this allows significant heat loss during the winter. Porcupines seem to reduce this heat loss by feeding in trees and by frequently using postures that reduce radiant heat loss (Clarke and Brander 1973).

Porcupines possess the chisellike incisor teeth characteristic of rodents. They are opportunistic feeders and eat a wide variety of vegetation (Earle 1978). During the summer, the porcupine's diet varies greatly over North America: in some areas porcupines feed largely on the leaves of deciduous trees, and in other areas they feed on a wide variety of terrestrial and aquatic herbaceous vegetation (Brander 1973; Dodge 1967). During the winter, the porcupine's preferred food is mostly the phloem of conifers and to a lesser extent the needles. Hemlocks and pines are generally favored (Brander 1973; Dodge 1967; Taylor 1935). In Upper Michigan, porcupines also eat the phloem of sugar maples, American elms, American basswoods, and yellow birches (Brander 1973). During the spring, herbaceous plants and grasses and the buds of several hardwoods are consumed (Earle 1978).

The porcupine's daily activities change with the seasons. Porcupines den in large hollow trees, hollow logs, and rockfalls during the winter (Figure 46). Dens are often used for many years in succession, and over the years porcupine excrement accumulates at the entrances of the dens. Porcupine excrement can be smelled from a considerable distance, at times even by humans (Powell 1977a, 1978a). Winter days are generally spent in the den, and winter nights are spent in nearby feeding trees (Brander 1973; Powell and Brander 1977). A porcupine travels from its den to its feeding tree in the evening and back to the den in the morning but may, on occasion, spend the entire day in a feeding tree. During the summer, feeding behavior is strongly diurnal (Brander 1973). Most of the day is spent in feeding trees, but much of that time is spent sleeping and resting. On summer

Figure 46. Porcupine winter dens. (A) Den in a large, hollow yellow birch; (B) den in a large, hollow log; and (C) den in a rockfall.

nights, porcupines travel to gathering sites, which are usually within 200 meters of their feeding trees. Many porcupines may gather at one site, and there is much interaction. Most activity takes place during the two or three hours before and after midnight. Porcupines cease coming to gathering sites coincident with the mating season in September and October (Brander 1973).

One and sometimes two offspring are born during the spring; parturition dates between March and June have been recorded (Taylor 1935). The young are born fully quilled, and it takes about 30 minutes for the quills to dry. The underfur is more apparent in young porcupines, and underfur and guard hairs may cover almost all of a young porcupine's quills (Taylor 1935), giving it a fuzzy appearance (Figure 47). Weight at birth is about 500 grams. Taylor (1935) repeated an American Indian legend that claims that a mother porcupine drives her baby from her as soon as it is born and never nurses it. Although the legend is not completely true, it is true to the extent that baby porcupines are never totally dependent on mother's milk or are so only for an extremely short period. Almost from birth, porcupines eat nonabrasive solid food and may be completely weaned when they are very young. The actual period between birth and weaning may be very long, however, and there are records of porcupines having nursed into the autumn (Taylor 1935). By autumn, though, young porcupines are quite capable of fending completely for themselves.

Porcupine quills are distributed to give the best protection against an attack from above or behind; they also protect a porcupine from being overturned. The quills are long and dense and are most apparent on the rump and tail of a porcupine, giving excellent protection from attacks oriented toward the back and from predators approaching from behind. The sides, back of the neck, and legs of porcupines are also well protected, providing protection from attacks to the back of the neck and from predators attempting to overturn them.

When attacked, a porcupine attempts to keep its back oriented toward the attacker. If the predator circles, the porcupine will circle with the predator, always keeping its back directed toward the predator. When possible, the porcupine tries to protect its face by facing a tree or a similar object (Figure 48). The porcupine flips its rump and tail in a humping motion when the predator gets too close (Powell 1978a; Powell and Brander 1977).

Figure 47. Porcupine approximately one week old. Baby porcupines are fully quilled with short quills about 1 centimeter long. Baby-pelage guard hairs are longer than quills at this age, giving the baby porcupine a fuzzy appearance.

Figure 48. Young porcupine utilizing a crevice in a tree to protect its face.

Fishers and Porcupines

There is evidence that porcupines and fishers have coexisted for many millennia. Both species are indigenous to North America and were part of the continental fauna by the Wisconsinan event of the Pleistocene, at least 10,000 years ago (Anderson 1970; Hibbard 1970). Ancient evidence of the interaction of porcupines and fishers is suggested by the comingling of their bones in caves used by archaic and woodland human cultures (900 BC to European settlement) in what is now Alabama and Missouri (Barkalow 1961; Parmalee 1971). Present ranges of the two species overlap extensively (Figures 26, 44), and it can be assumed that their ranges overlapped extensively in the past. Under these conditions, coevolution between a predator (the fisher) and its prey (the porcupine) can be expected.

The porcupine is subject to predation primarily by six carnivores: the wolf, the coyote, the mountain lion, the lynx, the bobcat, and the fisher. Porcupine remains have been found in the G-I tracts and scats of all six of these predators (Earle 1978). Of the six predators, the fisher appears to be best adapted morphologically and behaviorally for successful attacks on porcupines (Powell and Brander 1977), and porcupine remains are found more often and more consistently in the G-I tracts and scats of fishers than in those of the other predators.

Since porcupines spend approximately half of each day in the trees, canids are restricted to contacting porcupines when they are on the ground. Fishers are better adapted for arboreality and are more agile in trees than felids. Therefore, fishers are better adapted to taking advantage of encounters with porcupines in trees than are the other five predators (Powell and Brander 1977).

Both canid and felid predators are much taller than porcupines and, when they attack a porcupine, must make their major effort from above the porcupine. An attack made to the back of a porcupine's neck (a typical canid and felid killing technique [Ewer 1973]) encounters an area well protected by quills. Canids and felids do attempt biting attacks at porcupines' necks, and these attacks are known to be often unsuccessful (Figure 49).

Brander and I discounted large felids as frequent porcupine predators (Powell and Brander 1977). However, Earle (1978) pointed out

Figure 49. Bobcat found dead with its face full of quills. This animal also had numerous quills in its paws and shoulders. (*Wisconsin Department of Natural Resources*)

that, even though North American felids are longer legged than fishers, they have dexterous front legs and paws and are capable of wounding a porcupine's face with a blow from the front paws. Their short nasal bones would be a distinct disadvantage for attacking a porcupine's face, however, and may counteract any advantage of being able to attack with their front paws (Earle 1978).

Both the scientific and popular literature contain unsupported references to fishers overturning porcupines and attacking their bellies or attacking porcupines from under tree branches (Anthony 1928; Cahalane 1944, 1947; Coues 1877; Pringle 1964a; Seton 1937; Schoonmaker 1938). Coulter (1966) was the first to report observations that showed that the popular belief was an exaggerated myth. Brander and I have been able to reconstruct fishers' porcupine kills from tracks and signs in the snow in Upper Michigan (Powell and Brander 1977), and I have been able to reconstruct several more kills made by fishers both in the wild and in captivity and to observe one kill in captivity (Powell 1977a, 1978a). All of these recent observations show that fishers kill porcupines with repeated attacks on the face.

Pringle (1964a) was the first to point out that a porcupine is not an easy source of food for a fisher. An attacked porcupine attempts to keep its back toward the fisher and, when possible, faces a tree, log, or rock to protect its face. An attacking fisher repeatedly circles the porcupine, attempting to bite its face (Figure 50). When it finds a chance, the fisher jumps in (Figure 51), bites the porcupine's face, and jumps back again before the porcupine has a chance to turn and strike the fisher with its tail. Repeated wounds to the face over a period of 30 minutes or more finally kill or bewilder the porcupine so that the fisher can turn it over and begin feeding on its ventral surface. Most attacks to the face are unsuccessful, and a fisher often has to check an attack after it is started because the porcupine is able to move quickly enough to protect itself. Coulter (1966) and I both observed attacking fishers receiving a few quills in the head and shoulders, but these appeared to cause little or no trouble.

A porcupine being attacked by a fisher attempts to escape. I observed a captive porcupine attempting to climb a fence post to escape an attacking fisher. The fisher climbed the fence and got above the porcupine. From this advantage, the fisher was able to attack the porcupine's face from above, forcing the porcupine back down to the ground. Evidence from kill sites suggests that wild fishers utilize this technique to keep porcupines from climbing trees and to force them back from the protection of trees.

It is obvious that fishers are uniquely adapted to killing porcupines. Fishers are built low to the ground and at the level of a porcupine's face and can, therefore, make an attack directly at a porcupine's face. They are large enough to inflict a substantial wound when they have a chance to bite a porcupine's face, and yet they are small enough to be quick and agile and jump in and out at a porcupine's face and avoid a porcupine's tail. And fishers have arboreal adaptations that allow them to take advantage of trees and to reduce the protection afforded to porcupines by trees. No other predator possesses this array of characteristics, and so no other predator has the ability to attack and kill porcupines that a fisher has.

Figures 52 and 53 illustrate two sites where fishers killed porcupines. These kill sites are typical of those found by Brander and me in Michigan (Powell 1977a, 1978a; Powell and Brander 1977).

At the kill shown in Figure 52, fisher tracks led first to a hollow log, then to a porcupine den in a hollow log, and finally along a por-

Figure 50. Fisher circling a porcupine.

Figure 51. Fisher initiating a strike at a porcupine's face. Several wounds to the porcupine's face over the course of approximately 30 minutes are needed to kill the porcupine.

cupine trail to a porcupine den in a tree snag. The packed down snow covered with blood, urine, and quills at the base of the tree indicated the location of the actual kill site. Because the packed down area did not reach the den hole, the fisher must have somehow been able to keep the porcupine away from its den. The location of the packed down area next to the snag suggested that the porcupine tried to keep its face against the snag for protection. Scrapings on the tree and bark on the ground suggested that at least one animal climbed the snag. Tree climbing probably occurred in at least one of two situations: the fisher may have climbed the snag and come down headfirst toward the porcupine on the ground facing the tree trunk, or the porcupine may have climbed the tree and the fisher may have climbed above and forced it back to the ground. The drag mark with the fisher tracks showed that the fisher dragged the porcupine to a hollow log some time after the kill.

The kill shown in Figure 53 was made at the base of the porcupine's feeding tree. The location of the packed snow suggested that the porcupine put its face into the scar on the tree trunk for protection. Blood, urine, and quills in the packed down area adjacent to the tree identified the kill site. Bark scrapings suggested the same possibilities for tree climbing as described for the kill in Figure 52. The carcass found in the smaller packed down area indicated that the fisher dragged the porcupine a few meters before or while eating it.

Fishers always begin eating porcupines somewhere on their ventral surfaces (Figure 54). Internal organs such as the heart, liver, and lungs are usually eaten first. Fishers minimize contact with quills while eating, skinning porcupines neatly and leaving only a few large bones, feet, intestines (sometimes), and skin with quills.

There are several ways that porcupines can reduce the danger of being attacked by fishers. Coulter (1966) gave a captive female fisher opportunities to kill four porcupines. She was able to kill three porcupines that weighed approximately 8 kilograms each but was unable to kill the largest of the four, which weighed approximately 11 kilograms. He argued that fishers may not be able to kill very large porcupines. Brander and I made the same conclusion from evidence in the field (Powell and Brander 1977). We found a kill site where the fisher was able to kill a small, young porcupine with little struggle. But the kill site for a porcupine that weighed 7.7 kilograms after being partially eaten (Figure 53) showed signs of a great strug-

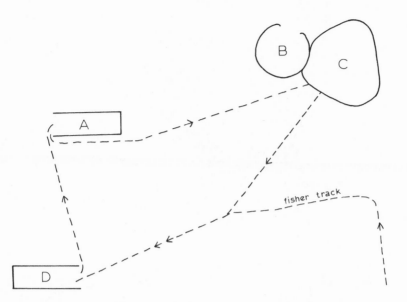

Figure 52. Map of porcupine kill site (not to scale). The porcupine was using a large, hollow log (A) and a large, hollow snag (B) as dens. One well-used porcupine trail led from A to B, and a few additional trails led from B to nearby feeding trees. There was a packed down area (C) at the base of the snag about 2 meters in diameter meeting the snag 90 degrees from the den hole. There were many claw scrapings around the lower 2 meters of the snag on the side where the kill took place. The entire area was littered with bark scrapings, quills, urine, and blood. Leading from the snag to another large, hollow log (D) was a drag mark with fisher tracks. The fisher and the dead porcupine were both in the hollow log (D) when the kill site was found. A to B is approximately 20 meters, D to B is approximately 40 meters. *(C. B. Powell)*

gle (Powell and Brander 1977). If large porcupines were free from predation by fishers, one would expect that the porcupine populations in areas with established fisher populations should have larger proportions of very large porcupines than porcupine populations in areas without fisher populations. Earle (1978) found that this is not the case. The porcupine population in the Ottawa National Forest in Upper Michigan had a lighter average weight than the porcupine population in the Hiawatha National Forest, also in Upper Michigan, which lacked a fisher population. In addition, there was not an excess of very heavy porcupines in the Ottawa National Forest. Earle concluded that female fishers may not be able to kill very large porcupines but that large male fishers are probably able to kill any porcupine, given the proper environmental conditions. This is in agreement with Coulter's (1966) observations. It is also possible that the fisher's predation on porcupines in the Ottawa National Forest is so

Figure 53. Photo of a site where a fisher killed a porcupine. The porcupine was killed at the base of an elm tree it had been using as a feeding tree. The area of packed snow was 1.5 meters in diameter and tangent to the tree at the site of a scar that formed an indentation. The packed snow was littered with bark scrapings, quills, urine, and blood. At the edge of the packed snow were two swish marks made by the fisher's tail. There were scattered tracks outside the packed area. The porcupine was found on its back in a smaller packed area about 3 meters from the tree. There were wounds on its face and a small hole in its chest cavity through which the heart, lungs, and part of one front leg had been eaten.

effective that no porcupines are able to reach a size that is too large for a fisher to kill. The maximum known longevity for wild porcupines is approximately 10 years (Brander 1971). Those porcupines just reaching a size too large for a fisher to kill at the time fishers were becoming reestablished in Upper Michigan would have died by the time of Earle's (1978) study. At present, there is no way to determine which is the case.

When a porcupine is able to find a tree, log, or rock pile with a properly shaped nook into which to face, a fisher is unable to make a successful attack. (See Figure 48.) Similarly, porcupines in dens are safe. When in its winter den, a porcupine faces in or upward, directing its back and tail toward the den's entrance (Figure 55). I have observed fisher tracks that show that the fisher approached a

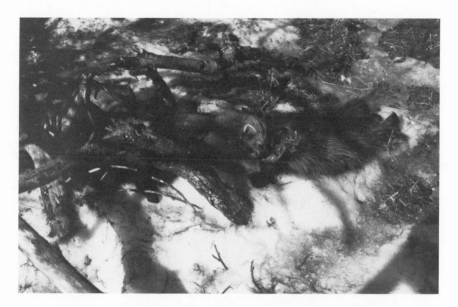

Figure 54. Adult female fisher eating a porcupine she killed. The porcupine is on its back, and the fisher is eating through a hole in the chest cavity.

Figure 55. Porcupine in its den with its back facing outward and with its tail protruding slightly from the den entrance. A porcupine is safe from a fisher's attack when in a den such as this.

Figure 56. Porcupine in a tree facing away from the trunk. When porcupines in trees face away from the trunk, they are safe from fishers' attacks.

porcupine's den in which there was a porcupine but left without making an attack. A den with only one entrance is completely safe from a fisher's attack (Powell and Brander 1977). Before the fisher's reintroduction to Upper Michigan during the early 1960s, porcupines sometimes used dens in hollow logs with holes at both ends (R. B. Brander, personal communication). Since the reestablishment of fishers in the upper peninsula, the use of such dens has ceased where there are fishers. This may be because porcupines have learned that such dens are not safe from fishers' attacks, but more probably it is because all the porcupines that used such dens have been killed, leaving only those porcupines that utilize dens with only one entrance.

Porcupines are also relatively safe from predation while they are in trees. On two occasions while I was working in the Ottawa Nation-

Figure 57. Fisher track in porcupine habitat. Fishers travel long distances with little or no change of direction when in porcupine habitat.

al Forest, I followed fisher tracks that showed that the fishers had climbed trees in which there were procupines but did not kill the porcupines. In both cases, the porcupines were facing out from the trunk of the tree when I came by several hours after the fisher (Figure 56). Out of 12 observations of porcupines in trees for which the direction the procupine faced was noted, the porcupine faced away from the trunk in 11 ($p < 0.01$, chi-square). If a porcupine were to face toward the trunk, a fisher could either attack its face or force it backward until it fell from the tree, and then the fisher could make a normal attack on the ground (Powell 1977a, 1978a).

In marked contrast to fishers' foragings for hares in lowland coniferous forests, fishers' foragings for porcupines in upland hardwood forests are characterized by long distances run with almost no changes in direction (Clem 1977; Powell 1977a, 1978a; Powell and Brander 1977). (See Figure 57 and Table 10.) Fishers change direction significantly less often in porcupine habitat than in hare habitat. I followed fisher tracks in Michigan that traveled up to 5 kilometers with little change in direction (Powell 1977a, 1978a).

Fishers' long upland travels often pass within a meter of one or more porcupine dens. Sometimes a fisher abruptly changes direction before going directly to a porcupine's den, as though the fisher had smelled the den. Some porcupine dens are visited by fishers several winters in succession, even when they are not active during all winters. Therefore, fishers appear to use olfaction and memory in locating porcupine dens.

There were 27 known porcupine dens in my Michigan study area that were active during at least one of the three winters I was doing my fieldwork (Figure 58). Table 11 summarizes the numerical relationships among these dens and the tracks of fishers that visited them. To see whether fishers hunting porcupines had a tendency to inspect several porcupine dens before going back to hunting snowshoe hares, the right-hand column in Table 11 was compared to a Poisson distribution. The number of dens visited by a fisher was significantly different from a Poisson distribution ($p < 0.02$), indicating that fishers visit several dens while foraging in porcupine habitat. This could be interpreted to mean that fishers specifically search for porcupine dens and do not simply pass dens on the way from one patch of hare habitat to another. However, several dens were close together (Figure 58); and, if those dens were considered as one den (a fisher might be able to smell other nearby dens from one den in a cluster), then the number of dens visited by a fisher (Table 11, third column, in parentheses) is not different from a Poisson distribution. Consequently, the interpretation that fishers specifically seek to visit several porcupine dens should be taken with some caution. Nevertheless, I feel that there is very suggestive evidence that resident fishers know the locations of active porcupine dens within their home ranges and direct their foraging in porcupine habitat toward those dens.

Fishers hunting porcupines exhibit many behaviors not used by weasels (Powell 1977a, 1978a). Porcupine dens are located far apart in habitat that offers little else as prey for a fisher. The typical musteline zigzag foraging behavior exhibited by fishers hunting

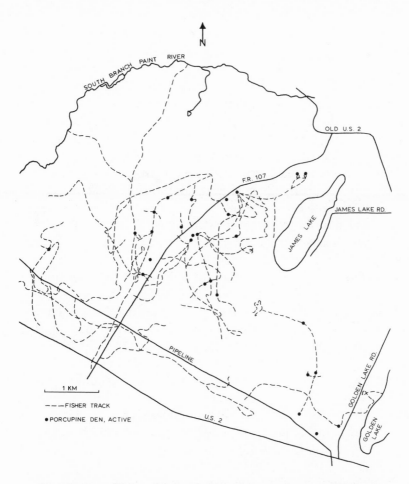

Figure 58. Map of fisher tracks in relation to known active porcupine dens in my study area in Upper Michigan. Several dens were visited by more than one track, and several tracks visited more than one den. (See Table 11.) (C. B. Powell)

Table 11. Numerical Relationships between Fisher Tracks and the Porcupine Dens They Visited in Michigan.

N	Number of Dens Visited by N Tracks	Number of Tracks Visiting N Dens[a]
0	3	13 (13)
1	14	7 (8)
2	4	3 (6)
3	2	4 (3)
4	4	3 (0)

Source: Powell 1977a.

[a] The numbers in parentheses were generated when dens close together were treated as a single den.

snowshoe hares in lowland coniferous forests would be highly un-productive in porcupine habitat. Also, because of its odor, a porcu-pine den can be located from farther away by smell than by direct inspection. Locations of porcupine dens can be learned and forag-ing can be directed toward them with little travel in other directions. There is an obvious selective advantage for fishers that minimize their energy expenditures and quickly locate possible food sources. Con-sequently, the typical musteline foraging behavior has been replaced by directional travel to porcupine dens (Powell 1977a, 1978a).

The fisher's attack behavior toward a porcupine involves a strategy that opens the porcupine's face to a bite. Repeated facial attacks have not been reported for other mustelids, but for long-tailed wea-sels (Allen 1938) and black-footed ferrets (Progulske 1969), "if prey is relatively large, a few preliminary bites delivered anywhere conve-nient may precede a definitive attack" (Ewer 1973, p. 177). I have observed the same behavior in European fitch ferrets attacking snow-shoe hares. If fishers also displayed preliminary bites "anywhere con-venient" when attacking larger prey, such behavior could easily have developed into repeated facial attacks on porcupines because the face is the only place convenient. The development of a successful and relatively safe technique for killing porcupines would have opened a new source of food, for which they had little competition, to fishers (Powell 1977a, 1978a).

The concurrence of all recent reports that fishers kill porcupines by attacking their faces does not mean that this is the only method employed by fishers. It is possible that some or all fishers have other techniques for killing porcupines. Pringle and Mech (1961) cited a report from a trapper who believed that fishers turn porcupines over by holding on to the face the first time a good bite to the face is achieved. It is possible that fishers sometimes overturn porcupines after securing a firm grip on their faces. Though such speculations may have merit, all the present evidence still strongly indicates that making repeated facial attacks is the primary killing method.

Fishers and Quills

Every long-term study of fishers to date has found quills in at least some wild fishers but no sign that these quills were causing infections or other complications. This fact and statements in the popular liter-ature have led to a common popular belief that fishers are somehow different from other animals and are not affected by porcupine quills (Balser 1960; Bradle 1957; Cook and Hamilton 1957; Hamilton 1957; Hardy 1899, 1907; and others). Nevertheless, there is no solid evidence to support these claims.

All mammals appear to react in the same manner to porcupine quills. Quills carry no poison or irritant and have no characteristics that should cause infection. Quick (1953b) looked at the incidence of quills in carcasses of mammals trapped in British Columbia and related this to the condition of the carcasses. Quills impaled in flesh appeared to drift about in the muscles and eventually became lodged against bones. Quick (1953b, p. 259) concluded that "ingested or injected quills are not necessarily lethal to mammals which prey upon porcupines." Coulter (1966) presented evidence showing that domestic dogs show no ill effects from quills that cannot be extracted. Therefore, there is nothing peculiar about quills that causes any animal harm other than the number of quills and the location of quills received during an encounter.

Fishers, like other animals, can suffer ill effects from quills under certain conditions. Coulter (1966), deVos (1952), Hamilton and Cook (1955), Morse (1961), and Pringle (1964a) all cited information gained from trappers that indicates that porcupine quills can blind or kill fishers when many become embedded in a fisher's face. One of my captive fishers somehow embedded a quill from a dead porcupine deep in her chest and acquired a bad infection in the wound. Had I not removed the quill and administered an antibiotic, she might not have survived.

There is good evidence that fishers are unlikely to receive a large number of quills in an area such as the face or paws that would hinder their hunting or killing prey or their defending themselves. Any predator with a mouth full of quills will have trouble killing prey and eating carrion and will be subject to starvation before the quills work their way to a harmless position. A predator with quills in its paws will have trouble running. Similarly, a face full of quills prevents an animal from properly defending itself against an attack from another predator. These problems combined with food deprivation should predispose animals with a large number of quills in a strategic area to high mortality from predation by other predators. Because fishers have developed a technique for killing porcupines that minimizes the chances of receiving a large number of quills, fishers are less likely than other predators to suffer serious problems from porcupine quills.

Long-Term Stability of the Fisher-Porcupine System

The reported association between increasing fisher populations and decreasing porcupine populations was discussed briefly in Chapter 4. Hamilton and Cook (1955, p. 29) wrote that "it seems probable that the increase of the fisher has had a part in the reduction of the once populous and destructive porcupine" in the Adirondack Mountains of New York. Using a Wisconsin county highway department's 12-year record of porcupines killed on highways, Olson (1966, p.22) concluded that "there is now good evidence that the fisher, restocked in the national forests of Wisconsin and Michigan, is becoming effective in controlling porcupines." Coulter (1966, p. 164) noted the decrease in the porcupine population in the Moosehead Plateau region in Maine concurrent with the increase in the fisher population during the 1950s, but he also found evidence that the high porcupine densities "were temporary and were associated with a population irruption." He (p. 164) concluded that "there is no conclusive evidence to indicate that fishers will control porcupine populations over a long period."

In 1975, Brander and I (Powell and Brander 1977) were the first to present quantitative data documenting the impact of predation by fishers on a porcupine population. Our data covered the porcupine population in part of my fisher study area from 1962 through 1975. Figure 59 shows porcupine population census data, plus the data through 1979. We reported that the porcupine population in our original study area declined from 21 porcupines in 1962 to 5 porcupines in 1975; this constituted a 76% reduction during the first 13 years after the fisher's reintroduction. The census for 1979 for the original study area showed 1 porcupine, indicating that the decline in the porcupine population had not ceased by that time. The census for a larger study area over a smaller number of years shows the same trends as those on our original study area.

Brander and I (Powell and Brander 1977) were unable to find any evidence that porcupine mortality factors other than the fisher (such as disease, predation by other predators, and human-related deaths) had increased during the 13 years for which we had data. There was some evidence that other mortality factors had decreased. Therefore, we concluded (p. 48) that "the fisher appears to be the sole

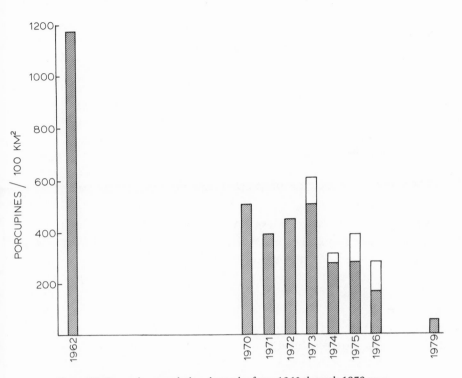

Figure 59. Porcupine population dynamics from 1962 through 1979 on a sample study area (1.79 square kilometers) in Upper Michigan, converted to porcupines per 100 square kilometers. Data are taken from Powell and Brander (1977, unpublished data) and Powell (1977, 1980a). The hollow histograms for 1973 to 1976 are population dynamics on an enlarged census area (2.83 square kilometers) encompassing the original census area. Porcupine populations were the same in the original and enlarged census areas in 1979. (*C. B. Powell*)

causal agent for the decline in porcupine population that we have documented."

Fieldwork done by Earle (1978) provided further evidence that fishers are responsible for the decrease in the porcupine density in the Ottawa National Forest. Earle compared the population densities, sex ratios, and weight distributions of the porcupine populations in the Ottawa and Hiawatha national forests in Upper Michigan. Although there were no differences in sex ratios and weight distributions for the two national forests, there was a significant difference in the population densities of porcupines in the forests. During a winter census of all porcupines in four study areas in each national forest, Earle found that the porcupine population density ranged from 2.3 to 4.6 porcupines per square kilometer in the Hiawatha National Forest but ranged from 0 to less than 1.0 porcupines per square kilometer in the Ottawa National Forest. The difference was highly significant ($p = 0.014$, Mann-Whitney U test). Similarly, Earle found a significant difference in the number of road-killed porcupines found per kilometer of road driven during the springs of 1976 and 1977; road-killed porcupines were found over twice as frequently in the Hiawatha National Forest as in the Ottawa National Forest both years ($p = 0.0011$ and $p = 0.0040$ in 1976 and 1977, respectively, Mann-Whitney U test).

Earle (1978) felt that the only significant difference between his study areas in the two national forests was the presence of the established fisher population in the Ottawa National Forest. Two measures of forest composition (distributions of importance values for the major tree species and proportions of cover types along highways) showed that the two national forests did not differ significantly ($p < 0.016$ and $p < 0.001$, respectively, Kendall rank correlation test). Therefore, Earle concluded that differences in habitat were not responsible for the difference seen in the porcupine population densities.

To date, no studies of fishers and porcupines have been carried on long enough to prove that the fisher can control porcupine populations over long periods of time. Such a study would have to cover at least 20 years, if not more. Evidence in the fossil and sub-fossil records of long-term coexistence of fishers and porcupines does not even support long-term porcupine control or a long-term stable relationship between fishers and porcupines. The fossil and sub-fossil record is not inconsistent with a scenario of repeated local extinctions and reestablishments of the species (Powell 1977a, 1980a). Therefore, Brander and I (Powell and Brander 1977) examined some factors that we believed would affect the long-term stability of the fisher-porcupine system. The long-term coexistence of the two species indicates that they have had a period over which to coevolve with each other and to establish some pattern of stability. The existence of several alternative prey for the fisher should stabilize the fisher-porcupine system by allowing fishers to "switch" prey preferences as relative prey populations change (Murdoch and Oaten 1975). And in Michigan there was much unoccupied habitat into which the fisher population could expand. Consequently, Brander and I concluded that a long-term stable relationship between fishers and porcupines can be expected.

Mathematical modeling and computer simulation of fisher-porcupine communities can give further insight into what the long-term
population dynamics might be. To address this problem I developed
from the literature five mathematical models that could be used to
investigate population dynamics and long-term community stability
in one-predator-one-prey and one-predator-three-prey model communities (Powell 1977a, 1980a). The model communities were based
on the fisher community present in the Ottawa National Forest. Because the porcupine has only one major predator—the fisher—I developed one-predator-one-prey communities containing only fishers
and porcupines. But, because fishers have other prey, I also developed one-predator-three-prey model communities containing fishers,
porcupines, snowshoe hares, and deer carrion. Each model community had for each community member species a difference equation
that provided the population size each year for that species, given the
population sizes of that and other species during the preceding year
and values for several other parameters that represented different
aspects of that species's biology. In all models, porcupine reproduction was assumed to resemble logistic growth; that is, porcupines had
an environmental carrying capacity such that, when their populations
were below this carrying capacity, reproduction exceeded mortality
and, when above, mortality exceeded reproduction. Snowshoe hares
were modeled in all models to have a 10 year population cycle, as
they do in real life. Fisher-related prey mortality or removal, and
fisher reproduction and mortality were modeled in a wide variety of
ways. In one model, prey losses were assumed to be proportional to
the product of the predator and prey population sizes (Lotka-Vol-
terra predator-prey model). In another model, prey losses were assumed to be proportional to the product of the predator and the
square root of the prey population sizes (Gause [1934] predator-prey
model). In the rest of the models, prey losses were modeled so as to
be influenced by predator interference, predator satiation, and maximum predation rates (Holling 1959; Ivlev 1961; Watt 1959). All of
the models attempted to represent the biology of the community
species accurately, but each model made slightly different assumptions about the species' biology and emphasized different aspects
of the species' biology. Five models were investigated both for fishers with one prey and for fishers with three prey to see whether
any of the assumptions made big differences in the results and to be

able to draw conclusions from consistencies among all the models. All of the models were explored for long-term stability of the community by using community matrices and computer simulations. A community matrix is a matrix whose elements represent quantified relationships among the species in the community. The magnitude and sign of an element are determined from the community model and represent the importance of the relationship and whether that relationship has positive or negative effects on the species involved. Computer simulations are simulations of the communities' population dynamics over many, many time intervals (in this case, years), assuming that the communities' member species are adequately represented by the mathematical equations put into the computer. The community matrices for all the models of the fisher community showed that the one-predator-one-prey fisher-porcupine community is stable and indicated that the one-predator-three-prey fisher-porcupine-hare-deer carrion community should be stable under real-life conditions. Computer simulations were run for the predicted long-term population dynamics of the model communities. Long-term community stability was defined as a fisher population that did not fall below 0.5 fishers per 100 square kilometers and a porcupine population that did not fall below 1.0 porcupines per 100 square kilometers in 100 years. Although there were quantitative differences between the models, all the models qualitatively predicted similar community population dynamics. In addition, I manipulated the values of the parameters in the models that represented different aspects of the species' biology. This work showed that the model communities remained stable over fairly large ranges of these parameter values. Consequently, I knew that errors in my original estimation of these parameter values would not greatly affect the conclusions I drew concerning the stability of the model communities.

I concluded from my models of the fisher predator-prey community in Michigan that neither fishers nor porcupines should become extinct or experience a population explosion, unless major disturbances are created by humans. This conclusion was not affected when species other than fishers and porcupines were included in the community. However, the possibility of either the fisher's or the porcupine's extinction is smaller when there are other species in the community.

Chapter 9

Ecological Energetics
of the Fisher

Most discussions of the food requirements of free-living wild mammalian predators deal with food consumption capacities or consumption rates calculated from observations of food intake (e.g., Burkholder 1959; Eaton 1974; Mech 1966, 1970, 1977a; Rudnai 1973; Schaller 1967). One cannot determine from such studies alone how closely the measured rates of food consumption compare with actual energy requirements or utilization. Mech (1977a) reported on a wolf pack for which he could show that the wolves were eating less than they required, but he needed extensive data on wolf blood in order to identify the deviant blood parameters in undernourished wolves. He still could not determine how much less than their requirements the wolves were eating.

There is information on the nutritional requirements of ranch minks and foxes (see Davison 1975 for a summary), but there is very little information available on the nutritional or energetic requirements of wild predators. Litvaitis and Mautz (1976) and Golley and co-workers (1965) discussed the energy requirements of captive wild foxes and bobcats, respectively, but were unable to gain much insight into the requirements of free-living wild predators. Golley (1960) and Moors (1974, 1977) assumed that the daily energy expenditure in the laboratory was the same as that in the field for least weasels and then modeled energy budgets for free-living weasels.

Table 12. Digestive and Metabolizable Efficiencies of Fishers Eating Different Prey and the Energy Available from Those Prey.

Prey Species	Digestive Efficiency	Metabolizable Efficiency	Meal Size	Digestible kcal/Meal	Metabolizable kcal/Meal	Source[a]
Snowshoe hare	83%[b]	–	1.25 kg	1440	–	Powell 1981
Snowshoe hare	83%	–	1.25 kg	1440	–	Clements 1975
Snowshoe hare	91%	77%	1.25 kg	1590	1350[c]	Davison 1975 and Davison, Mautz, and Hayes 1978
Porcupine[d]	–	85%	4.35 kg	–	7050	Powell 1979a
Deer carrion	97%[e]	–	1.00 kg	1710	–	Powell 1981
Deer carrion	93%	86%	1.00 kg	1640	1520	Davison 1975 and Davison, Mautz and Hayes 1978
Red squirrel	84%[f]	–	380 g	520	–	Powell 1981
Squirrels[d]	–	75%	380 g	–	470	Powell 1979a
Small mammals[g]	81%	74%	25 g	33	30	Davison 1975 and Davison, Mautz and Hayes 1978
Coturnix quail	91%	87%	125 g	221	211	Davison 1975 and Davison, Mautz, and Hayes 1978

[a] Source of measurement of digestive and/or metabolizable efficiency; digestible and metabolizable kcal/meal are calculated in Powell (1981).
[b] Values for percentage dry weight and kcal/g dry weight are averaged from Davison (1975), Davison, Mautz, and Hayes (1978), Golley et al. (1965), and Litvaitis and Mautz (1980).
[c] This value was incorrectly calculated in Powell (1979a); the correct value for a 1.25-kilogram hare is given here.
[d] Estimated.
[e] Values for percentage dry weight and kcal/g dry weight are averaged from Davison (1975), Davison, Mautz, and Hayes (1978), Golley et al. (1965), and Litvaitis and Mautz (1976, 1980).
[f] Values for percentage dry weight and kcal/g dry weight are averaged over values for hares and small mammals given in Davison (1975), Davison, Mautz, and Hayes (1978), Golley et al. (1965), and Litvaitis and Mautz (1976, 1980).
[g] Included are *Microtus*, *Peromyscus*, and *Blarina*; digestible kilocalories per meal are calculated for *Microtus* and *Peromyscus* only.

Direct measurement of the energy expenditure of free-living mammals has only been carried out for rodents (Mullen 1970, 1971a, 1971b; Mullen and Chew 1973).

Energy Acquisition and Expenditure

Considering the small amount of research that has been done on fishers, there is a surprising amount of information available on their ecological energetics. This is because two studies have concentrated on the fisher's energetics. Davison and co-workers (Davison 1975; Davison et al. 1978) studied the efficiency of food utilization by fishers and the energy requirements of captive fishers. I studied the energy requirements of free-living fishers (Powell 1977a, 1979a, 1981). The information gained from these studies also provides new insight into the fisher's sexual dimorphism in body size and into the fisher's foraging strategies.

Table 12 summarizes the energy available to fishers from different prey species. Davison and co-workers (Davison 1975; Davison et al. 1978) maintained four female fishers on four different diets to determine their gross energy intake, the digestibility of nutrients, the partitioning of dietary energy, the partitioning of dietary nitrogen, and the net maintenance energy requirements. Clements (1975) studied the digestive efficiency of fishers eating snowshoe hares, and I have done research on fishers eating three different diets (Powell 1981). For Table 12, digestive efficiency was determined by subtracting the energy lost in excrement and uneaten parts of prey from the total energy available from a member of a prey species. Metabolizable efficiency is determined by further subtracting the energetic cost of digestion.

The porcupine is the only major prey of the fisher for which direct measurements of energy available are lacking. A fisher takes several days to eat a porcupine, and it is difficult to collect all of the uneaten material in feeding experiments. Therefore, the energy available to fishers from porcupines has had to be estimated. From observations of more than 20 porcupines eaten by fishers, I have determined that fishers usually eat only the meat, fat, internal organs, and very small bones of porcupines and leave the skin, quills, feet, leg bones, backbone, and skull. I dismembered five porcupines of known weight in a manner simulating the fisher's eating habits and estimated that fishers eat roughly 75% (a range of 72% to 79%) of the wet weight of a porcupine. That part of a porcupine that is eaten is roughly of the same composition as the deer used by Davison (1975). Consequently, the values for the percentage of metabolizable energy, the kilocalories per dry gram, and the ratio of dry weight to wet weight were assumed to be the same for porcupines as they are for deer for the figures in Table 12. The weights for porcupines and hares listed in Table 12 are average weights for those species in the Ottawa National Forest, but they are representative of the weights of those species anywhere. The weights for squirrels and mice are approximate median weights taken from the literature.

The digestive and metabolizable efficiencies are both lower for mammalian prey with relatively large amounts of hair and bones (small mammals and squirrels) than for prey of which fishers eat mostly meat and viscera (deer carrion and porcupines). The metabolizable energy available from prey items ranges from 30 kilocalories for a mouse to 7050 kilocalories for a porcupine. Table 12 shows that there is some variation in digestive efficiency values found for fishers eating snowshow hares and deer carrion in different studies. The similarity of the values suggests that the trends shown in the table are correct; but the variation indicates that, in addition to measurement error, there may be differences in energy values from different populations or individuals of a given prey species.

Davison and co-workers (Davison 1975; Davison et al. 1978) did not know whether or not the information obtained for Coturnix quail is similar to that which would be obtained from other birds that are natural prey of the fisher. Unfortunately, these quail were the only birds Davison could obtain in sufficient quantity to do the work. Quail and grouse are both in the order Galliformes but are very different in size, so whether the results for quail can be extrapolated to grouse is unknown.

High energy digestibility similar to that found for fishers has been reported for badgers (Jense 1968), bobcats (Golley et al. 1965), coyotes (Litvaitis and Mautz 1980), least weasels (Golley 1960; Moors 1974, 1977), minks (Roberts and Kirk 1964), and red foxes (Litvaitis and Mautz 1976).

Davison and co-workers estimated the daily maintenance energy requirements of captive fishers under laboratory conditions. They arrived at the figure of $172 \text{ kcal}/W^{.75}/\text{day}$ (W = weight in kilograms). This is equivalent to 660 kilocalories for a 6-kilogram male fisher, 490 kilocalories for a 4-kilogram male fisher, and 290 kilocalories for a 2-kilogram female fisher.

In order to estimate the energy expenditures of free-living fishers, I developed a model for the daily energy expenditures of free-living solitary mammals (Powell 1977a, 1979a). The model can be applied to any mammal that does not spend much time in activities other than sleeping and running. From estimates of daily energy expenditures, daily food requirements can be calculated. The model was derived in the following way.

The total energy expenditure (X) of an animal can be expressed as the sum of the energies expended in different activities and can be represented by a statement of the form:

$$X = \Sigma X_i$$

where X_i is the energy expended in activity i and is a function of the time for which i occurs and the ambient temperature. Activities i must be exhaustive and mutually exclusive.

There are only three important nonreproductive activities for fishers: sleeping, running, and capturing prey. Fishers do not often climb trees, remain solitary except for a brief mating period, and hunt during a small number of periods each day that are separated by sleep. (See Chapters 3 and 5.) Thus, fishers spend almost all of their time sleeping or running on the ground while hunting, the energy expenditures of which are symbolized as X_1 and X_2, respectively. Prey capture is infrequent (Powell 1977a, 1978a), but, when it occurs, energy is expended at a high rate. The energy expended during prey capture is symbolized as X_3.

The sleeping metabolic rate (X_1) of a healthy mammal in its thermoneutral zone is roughly the same as its basal metabolic rate (BMR). Kleiber (1961, empirical) and McMahon (1973, theoretical) have shown that (letting the BMR equal X_1/t_1):

$$\frac{X_1}{t_1} = k_1 W^{.75} ;$$

thus:

$$X_1 = k_1 t_1 W^{.75} \tag{1}$$

where k_1 is a constant, W is the weight of the mammal, and t_1 is the time spent sleeping. For mammals in general, Kleiber (1961) gave a value of 3 for k_1 (in kcal/kg$^{.75}$/hr).

Running metabolism (X_2) can be predicted from a mammal's weight. For a wide variety of mammals, Schmidt-Nielsen (1971), Taylor (1973), Taylor, Schmidt-Nielsen, and Rabb (1970), Wunder (1975), and Yousef and co-workers (1973) have shown that the metabolic rate increases in a straight-line fashion with running speed. The relationship is:

$$\begin{array}{l} running \\ metabolic = k_2 W^{.75} + k_3 W^{.6} s, \\ rate \end{array}$$

where k_2 and k_3 are constants, $k_3 W^{.6}$ is the rate of increase of metabolic rate with running speed, and s is running speed.

Because of this straight-line relationship, average running speed can be used to obtain average metabolic rate and energy expenditure during the time spent running (t_2). Average running metabolic rate is X_2/t_2, and the expression for energy expenditure becomes:

$$X_2 = k_2 t_2 W^{.75} + k_3 W^{.6} s t_2.$$

Since the distance run (d) is equal to $s t_2$:

$$X_2 = k_2 t_2 W^{.75} + k_3 d W^{.6}. \tag{2}$$

Running speed is not even needed. The energy expended can be calculated from the time spent running and the distance run.

The metabolic rate of a carnivore capturing prey (X_3) depends on the methods of capture, but for most carnivores (including fishers [Powell 1977a, 1978a]), energy is expended at a high rate, and a primary part of prey capture is running. A reasonable estimate of the metabolic rate during prey capture is the metabolic rate at maximum running speed. Thus:

$$\frac{X_3}{t_3} = k_2 W^{.75} + k_3 W^{.6} s_m,$$

and:

$$X_3 = k_2 t_3 W^{.75} + k_3 s_m t_3 W^{.6}, \tag{3}$$

where t_3 is capture time and s_m is maximum running speed. Errors introduced by using this estimate are minimized by the infrequency or prey capture.

Adding equations 1, 2, and 3 yields a general equation for the energy expenditure of a fisher in its thermoneutral zone:

$$X = (k_1 t_1 + k_2(t_2 + t_3))W^{.75} + k_3(d + s_m t_3)W^{.6} \qquad (4)$$

Equation 4 holds for ambient temperatures (T_a) above a mammal's lower critical temperature (T_c). When T_a is less than T_c, the metabolic rate is increased by the amount $mW^{1/2}(T_c - T_a)$, where the value of the constant m depends on the units used (Herreid and Kessel 1967).

After I taught two fishers to run on a treadmill, I determined the relationship between running speed and metabolic rate and the constants k_1, k_2, k_3, and s_m for fishers (Powell 1977a, 1979a). I also estimated T_c for fishers. The completed equation 4 for fishers is:

$$X = (3.0 \cdot t_1 + 5.4(t_2 + t_3))W^{.75} + 3.3(d + 12.5t_3)W^{.6}, \qquad (5)$$

where the units used are kilocalories, kilograms, and hours. Estimated T_c's were -30°C and -20°C for active male and female fishers, respectively, and -80°C and -40°C for male and female fishers curled up for sleeping.

Figure 60 shows the predicted daily energy expenditures of fishers of different weights and different activity schedules. The predicted daily energy expenditures range from about 130 kilocalories for a female fisher who sleeps all day to about 450 kilocalories for a large male fisher who is active 40% of the day and travels 8 kilometers.

Figure 61 shows the predicted energy expenditures from equation 3 for fishers of different weights that handle and kill a porcupine and a snowshoe hare. The more energy expended while capturing the prey, the more important that energy expenditure becomes compared to the energy obtained from the prey. Therefore, it is best to look at a high estimate of energy expenditure for handling prey in order to see whether handling energy expenditure is important and, when it is, how important it can potentially be. The maximum running speed on the treadmill was used for s_m. A handling time of 45 minutes (1.5 times the handling times found by Coulter [1966]) was used to calculate porcupine-handling energy expenditure, and 5 minutes (far in excess of the one handling time obtained during my study [Powell 1977a, 1978a]) was used to calculate the expenditure for hares. Prey-handling energy expenditures range from approximately 40 kilocalories to 100 kilocalories for porcupines and from approximately 5 kilocalories to 10 kilocalories for hares. It can be seen in both cases that the prey-handling energy expenditures are very small in

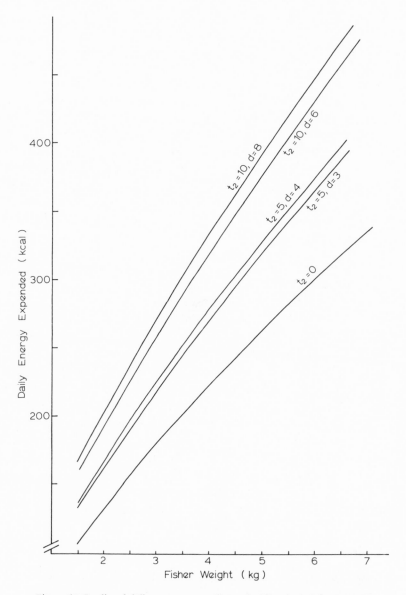

Figure 60. Predicted daily energy expenditure (in kilocalories) from equation 5 for fishers of different weights and different activity regimes that do not catch prey. Lines are labeled for fishers that were active 0%, 20%, and 40% of 24 hours and that traveled 0, 3, 4, 6, 8 kilometers.

relation to the energy acquired from the prey (Table 12) and that handling expenditures are even small compared to expected daily energy expenditures excluding prey handling (Figure 60).

Using radiotelemetric collars that told me whether a fisher was active or inactive, I was able to estimate the energy expenditures of free-living fishers. On five occasions I was able to maintain continuous radio contact with a fisher for periods of 8 to 26 hours and then measure how far the fisher had run while it had been monitored. The data I recorded are summarized in Table 13. The estimated energy

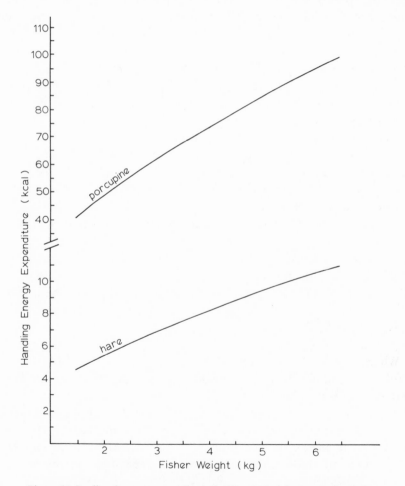

Figure 61. Predicted energy expenditure (in kilocalories) from equation 3 for for fishers of different weights killing porcupines and a snowshoe hares.

expended adjusted to 24 hours ranged from 206 kilocalories for a female fisher to 447 kilocalories for a male fisher.

There are two other sources of activity data that have been used to estimate the daily energy expenditures of fishers (Powell 1981). Kelly (1977) collected data on fishers' activities and distances traveled in New Hampshire. Distances between radiotelemetric locations on two consecutive days were determined a total of 136 times for 31 fishers; distances traveled were categorized by sex, age, and season. These data have been inserted into equation 5 to estimate the daily energy expenditures of the fishers studied by Kelly (Powell 1981). The estimated daily energy expenditures ranged from 191 kilocalories for females during the winter to 454 kilocalories for adult males during the entire year. The low value for females during the winter was due to their small average weight and the small amount of time they were active. The high value for adult males averaged over the whole year was due to a combination of their large size, long distances traveled, and high level of activity.

Leonard (1980b) collected data on a fisher in Manitoba that also can be used to estimate daily energy expenditures. Leonard maintained continuous radiotelemetric contact with a female fisher for 19 days of the 7-week period during which she had kits in a maternal den. He was able to determine her time spent at the den, her time spent away from the den, and the general route of travel she followed while away from the den. When Leonard's data are inserted into equation 5, the estimated nonreproductive energy expenditures of this female ranged from 211 kilocalories (on a day when the kits were very small and the female stayed with them much of the day) to 337 kilocalories (on a day when the kits were growing quite fast and the female spent much time away from the den hunting [Powell 1981]).

When one looks at 123 kilometers of measured fisher tracks I followed and assumes that the fishers who made the tracks had two active periods per day, traveled approximately 3 kilometers between sleeping sites, and averaged 0.8 kilometers per hour while hunting (Table 13), then another estimate of fishers' daily energy expenditures can be made. (See Chapter 5.) This estimate ranges from 200 kilocalories to 480 kilocalories per day, depending on the fisher's weight.

Although Davison's estimates (Davison 1975; Davison et al. 1978)

Table 13. Fisher Watches: Activity, Distance, and Energy Expended.

Watch Number	Fisher	Sex	Weight (kg)	Hours Inactive (t_1)	Hours Active (t_2)	Length of Watch $(t_1 + t_2)$[a]	Total Distance Run (km)	Total kcal Expended	kcal Expended per 24 Hours
1	A	M	4.7	24.0	0	24.0	0	253	253
2	B	F	2.4	17.1	7.6	24.7	4.65	212	206
3	C	M	5.1	21.2	4.8	26.0	3.20	351	324
4	C	M	5.1	5.8	2.8	8.6	3.00	140	391
5	C	M	5.1	9.8	11.2	21.0	9.50	390	447

Sources: Powell 1977a; R. A. Powell, 1979, Ecological energetics and foraging strategies of the fisher (*Martes pennanti*). J. Anim. Ecol. 48: 195-212, used by permission of the publisher.

[a] Hours prey capture (t_3) = 0 for all watches.

of daily maintenance energy requirements (290 kilocalories to 660 kilocalories per day) and the several estimates of daily energy expenditures of fishers in the field using equation 5 (130 kilocalories to 480 kilocalories per day) are broadly overlapping, the model estimates are consistently smaller than Davison's. There are two probable reasons for this discrepancy. First, free-living fishers spend a great deal of time sleeping, whereas captive fishers are very active (Davison 1975; Powell, personal observation). Also, as Table 13 shows, the average speed of a hunting fisher is very slow, but fishers pacing in cages usually move quickly (Powell, personal observation). Consequently, because Davison used captive fishers, his estimate is biased to overestimate maintenance energy requirements. Second, my model may underestimate the energy expenditures of free-living fishers. My model does have many sources of error: several constants had to be determined, and each determination is subject to error; the constants were determined under laboratory conditions that did not always duplicate those in the field; and field measurements are always subject to error. However, Davison's estimates are also subject to error for many of the same reasons. I believe all of these estimates together provide a good understanding of the fisher's daily energy expenditures.

The frequencies at which fishers with different daily energy expenditures must catch prey are given in Table 14. Davison (Davison 1975; Davison et al. 1978) and I (Powell 1977a, 1979a) have both measured and estimated fishers' actual food consumption. Under laboratory conditions, Davison measured a consumption of metabolizable energy ranging from 260 kilocalories per day to 450 kilocalories per day for the four female fishers on different diets. These estimates agree closely with the estimated maintenance energy found by Davison for these fishers: 440 kilocalories per day for each fisher weighing 3.5 kilograms. On a $kcal/W^{.75}$ basis, Davison's estimates are similar to the consumption of metabolizable energy of minks reported by Cowan, Wood, and Kitts (1957) but less than that found by Farrell and Wood (1968).

Along 123 kilometers of measured fisher tracks, I found 14 kills and scavenges (Powell 1977a, 1978a, 1979a). These and their estimated kilocalories available to fishers are shown in Table 15. The average number of kilocalories available from each kill-scavenge is approximately 1250. This estimate adjusts to approximately 860

Table 14. Days of a Fisher's Food Requirements That are Met by Acquisition of an
Individual or Amount of a Given Prey Type at Different Daily Energy Expenditures.

Food Item	Amount Eaten	Daily Energy Expenditure (kcal)					
		200	300	400	500	600	700
Deer carcass	1.0 kg	8.1	5.4	4.1	3.2	2.7	2.3
Porcupine	4.4 kg	41	28	21	16	14	12
Snowshoe hare	1.2 kg	8.0	5.4	4.0	3.2	2.7	2.3
Squirrel	380 g	2.4	1.6	1.2	0.9	0.8	0.7
Mouse	25 g	0.14	0.10	0.07	0.06	0.05	0.04
Coturnix quail	125 g	1.1	0.7	0.5	0.4	0.4	0.3

kilocalories acquired per day on the average, with the same assumptions about activity periods, distance between rests, and running speed made on p. 170. The average number of kilocalories expended between each kill-scavenge ranges from about 300 to about 700, depending on the fisher's weight. Thus, the estimated number of kilocalories expended between kill-scavenges is of the same order of magnitude as the number of kilocalories available from each kill-scavenge.

There are three likely explanations for the difference between the estimates of energy expenditure and consumption that do occur. First, the estimates of energy expenditure from my model may underestimate the amount of energy expended between kill-scavenges. Second,

Table 15. Energy Available from Each of the 14 Kills and Scavenges Made along
123 Kilometers of Measured Tracks in Michigan and Average Energy Available
per Kill or Scavenge.

Kills and Scavenges	Energy Available (kcal)	Conservative Estimate of Energy Available (kcal)
1 porcupine	7050	3500
1 snowshoe hare	1350	1350
2 squirrels	940	940
2 mice	60	60
7 small scavenges	210	0
½ deer carcass	8000	4000
Average kcal per kill or scavenge	1258	704

Source: Powell 1977a.

Note: The third column is a conservative estimate of the energy a fisher is actually able to obtain from kills or scavenges since it shares large kills with other predators and scavengers.

it is possible that the amount of energy acquired from kill-scavenges has been overestimated. Porcupines and deer carcasses are large and are probably shared with scavengers, and many scavenges are scanty and probably of no energy value to a fisher. With these facts in mind, recalculating the average energy acquisition yields approximately 700 kilocalories per kill-scavenge; this estimate is shown in the far-right-hand column of Table 15. The calculations listed in this column assume that a fisher shares half of the large food items such as deer carcasses and porcupines with scavengers; that hares, squirrels, and mice are eaten in one meal; and that small scavenges are of no energy value to a fisher. Seven hundred kilocalories per kill-scavenge (490 kilocalories acquired per day) is almost exactly the estimated energy expenditure between kill-scavenges.

The third possibility is that the fishers that made the tracks I followed were actually able to acquire more food than they needed to replace the energy they expended. Under such conditions, fishers might be expected to gain weight and not to eat all of the large food items. Of the 18 fishers I handled during my study, all were in excellent health and 11 were well padded with fat over the pelvis and ribs. It was impossible to determine whether fishers did not eat all food available from porcupines and deer carcasses. Fishers always left porcupine kills shortly after I found them, probably because I disturbed them. Nor was it possible to determine how much of the large food items were eaten by fishers; tracks of foxes, coyotes, bobcats, and weasels were seen around the large food items eaten by fishers. Further evidence that the fishers in my study area were able to obtain more than an adequate food supply is in the sexual dimorphism of the body size of fishers in Michigan.

Sexual Dimorphism in Body Size and Energetics

Moors (1974) concluded from his work on the energetics of least weasels that sexual dimorphism in body size is maintained by conflicting selective pressures. There is selective pressure for weasels to be large because large weasels are able to exploit a wider range of prey sizes and thus have more potential prey. There is also selective pressure among weasels for small size because small weasels have lower daily energy requirements. One would assume that the size range of a species is determined by these factors and by competition for food with other predators of different sizes. In addition, female weasels are under selective pressure for small size to reduce maintenance energy requirements during gestation, lactation, and weaning. Moors (1974) has calculated that, compared to a normal-size female, a female least weasel the size of a male would have 25% higher maintenance energy requirements during reproduction. This is approximately the equivalent of 1 additional mouse per day during the period of gestation through weaning, or approximately 50 mice for the entire period. This is a sizable increase in the amount of food required.

This argument for weasels applies equally well to fishers because of the many similarities between weasels and fishers. Fishers and weasels are both long and skinny, with high surface to volume ratios. This means that both species have high convective heat loss and high energy requirements (Brown and Lasiewski 1972; Powell 1977a, 1979a).

There are two correlates to Moors's (1974) hypothesis: during extended periods of abundant food, males should (1) show an increase in average body size (because size is no longer limited by nutrition and fishers can approach maximum size; this has been generally predicted by the cost-benefit analysis made by Schoener 1969) and (2) show an increase in size variance (because males do not reach full size immediately). Females should not show such increases in size and variance in size because their maximum size is much smaller and more easily attained with limited food supplies.

The average weight of male fishers in Michigan *did* increase significantly during the 15 years between their introduction to the area and my study. (See Table 1 in Chapter 1.) Fishers in Michigan were released into an area with a food supply (porcupines) unexploited by other predators, and populations of that food supply were at high levels (Brander and Books 1973; Powell and Brander 1977). Since their release, fishers have exploited the porcupine population (Brander and Books 1973; Powell 1977a, 1978a; Powell and Brander 1977). The average weight of male fishers from Minnesota released in Michigan during the early 1960s was 3.98 kilograms. Since that time the weight of male fishers in Minnesota has remained stable. The average weight of males in Michigan is 4.98 kilograms. This weight is significantly higher than that of the introduced males. The difference in weights was not caused by a disproportionate number of juveniles in the released population (Irvine 1961, 1962). The average weight of females in Michigan is the same as that of the females released. (See Table 1 in Chapter 1.)

Thus, the patterns of sexual dimorphism seen in fishers support Moors's (1974) hypothesis that sexual dimorphism in body size in mustelids is maintained by energetic considerations (Powell 1979b). In addition, these patterns indicate that the fisher population I studied in Michigan may actually have been able to acquire more food than was required to replace the energy expended in daily activities.

Energy Expenditure and Reproduction

Richard Leonard and I (Powell and Leonard, submitted) have developed a model to estimate the energy expenditure of a female fisher with kits, and we have used this model to estimate the energy expenditure of a female fisher Leonard followed radiotelemetrically in Manitoba. This female had a litter of four kits in a den in a quaking aspen tree in April 1977. Her kits remained in this den tree for about 7 weeks, during which time continuous radiotelemetric contact was maintained during 22 days. We were able to calculate the distance the female traveled each time she left the den tree and the amounts of time she spent with the kits (time spent inactive or sleeping) and she spent away from the den tree (time spent active or hunting) for each of those 22 days. From weights of this female known at two other times, we estimated that her weight during this period was 2.64 kilograms.

We believe that seven categories of energy expenditure are important to a female fisher during lactation: (1) maintenance energy, (2) energy for running (hunting), (3) energy for capturing prey, (4) lactation energy, (5) copulation energy, (6) energy to climb the den tree, and (7) energy for thermoregulation. We estimated these energy expenditures for our female fisher.

To estimate the maintenance, hunting, and prey-capturing categories of energy expenditure, we used equation 5 (p. 167). Lactation energy (L) has been estimated for other mustelines by estimating the energy kits require for growth and maintenance (Moors 1974). Thus:

$$L = \frac{\text{(litter size) (kit growth energy + kit maintenance energy)}}{\text{(efficiency of lactation) (efficiency of milk assimilation)}}.$$

We used a litter size of four because our female fisher had litters of four for three years in a row. We estimated kit growth energy (11.2 kilocalories per day) from kit growth rates (6.8 grams per day, starting at 40 grams) recorded by Coulter (1966) and me (Figure 25) and from energy content per unit weight of other mustelines (energy content per unit weight of fishers is not known). The efficiency of milk production was assumed to be 0.90 (Brody 1945); and the efficiency of lactation, to be 0.95 (Moors 1974). Lactation energy was estimated as:

$$L = \frac{(4)\,(11.2 + 77(0.040 + (\text{kit age}) \cdot 0.0068)^{.75})}{(0.90)\,(0.95)}$$

$$= 52.4 + 360.2(0.040 + 0.0068 \cdot (\text{kit age}))^{.75}.$$

Because fishers are awake during copulation but are generally inactive (in that they remain in the same place), we estimated copulation energy as running energy (equation 2, p. 167), with the distance traveled set equal to 0. Copulation occurs during a female fisher's active hours away from her den and occurs at a time when she would be hunting if she were not copulating. This means that on those days when our female copulated, the time spent copulating was part of the calculated time spent active. Therefore, copulation energy is estimated within equation 5 as part of the energy spent while hunting.

We estimated the energy expended to climb the den tree by determining the change in potential energy required to move an object the weight of a fisher up to the den entrance and then down to the den floor, plus the kinetic energy required to move a fisher that same distance horizontally. This turned out to be approximately 1 kilocalorie per day, with the assumption that the female left and returned to the den only once per day.

We estimated thermoregulation energy expenditure by using the equation presented earlier in this chapter. This energy expenditure turned out not to be a factor.

The estimated total energy expenditure of our female fisher with kits ranged from 342 kilocalories on a day when her kits were small and she spent 21 hours with them to 544 kilocalories on a day when the kits were large and she spent 23 hours hunting. A linear regression of the total energy expenditure (E) of our female versus the age of the kits (age) is:

$$E = 4.42(\text{age}) + 312.$$

The correlation coefficient (r) for this equation is 0.94.

The average daily energy expenditure for our female was 435 kilocalories; the average daily maintenance energy expenditure before parturition was 228 kilocalories. When the female moved the kits from the den in the quaking aspen, there were still a few weeks remaining before the kits were weaned. Therefore, we estimated that the total energy expenditure of our female fisher would increase to about 600 or 700 kilocalories per day before leveling off or decreasing. This is an approximate trebling of the female's calculated maintenance expenditure before parturition. A similar increase in energy expenditure was found for a female least weasel during lactation by East and Lockie (1964).

Energetics and Foraging Strategies

I used my energy-budget model (equation 5) to investigate the foraging strategies of the fisher in Upper Michigan (Powell 1977a, 1979a). Many theoretical models of the foraging strategies of predators and parasites have been proposed (reviews in Charnov 1976; Krebs 1973; MacArthur 1972; Murdoch and Oaten 1975; Schoener 1971). Most involve the rate of energy intake for a predator choosing between food types or habitat patches and assume a goal of maximizing the rate of energy intake. This is probably a reasonable assumption, because most predators have evolved under conditions of periodic food shortages when it would be advantageous to maximize utilization of food supplies.

The models of optimal foraging strategies deal with gross energy gain, energy expenditure, and net energy gain from different food types. All of these categories have been estimated for fishers in the preceding sections of this chapter. If a predator does not have specific nutritional requirements supplied by only a limited number of prey items, then the predator's optimal choice of food depends on the rate of energy gain available from each of its prey types:

$$E_j = \frac{A_j - X_{sj} - X_{hj}}{t_{sj} - t_{hj}}$$

where E_j is the net rate of energy gain from prey type j; A_j is the metabolizable energy available from a food item of prey type j; X_{sj} and X_{hj} are the energetic costs of searching for and handling a prey item of type j; and t_{sj} and t_{hj} are search and handling times for a prey item of type j.

Charnov (1976) presented a theorem for the inclusion of prey types in a predator's optimal diet. The theorem is derived from a multispecies version of the Holling disk equation (Holling 1959). The assumptions made for the theorem apply to fishers, except that all prey types may not be available to fishers at one time. For example, porcupine and snowshoe hare habitats were the two distinct major habitats in my study area in Upper Michigan; therefore, only one of these prey types is available to a given fisher at any time. When each habitat is treated separately, however, it follows from the theorem that Upper Michigan fishers should eat all prey types found in a particular habitat (listed in Table 9) under my study. Dead deer, squirrels, and small mammals are found in both porcupine habitat and hare habitat and are eaten by fishers when they are encountered. Therefore, modeling fishers' foraging strategies in Upper Michigan is reduced to modeling fishers foraging in porcupine habitat or hare habitat. Because the density of deer carcasses is very low and the energy returns from squirrels and small mammals are low, this strategy is equivalent to foraging for either porcupines or hares.

When a fisher in Upper Michigan attempts to maximize its caloric intake, its decision to hunt for porcupines or hares is determined by whether E_p (for porcupines) or E_h (for hares) is larger. Reasonable estimates for all variables in equation 6, except t_{sj}, can be obtained from Table 12, Figures 60 and 61, fisher tracking data, and observations on captive fishers (Powell 1977a). Let $d = st_{sj}$ in X_{sj}.

$A_p = 7050$ kcal (Table 12)

$X_{hp} = 45$ to 100 kcal (Figure 61)

$X_{sp} = (3.0)(0.8)W^{.6}t_{sp} + (5.4)W^{.75}t_{sp}$ (equation 2)

$t_{hp} = 0.75$ hours (Figure 61)

$A_h = 1350$ kcal (Table 12)

$X_{hh} = 5$ to 10 kcal (Figure 61)

$X_{sh} = (3.0)(0.8)W^{.6}t_{sh} + (5.4)W^{.75}t_{sh}$ (equation 2)

$t_{hh} = 0.083$ hours (Figure 61)

A fisher should hunt porcupines when $E_p > E_h$. To two decimal places, this inequality reduces to the same criterion for fishers of any weight between 2 and 6 kilograms:

$$t_{sh} > 0.19 \cdot t_{sp} + 0.09.$$

Because:

$$\frac{A_h}{A_p} = 0.19,$$

the above inequality can be expressed as:

$$t_{sh} > \left(\frac{A_h}{A_p}\right) t_{sp} + 0.09.$$

A fisher should begin hunting porcupines only when the expected search time to find a hare is greater than the ratio A_h/A_p (which is about one-fifth) times the expected search time to find a porcupine plus 0.09 hours (about 5 minutes). For a fisher hunting porcupines or hares, the critical relationship between t_{sp} and t_{sh} is roughly the ratio of A_p to A_h and the relationship between the E_j's is roughly the relationship between the $(A_j t_{sj})$'s. Even though the energy cost of handling a porcupine is much greater than that for a hare, energy cost of handling a porcupine is only a small percentage of the metabolizable energy available from a porcupine. The difference between the X_{sj}'s, X_{hj}'s, and t_{hj}'s for porcupines and hares reduces to an adjustment of 5 minutes in expected t_{sj}'s. Fishers may shift between hunting porcupines and hares several times in a day, and yet the interval between kills is on the order of days. Therefore, the 5-minute adjustment in t_{sj}'s can be ignored. A_j and t_{sj} are by far the most important components in E_j for fishers in Upper Michigan. A fisher in Upper Michigan should hunt in porcupine habitat when the ratio of the energy acquired from each prey is greater than the ratio of expected search times:

$$\frac{A_p}{A_h} > \frac{t_{sp}}{t_{sh}}.$$

The addition of other prey found in Upper Michigan and eaten by fishers does not complicate the decision for a fisher. For other prey types, t_{sj} is so large and E_j is so small that none would be worth considering by itself if it had to be found in a separate habitat. But all the other prey types are found in both porcupine and hare habitats, and fishers do eat them. This indicates that fishers take them when they are available but do not search for them specifically; this makes the search time for them zero.

In Chapters 7 and 8 it was pointed out that fishers use two distinctly different foraging techniques to hunt hares and porcupines. Hunting in hare habitat is typical of the Mustelinae and involves frequent changes in direction and much zigzagging to look for hares; hunting in porcupine habitat involves running in nearly straight lines from one porcupine den to another. The actual distance a fisher travels between two points is approximately 1.5 times farther in hare habitat than in porcupine habitat (Table 10).

If fishers hunted in porcupine habitat the same way they hunt in hare habitat, the energy expenditure in porcupine habitat would increase by approximately 50%. Hunting success would be unchanged, however, because the only major source of food for a fisher in porcupine habitat is porcupines, which are found only near porcupine dens. Thus, fishers appear to have made a major energetic savings by developing a new hunting method to hunt porcupines (Powell 1979a).

Chapter 10

Conservation and the Fisher's Relationship to Humans

Evolution has molded the fisher into a predator keenly adapted to its environment. The fisher can survive the climate of northern North America, it can travel long distances in short periods of time, and it can hunt and capture a wide variety of prey animals, including the porcupine. The forces that have molded the fisher in the past should keep the fisher adapted to the natural conditions in the forests of North America for millennia to come.

Yet, the fisher's future does not lie with evolution and the forces that have molded its evolutionary past. Today, the fisher's interactions with humans are probably as important as any aspect of the fisher's biology, for humans have the capacity to affect every aspect of the fisher's environment.

Interactions with Humans

Our interest in fishers and our interactions with them fit into five general categories. First, since the time of its discovery, the fisher has been valued for its pelt. Fishers have always been considered furbearers and have always been subject to trapping and, to a lesser extent, fur farming. Second, humans have an important influence on fisher populations through their logging practices and other activities that result in the alteration of the fisher's habitat. Third, some hunters of small game fear that fishers have an adverse effect on populations of small game such as rabbits, hares, and grouse. Fourth, within the last two decades, foresters have acquired and promoted an interest in the fisher as a tool for managing porcupine populations. And, fifth, the fisher is a creature of natural beauty. Many people are interested in the fisher because it is a part of our native fauna; they feel that its preservation is an end in itself aside from the pleasure they gain from a fleeting glimpse of a wild fisher.

The fisher's reaction to humans in all of these interactions is one of avoidance and fear. Even though mustelids as a group appear to be curious by nature, fishers seldom linger when they become aware of the immediate presence of a human.

Trapping

In the past, trapping has been one of the two most important factors influencing fisher populations. As discussed in Chapter 4, the value of fisher pelts has created trapping pressure at times great enough to exterminate fishers completely from large geographic areas. Trapping still has an important impact on fisher populations. In some parts of the fisher's present range, trapping is a primary cause of death. In all parts of the fisher's present range where fishers are trapped, the interest in trapping requires management of fisher populations that guarantees the maintenance of fisher populations. Unfortunately, recent management practices have not always been completely successful. Kelly (1977), Wood (1977), and Young (1975) noted a decrease in fisher populations in New Hampshire during the mid-1970s and attributed the decrease to overtrapping. During the 1977-1978 trapping season, New York, New Hampshire, and Maine were forced to limit or close completely fisher trapping in order to allow populations to build back up. Total trapping returns for the 1977-1978 trapping season were lower than for the previous season (Max Bass, personal communication), but whether that was due to decreased populations, reduced prices offered for pelts, or reduced trapping area can not be determined.

The fisher is well known for being easily trapped and for frequently being trapped in sets for other furbearers (Coulter 1966; Young 1975). Coulter (1966) stressed that, in areas where fishers are scarce, the populations can be seriously affected by fox trapping. I have released fishers accidently captured in coyote sets in Michigan. The number of fishers crippled by being caught in fox and coyote traps can be significant (Powell, unpublished data). In light of this fact, Wisconsin designated fisher wildlife management areas in the Nicolet and Chequamegon national forests (approximately 55,000 hectares and 100,000 hectares, respectively) where land sets for all furbearers were prohibited (Petersen, Martin, and Pils 1977).

Fisher populations are very sensitive to pressures from trapping. In addition to the clear evidence from past population declines, there is evidence from recent changes in trapping regulations in New York and Ontario and theoretical evidence that small changes in mortality due to trapping can greatly affect fisher populations.

The fisher-trapping season in New York during the 1970s was during October (in part), November, and December. During the first half of the decade, annual returns remained approximately constant at about 900 to 1100 fishers (Parsons 1980). The 1976 harvest, however, was approximately 50% greater than the harvests of the preceding few years. Because of this increase, the fisher season was closed for 1977, resulting in an estimated 70% decrease in the deaths of fishers from trapping (the estimated 30% remaining was accounted for by the deaths of fishers captured in sets meant for other furbearers). In 1978, there was again an open fisher season, and the harvest went back to pre-1976 levels.

The age structure of the fisher populations, as indicated in the harvests of 1978 compared to previous years, showed an immediate response to the season's closure. Population models indicate that the New York fisher population was seriously decreased after the 1976 trapping season. Had a harvest similar to 1976 or even previous years been allowed in 1977, the fisher population would have dropped even lower. Closure of the season for one year allowed the population to regain its losses from the previous trapping season because the trapping season in New York is timed to harvest mostly juveniles, leaving adults for future reproduction (Parsons 1980; Strickland 1980). The 1977 age structure indicated that good reproduction had occurred during the closed season and that an increased number of fishers survived to adulthood that year. The management of fisher trapping in New York in the future will be aimed toward stabilizing the annual harvest at around 1200 fishers.

Prior to the 1975-1976 fisher-trapping season, fishers could be harvested in Ontario from 25 October through 28 February (Strickland and Douglas 1978). During the early 1970s, the fisher population in the Algonquin region was declining and 6% to 8% of the adult females were not reproducing. Strickland and Douglas (1978) found that, during the first half of the trapping season (through December), roughly 80% of the male fishers trapped were juveniles (the young of the year) but that later in the season adult males were more commonly captured. They believed that the high mortality rate of adult males resulting from trapping was causing the barrenness in adult females that should have been breeding (Douglas and Strickland 1977; Strickland and Douglas 1978). (See Chapter 3.) In 1975, the fisher season in the Algonquin region was shortened, to end on 31 December; this effectively reduced the trapping pressure on adult males. During succeeding years, the females' barrenness disappeared and the population began to increase (Strickland and Douglas 1978). By 1978, the anticipated harvest was equal to that of the 1973-1974 high. Therefore, a slight change in the length of the trapping season resulting in a change in mortality rates for adult male fishers appears to have had a significant effect on the fisher population in the Algonquin region of Ontario.

Working with the five one-predator-one-prey and one-predator-three-prey population models for the fisher community in Michigan, I found that a very small increase in mortality might reexterminate the fisher population. (See Chapter 8.) The amount of increased mortality that would eliminate the fisher population from the model communities ranged from 3% to 98% of the equilibrium mortality rates for the models without trapping, depending on which model was used. All models were consistent in that none could tolerate an increased mortality greater than about one to four fishers per 100 square kilometers. Quantitative extrapolation of these results to fisher populations in areas other than Upper Michigan is not recommended because of the many differences in habitat and prey and logging and trapping practices throughout the fisher's range. However, the qualitative results reinforce the knowledge gained from past population declines. Fisher management policies in the future must acknowledge that past fisher population declines were not a unique event and could be repeated. All fisher trapping must be closely managed so that trapping pressure can be immediately eased as soon as populations begin to decline (Powell 1979c).

Logging

Logging has had the other major impact on fisher populations. As discussed in Chapter 5, fishers prefer forests with continuous canopy. Clear-cut logging has the greatest effect on forest canopy and thus on fishers' habitats and populations. Clear-cut logging involves removing all of the trees in an area and is sometimes followed by a controlled fire that burns away the slash (branches and debris left after the logging is finished). Extensive clear-cuts are avoided by fishers during the winter and selectively cut areas are not. The extensive clear-cutting done during the late 1800s and early 1900s, together with trapping, decimated fisher populations all over the continent.

Clear-cutting is still commonly practiced in many areas of the United States and Canada. Aspen and many types of coniferous forests are most commonly clear-cut. Such forests are found over most of the fisher's present range. So, fishers must still contend with the destruction of their habitat through clear-cut logging practices.

Because fishers do utilize clear-cuts during the summer when the cover formed by ground vegetation and young trees is dense and do utilize young-growth forests, the extent of clear-cutting in an area is of importance. Small clear-cuts interspersed with uncut areas may not seriously affect fisher populations. Large clear-cuts, however, can seriously limit the available foraging area for a fisher population during the winter and thus limit the population size.

The fisher's habitat can recover from logging; second-growth forests are the most common habitat of fishers in the United States today. However, in order for a fisher population to reestablish itself, there must be either a healthy nearby fisher population that can immigrate to the recovered forest or a reintroduction program implemented by humans.

Effects of the Fisher's Predation on Other Animals

There is no evidence that predation by fishers has an important effect on any prey other than porcupines. Fisher populations have been found to cycle in response to snowshoe hare population cycles (Bulmer 1974, 1975), and the total effect of predation by all predators on snowshoe hares has been found to do little other than to speed up population declines (Keith and Windberg 1978). So, the fears of hunters that fisher populations may seriously affect the populations of game animals are unsubstantiated and partially refuted.

Fishers and Porcupines

There is a growing body of evidence that indicates that fishers may have long-term effects on porcupine populations. (See Chapter 8.) Fishers definitely can have short-term effects on porcupine populations (Coulter 1966; Hamilton and Cook 1955; Powell and Brander 1977). Declines in porcupine populations following increases in fisher populations have been reported in New York, Maine, and Wisconsin and have been documented in Michigan. My work with model communities and computer simulations indicated that the short-term effects of a new fisher population on an extremely high porcupine population may be greater or at least more dramatic than the long-term effects (Powell, unpublished data). The modeling work also indicated that in the long run porcupine populations will be lower with fishers in the community than without them.

Thus, it appears that fishers may be used successfully as a forest-management tool to limit extremely high porcupine populations. It must be remembered, however, that there is no evidence that fishers will eliminate porcupines in any local area. Also, there is evidence that porcupine populations may cycle in response to fisher and snowshoe hare populations and periodically reach population levels at which they may concern foresters. The success of fishers in reestablishing themselves in areas from which they have been eliminated and in which porcupine populations have reached high densities is also dependent on local logging and trapping practices. Even with an abundant food supply, fishers can be exterminated because of high trapping pressure and extensive clear-cut logging practices.

The Fisher as a Part of Our Native Fauna

During recent years, there has been an increased awareness of the value of natural communities of animals and plants beyond any economic value individual animals and plants may have for humans. There is a beauty in the way that many organisms can live together and all survive as species for long periods of time. Fishers certainly fit into "this view of life" as part of the native fauna of North America.

There is also no doubt that the fisher itself is a creature of beauty. Beyond its beautiful fur, the graceful movements of a fisher are also beautiful. Seeing a wild fisher free in the woods is a thrill. For an increasing number of people, simply knowing that fishers can be found wild in an area is rewarding, even though they seldom see them.

The Value of the Fisher

The fisher is valued differently by different people. Foresters and loggers are interested in maintaining fisher populations in order to limit porcupine populations and thus limit any damage porcupines might do to timber crops. The influence of logging practices on fisher populations will probably be taken into more consideration in the future now that it is known that fishers can limit porcupine populations to some degree. State game agencies are interested in maintaining fisher populations for trappers on a long-term and sustained-yield basis.

There are areas of conflict, however. Despite evidence to the contrary, some people still believe that fishers can have a detrimental effect on game animals. The conflict between these people and those people who wish to maintain fisher populations can best be resolved through education.

Probably the greatest disagreement arises between those people who wish to protect animal populations totally, especially those of such aesthetic value as the fisher, and those people who wish to harvest the populations. Because this conflict is an emotional one, its resolution may be slow and difficult. The fisher, however, is in a better position in this conflict than other animals because the people wishing to eradicate the fisher are few in number. Most of the people who want to harvest fisher populations are also concerned with maintaining fisher populations at harvestable levels over long periods of time. Thus, the fisher may be the subject of some controversy, but the level of the controversy will never be as great as the level of the controversy surrounding other predators, such as wolves and coyotes.

Fishers in Captivity

Fishers have been maintained in captivity for extended periods of time (Hodgson 1937; Laberee 1941; Bronx Zoo, New York Zoological Society, unpublished files); however, this has never been an important aspect of the fisher's relationship with humans. Despite the value of their fur, fishers have never been raised extensively on fur farms (Hodgson 1937; Laberee 1941). The reason for this may lie in the fisher's reproductive cycle, with the long-delayed implantation and consequent delay in knowing whether a female fisher has conceived. This, in turn, affects the decision whether a female's pelt can be harvested during a particular year. Both zoos and fur farms have had difficulty breeding fishers, though fur farms have had some success (Hodgson 1937; Laberee 1941; Bronx Zoo, New York Zoological Society, unpublished files). Some zoos have even had difficulty keeping fishers alive because of their susceptibility to many diseases in captivity (Brookfield Zoo, Chicago Zoological Society, unpublished files). In addition, because there are numerous healthy populations of wild fishers, there is no pressure to develop a dependable program for maintaining and breeding fishers in captivity.

The Fisher's Future

The future of the fisher looks brighter and less controversial than do the futures of many other carnivores. Wolves, coyotes, and mountain lions, for example, frequently come into direct conflict with humans over livestock and big game (Cahill 1971; Hendrickson, Robinson, and Mech 1975; Koford 1978; Mech 1970, 1977b; Morgan 1977; Pitts 1977; Reardon 1977; Robinson and Smith 1977; Vogt 1977; Weise et al. 1975). Smaller carnivores, such as the red fox and the bobcat, have been subjected to bounty hunting because of the belief that they depress the populations of small game animals. All of these carnivores are also harvested for their pelts, though their pelts at times may be of less value than their bounties. The fisher is perhaps unique because of its relationship to the porcupine. Thus, even though fishers are trapped for their fur, there is a widespread interest in maintaining fisher populations. In addition, the recent activities of conservation and preservation groups have helped the fisher.

I do not wish to end by describing too rosy a picture. Fisher populations are adversely affected by both trapping and logging practices. Trapping seasons and logging practices are often determined by people who do not have a direct interest in the fisher's welfare or who do not have enough knowledge of the fisher's habits. When this happens, fisher populations can be seriously overharvested and the fisher's habitat can be extensively damaged. The future of the fisher does look good, but that future depends upon proper management. The future of the fisher is completely in our hands.

References

References

Aldous, S. E., & J. Manweiler. 1942. The winter food habits of the short-tailed weasel in northern Minnesota. J. Mammal. 23: 250-55.

Allen, D. L. 1938. Notes on the killing technique of the New York weasel. J. Mammal. 19: 225-29.

Anderson, E. 1970. Quaternary evolution of the genus *Martes* (Carnivora, Mustelidae). Acta Zool. Fenn. No. 130.

Anonymous. 1977a. Hudson's Bay Company fur auction. News of the North (Yellowknife, N.W. T., Canada). 16 February 1977.

Anonymous. 1977b. North Dakota fisher. North Dakota Outdoors 39(8): 20.

Anonymous. 1978. Fur production. Statistics Canada, Agric. Div., Livestock & Animal Production Sec. Ottawa, Ontario.

Anthony, H. E. 1928. Field Book of North American Mammals. G.P. Putnam's Sons. New York.

Archibald, H. L. 1977. Is the 10-year wildlife cycle induced by a lunar cycle? Wildl. Soc. Bull. 5: 126-29.

Audubon, J. J., & J. Bachman. 1845-1848. The Viviparous Quadrupeds of North America. Publ. by J. J. Audubon. New York. 3 vols.

Baldwin, H. I. 1934. Some physiological effects of girdling northern hardwoods. Bull. Torrey Bot. Club 61: 249-57.

Balser, D. S. 1960. The comeback of the furbearers. Conserv. Volun., Minn. Div. Game & Fish 23(134):57-59.

Balser, D. S., & W. H. Longley. 1966. Increase of fishers in Minnesota. J. Mammal. 47: 342-47.

Banville, D. 1980. *In* C. W. Douglas & M. A. Strickland (eds.), pp. 133-35. Trans. 1979 fisher conf. Ontario Min. Nat. Res. unpubl. rep.

Barkalow, F. S. 1961. The porcupine and fisher in Alabama archeological sites. J. Mammal. 42: 544-45.

Bashore, T. L. 1978. Highway deer mortalities: A non-random occurrence. *In* M. H. Smith (chairman), p. 79. Abstr. Tech. Papers, 58th Ann. Meeting Amer. Soc. Mammal. Publ. by the local committee, Univ. Georgia, Athens.

Bensen, D. A. 1959. The fisher in Nova Scotia. J. Mammal. 40: 451.

Blanchard, H. 1964. Weight of a large fisher. J. Mammal. 45: 487-88.

Boise, C.M. 1975. Skull measurements as criteria for aging fishers. N.Y. Fish & Game J. 22: 32-37.

Bradle, B. J. 1957. The fisher returns to Wisconsin. Wisconsin Conserv. Bull. 22(11): 9-11.

Brander, R. B. 1971. Longevity of wild porcupines. J. Mammal. 52: 835.

Brander, R. B. 1973. Life history notes on the porcupine in a hardwood-hemlock forest in Upper Michigan. Michigan Academician 5(4): 425-33.

Brander, R. B., & D. J. Books. 1973. Return of the fisher. Natur. Hist. 82(1): 52-57.

Brody, S. 1945. Bioenergetics and Growth. Reinhold. New York.

Brown, J. H., & R. C. Lasiewski. 1972. Metabolism of weasels: The cost of being long and thin. Ecology 53: 939-43.

Brown, L. N. 1965. The fisher, *Martes pennanti*, in Sheridan County (Wyoming). S. West Natur. 10: 143.

Brown, M. K., & G. Will. 1979. Food habits of the fisher in northern New York. N.Y. Fish & Game J. 26: 87-92.

Buck, S., C. Mullis, & A. Mossman. 1978. Annual Report: Corral Bottom-Hayfork Bally fisher study, 1 October 1977-1 October 1978. unpubl. report, Forest Service, U.S.D.A. and Humboldt State University, Arcata, Calif.

Buck, S., C. Mullis, & A. Mossman. 1979. A radio telemetry study of fishers in northwestern California. Cal.-Nev. Wildl. Trans. 1979: 166-72.

Buffon, G. L., & J. M. D'Aubenton. 1765. Historie Naturelle. Vol. 13. Imprimerie Royale. Paris.

Bulmer, M. G. 1974. A statistical analysis of the 10-year cycle in Canada. J. Anim. Ecol. 43: 701-18.

Bulmer, M. G. 1975. Phase relations in the ten-year cycle. J. Anim. Ecol. 44: 609-22.

Burkholder, B. L. 1959. Movements and behavior of a wolf pack in Alaska. J. Wildl. Mgt. 23: 1-11.

Burt, W. H., & R. P. Grossenheider. 1964. A Field Guide to the Mammals. Hougton Mifflin. Boston.

Cahalane, V. H. 1944. Meeting the Mammals. Macmillan. New York.

Cahalane, V. H. 1947. Mammals of North America. Macmillan. New York.

Cahill, J. L. 1971. Puma. Sierra Cl. Bull. 56: 18-22.

Charnov, E. L. 1976. Optimal foraging: Attack strategy of a mantid. Amer. Natur. 110: 141-51.

Charnov, E. L., G. H. Orians, & K. Hyatt. 1976. Ecological implications of resource depression. Amer. Natur. 110: 247-59.

Chitwood, B. G. 1932. Occurrence of *Uncinaria stenocephala* from the fisher. J. Parasit. 18: 307.

Clark, T. W., & T. M. Campbell. No date. Population organization and regulatory mechanisms of pine marten in Grand Teton National Park, Wyoming. Unpubl. ms.

Clarke, S. H., & R. B. Brander. 1973. Radiometric determination of porcupine surface temperature under two conditions of overhead cover. Physiol. Zool. 46: 230-37.

Clem, M. K. 1977. Food habits, weight changes and habitat selection of fisher during winter. M.S. thesis, Univ. Guelph. Guelph, Ontario.

Clements, B. 1975. A report on subproject 2 of a proposal for an integrated study of wildlife resources of northeastern Minnesota. Unpubl. rep. North Central Forest Experiment Station, Forest Service, U.S.D.A., St. Paul.

Colbert, E. H. 1969. Evolution of the Vertebrates. 2nd ed. John Wiley & Sons. New York.

Cook, D. E., & W. J. Hamilton, Jr. 1957. The forest, the fisher, and the porcupine. J. Forest. 55: 719-22.

Cottrell, W. 1978. The fisher (*Martes pennanti*) in Maryland. J. Mammal. 59: 886.

Coues, E.   1877. Fur-bearing mammals: A monograph of North american mustelidae. U.S.D.I. Misc. Publ. no. 8.

Coulter, M. W. 1966. Ecology and management of fishers in Maine. Ph.D. thesis. St. Univ. Coll. Forest., Syracuse Univ. Syracuse, N.Y.

Cowan, I. McT., A. J. Wood, & W. D. Kitts. 1957. Feed requirements of deer, beaver, bear, and mink for growth and maintenance. Trans. North Amer. Wildl. Conf. 22: 179-88.

Craighead, J. J., & F. C. Craighead. 1956. Hawks, Owls and Wildlife. Stackpole, Harrisburg and Wildlife Management Institute. Washington, D.C.

Cronquist, A. 1961. Introductory Botany. Harper & Row. New York.

Crowe, D. M. 1975. Aspects of aging, growth, and reproduction of bobcats from Wyoming. J. Mammal. 56: 177-98.

Crowe, D. M., & M. A. Strickland. 1975. Dental annulation in the American badger. J. Mammal. 56: 269-72.

Curtis, J. D. 1941. The silvicultural significance of the porcupine. J. Forest. 39: 583-94.

Curtis, J. D. 1944. Appraisal of porcupine damage. J. Wildl. Mgt. 8: 88-91.

Curtis, J. D., & A. K. Wilson. 1953. Porcupine feeding on ponderosa pine in central Idaho. J. Forest. 51: 339-41.

Daniel, J. C., Jr. 1970. Dormant embryos in mammals. Biosci. 20: 411-15.

Davis, D. D. 1949. The shoulder architecture of bears and other carnivores. Fieldiana Zool. 31: 285-305.

Davison, R. P. 1975. The efficiency of food utilization and energy requirements of captive fishers. M.S. thesis. Univ. New Hampshire. Concord, N.H.

Davison, R. P., W. W. Mautz, H. H. Hayes, & J. B. Holter. 1978. The efficiency of food utilization and energy requirements of captive female fishers. J. Wildl. Mgt. 42: 811-21.

deVos, A. 1951. Recent findings in fisher and marten ecology and management. Trans. North Amer. Wildl. Conf. 16: 498-507.

deVos, A. 1952. Ecology and management of fisher and marten in Ontario. Tech. Bull. Ontario Dept. Lands and Forests.

Dick, L. A., & R. D. Leonard. 1979. Helminth parasites of fisher *Martes pennanti* (Erxleben) from Manitoba, Canada. J. Wildl. Diseases 15: 409-12.

Dodds, D. G., & A. M. Martell. 1971. The recent status of the fisher, *Martes pennanti* (Erxleben), in Nova Scotia. Can. Field-Natur. 85: 62-65.

Dodge, W. E. 1967. The biology and life history of the porcupine (*Erethizon dorsatum*) in western Massachusetts. Ph.D. thesis. Univ. Massachusetts Amherst, Mass.

Dodge, W. E. 1977. Status of the fisher (*Martes pennanti*) in the conterminous United States. Unpubl. rep. submitted to U.S.D.I.

Douglas, C. W., & M. A. Strickland. 1977. Age class distribution and reproductive biology in the management of fisher, *Martes pennanti*. Ecology Coll., Univ. West. Ontario. Unpubl. ms.

Douglas, W. O. 1943. Fisher farming has arrived. Amer. Fur Breeder 16: 18, 20.

Drew, J. V., & R. E. Shagg. 1965. Landscape relationships of soils and vegetation in the forest-tundra ecotone, Upper Firth River Valley, Alaska-Canada. Ecol. Monogr. 35: 285-306.

Eadie, W. R., & W. J. Hamilton, Jr. 1958. Reproduction of the fisher in New York. N.Y. Fish & Game J. 5: 77-83.

Ealey, E. H. M. 1963. The ecological significance of delayed implantation in a population of the hill kangaroo (*Macropus robustus*). *In* A. C. Enders (ed.), pp. 33-48. Delayed Implantation. Univ. Chicago Press. Chicago.

Earle, R. D. 1978. The fisher-porcupine relationship in Upper Michigan. M.S. thesis, Mich. Tech. Univ. Houghton, Mich.

East, K., & J. D. Lockie. 1964. Observations on a family of weasels (*Mustela nivalis*) bred in captivity. Proc. Zool. Soc. Lond. 143: 359-63.

East, K., & J. D. Lockie. 1965. Further observations on weasels (*Mustela nivalis*) and stoats (*Mustela erminea*) born in captivity. J. Zool. Lond. 147: 234-38.

Enders, R.K., & A. C. Enders. 1963. Morphology of the female reproductive tract during delayed implantation in the mink. *In* A. C. Enders (ed.), pp. 129-40. Delayed Implantation. Univ. Chicago Press. Chicago.

Enders, R.K., & O. P. Pearson. 1943. The blastocyst of the fisher. Anat. Rev. 85: 285-87.

Erickson, A. B. 1946. Incidence of worm parasties in Minnesota Mustelidae and host lists and keys to North American species. Amer. Midl. Natur. 36: 494-509.

Erlinge, S. 1974. Distribution, territoriality and numbers of the weasel *Mustela nivalis* in relation to prey abundance. Oikos 25: 308-14.

Erlinge, S. 1977. Spacing strategy in stoat *Mustela erminea*. Oikos 28: 32-42.

Erlinge, S., B. Bergsten, & A. Kristiansson. 1974. Hermelinen och des bute – Jaktbeteende och flykreaktioner. Fauna och flora 69(6): 203-11.

Erlinge, S., & P. Widen. 1975. Hermilinens aktivitetsmönster under hösten. Fauna och flora 70(4): 137-42.

Errington, P. L. 1943. An analysis of mink predation upon muskrats in north central United States. Agr. Exp. Sta. Iowa St. Coll. Agr. & Mech. Arts. Res. Bull. No. 320: 797-924.

Errington, P. L. 1967. Of Predation and Life. Iowa St. Univ. Press. Ames, Iowa.

Ewer, R. F. 1973. The Carnivores. Cornell Univ. Press. Ithaca, N.Y.

Farrell, D. J., & A. J. Wood. 1968. The nutrition of the female mink (*Mustela vison*). II. The energy requirement for maintenance. Can. J. Zool. 46: 47-52.

Floyd, T.J., L. D. Mech, & P. A. Jordan. 1978. Relating wolf scat content to prey consumed. J. Wildl. Mgt. 42: 528-32.

Fogl, J. G., & H. S. Mosby. 1978. Aging gray squirrels by cementum annuli in razor-sectioned teeth. J. Wildl. Mgt. 42: 444-48.

Fox, M. L. 1978. The Dog: Its Domestication and Behavior. Garland STPM Press. New York.

Fries, S. 1880. Uber die Fortpflanzung von *Meles taxus*. Zool. Anz. 3: 486-92.

Fries, S. 1902. Zur Nahrung Fortpflanzung, sowie zur Schonzeit des duches. Deutsche Jager-Zug. 39.

Forthingham, E. H. 1915. The eastern hemlock. U.S.D.A. Bull. 152.

Gambaryan, P. P. 1974. How Mammals Run. Halsted Press, Wiley. New York.

Gaughran, G. R. L. 1950. Domestic cat predation on short-tailed weasel. J. Mammal. 31: 356.

Gause, G. F. 1934. The Struggle for Existence. Williams and Wilkins. Baltimore.

Gerell, R. 1970. Home range and movements of the mink *Mustela vison* Schreber in southern Sweden. Oikos 21: 160-73.

Getz, L. L. 1961. Home ranges, territoriality, and movements of the meadow vole. J. Mammal. 42: 24-36.

Gillingham, B. J. 1978. A quantitative analysis of prey killing and its ontogeny in the ermine *Mustela erminea*. M.S. thesis. Univ. Montana. Missoula, Mont.

Glover, F. A. 1942. A population study of weasels in Pennsylvania. M.S. thesis, Pennsylvania St. Coll., University Park, Pa.

Glover, F. A. 1943. Killing techniques of the New York weasel. Penn. Game News 13(10): 11.

Goldman, F. A. 1935. New American mustelids of the genera *Martes, Gulo,* and *Lutra* Proc. Biol. Soc. Wash. 48: 175-86.

Golley, F. B. 1960. Energy dynamics of a food chain of an old field community. Ecol. Monogr. 30: 187-206.

Golley, F. B., G. A. Petrides, E. L. Rauber, & J. H. Jenkins. 1965. Food intake and assimilation by bobcats under laboratory conditions. J. Wildl. Mgt. 29: 442-47.

Goszczynski, J. 1976. Composition of the food of martens. Acta Ther. 21(36): 527-34.

Grafen, A. 1980. Opportunity, cost, benefit and degree of relatedness. Anim. Behav. 28: 967-68.

Grenfell, W. E., & M. Fasenfest. 1979. Winter food habits of fishers, *Martes pennanti*, in northwestern California. Calif. Fish & Game 65: 186-89.

Grigoriev, N. D. 1938. [On the reproduction of the stoat.] Zool. Zhur. 17: 811-14.

Grinnell, J., J. S. Dixon, & L. M. Linsdale. 1937. Fur-Bearing Mammals of California: Their Natural History, Systematic Status and Relations to Man. Vol. 1. Univ. Calif. Press. Berkeley, Calif.

Hagmeier, E. M. 1955. The genus *Martes* (Mustelidae) in North America, its distribution, variation, classification, phylogeny and relationship to Old World forms. Ph.D. thesis, Univ. British Columbia. Vancouver, B. C.

Hagmeier, E. M. 1956. Distribution of marten and fisher in North America. Can. Field-Natur. 70: 149-68.

Hagmeier, E. M. 1959. A re-evaluation of the subspecies of fisher. Can. Field-Natur. 73: 185-97.

Hagmeier, E. M. 1961. Variation and relationships in North American marten. Can. Field-Natur. 75: 122-37.

Hahn, E. W., & R. C. Wester. 1969. The biomedical use of ferrets in research. Publ. by Marshall Research Animals, Inc. North Rose, N.Y.

Haley, D. 1975. Sleek & Savage: North America's Weasel Family. Pacific Search. Seattle.

Hall, E. R. 1942. Gestation period of the fisher with recommendation for the animal's protection in California. Calif. Fish & Game 28: 143-47.

Hall, E. R. 1951. American Weasels. Univ. Kansas Publ. Mus. Nat. Hist. no. 4.

Hall, E. R. 1974. The graceful and rapacious weasel. Nat. Hist 83(9): 44-50.

Hamilton, G. T. 1957. Resurgence of the fisher in New Hampshire. Appalachia 31: 485-90.

Hamilton, W. J., Jr. 1933. The weasels of New York. Amer. Midl. Natur. 14: 289-344.

Hamilton, W. J., Jr. 1943. The Mammals of Eastern United States. Comstock Publ. Co. Ithaca, N.Y.

Hamilton, W. J., Jr., & A. H. Cook. 1955. The biology and management of the fisher in New York. N.Y. Fish & Game J. 2: 13-35.

Hamlett, G. W. 1935. Delayed implantation and discontinuous development in the mammals. Quart. Rev. Biol. 10: 432-47.

Hardy, M. 1899. The fisher. Shooting & Fishing 25: 526.

Hardy, M. 1907. The fisher. Forest & Stream 68: 692-93.

Hawley, V. D., & F. E. Newby. 1957. Marten home ranges and population fluctuations. J. Mammal. 38: 174-84.

Heidt, G. A. 1970. The least weasel, *Mustela nivalis* Linnaeus: Developmental biology in comparison with other North American *Mustela*. Publ. Mus. Mich. St. Univ., Biol. Ser. 4(7): 227-83.

Heidt, G. A., M. K. Petersen, & G. L. Kirkland, Jr. 1968. Mating behavior and development of least weasels (*Mustela nivalis*) in captivity. J. Mammal. 49: 413-19.

Henderson, F. R., P. F. Springer, & R. Adrian. 1969. The Black-Footed Ferret in South Dakota. S.D. Dept. Game, Fish & Parks. Brookings, S.D.

Hendrickson, J., W. L. Robinson, & L. D. Mech. 1975. Status of the wolf in Michigan, 1973. Amer. Midl. Natur. 94: 226-32.

Herreid, C. F., & B. Kessel. 1967. Thermal conductance in birds and mammals. Comp. Biochem. Physiol. 21: 405-14.

Hibbard, C. W. 1970. Pleistocene mammalian local faunas from the Great Plains and Central Lowland Provinces of the United States. *In* W. Dort, Jr., & J. K. Jones, Jr. (eds.), pp. 395-433. Pleistocene and recent environments of the Central Great Plains. Univ. Kansas Dept. Geol. Spec. Publ. no. 3.

Hildebrand, M. 1974. Analysis of Vertebrate Structure. John Wiley & Sons. New York.

Hillman, C. N. 1968. Field observations of black-footed ferrets in South Dakota. Trans. N. Am. Wildl. Conf. 33: 433-43.

Hine, R. L. 1975. Endangered animals in Wisconsin. Unpubl. rep., Wisc. Dept. Nat. Res. Madison.

Hodgson, R. G. 1937. Fisher Farming. Fur Trade J. Can. Toronto.

Holland, G. P. 1950. The Siphonaptera of Canada. Science-Service, Div. Entomol., Livestock Insect Lab., Kamloops, B.C.

Holling, C. S. 1959. Some characteristics of simple types of predation and parasitism. Can. Entomol. 91: 385-98.

Ingram, R. 1973. Wolverine, fisher and marten in central Oregon. Central Reg. Admin. Rep. No. 73-2. Ore. St. Game Comm. Salem, Ore.

Irvine, G. W. 1960a. Preliminary report on the porcupine problem on the Ottawa National Forest. Unpubl. rep., Ottawa National Forest, Forest Service, U.S.D.A. Ironwood, Mich.

Irvine, G. W. 1960b. Progress report on the porcupine problem on the Ottawa National Forest. Unpubl. rep., Ottawa National Forest, Forest Service, U.S.D.A. Ironwood, Mich.

Irvine, G. W. 1961. Fisher restoration project, 1961. Unpubl. rep., Ottawa National Forest, Forest Service, U.S.D.A. Ironwood, Mich.

Irvine, G. W. 1962. Fisher restoration project: Progress report, 1962. Unpubl. rep., Ottawa National Forest, Forest Service, U.S.D.A. Ironwood, Mich.

Irvine, G. W., B. J. Bradle, & L. T. Magnus. 1962. The restocking of fisher in lake states forests. Midw. Fish & Wildl. Conf. 24.

Irvine, G. W., & R. B. Brander. 1971. Progress report on a fisher-porcupine study on the Ottawa National Forest. Unpubl. rep., N. Cen. For. Exp. Sta., Forest Service, U.S.D.A. St. Paul.

Irvine, G. W., L. T. Magnus, & B. J. Bradle. 1964. The restocking of fishers in lake states forests. Trans. N. Am. Wildl. Nat. Res. Conf. 29: 307-15.

Ivlev, V.S. 1961. Experimental ecology of feeding of fishes. Yale Univ. Press. New Haven, Conn.

Jackson, H. H. T. 1961. Mammals of Wisconsin. Univ. Wisc. Press. Madison.

Jense, G. K. 1968. Food habits and energy utilization of badgers. M.S. thesis. S.D. State Univ. Brookings.

Jensen, A., & B. Jensen. 1970. Husmaaren (*Martes foina*) og maarjagten i Danmark. Danske Vildtundersøgelser, Hefte 15. Vildtbiologisk Station.

Joliceous, P. 1963a. The degree of generality of robustness in *Martes americana*. Growth 27: 1-27.

Joliceous, P. 1963b. Bilateral symmetry and asymmetry in limb bones of *Martes americana* and man. Rev. Can. Biol. 22: 409-32.

Jonkel, C., & R. P. Weckwerth. 1963. Sexual maturity and implantation of blastocysts in wild pine marten. J. Wildl. Mgt. 27: 93-98.

Kebbe, C. E. 1961. Return of the fisher. Ore. St. Game Comm. Bull. 16: 3-7.

Keith, L. B. 1963. Wildlife's Ten-Year Cycle. Univ. Wisc. Press. Madison.

Keith, L. B. 1966. Habitat vacancy during a snowshoe hare decline. J. Wildl. Mgt. 30: 828-32.

Keith, L. B., & L. A. Windberg. 1978. A demographic analysis of the snowshoe hare cycle. Wildl. Monogr. 58.

Kelly, G. M. 1977. Fisher (*Martes pennanti*) biology in the White Mountain National Forest and adjacent areas. Ph.D. thesis. Univ. Mass. Amherst, Mass.

Kelsey, P. 1977. The return of the fisher. N.Y. St. Environ. 6(8): 10.

King, C.M. 1975. The home range of the weasel (*Mustela nivalis*) in an English woodland. J. Anim. Ecol. 44: 639-68.

Kleiber, M. 1961. The Fire of Life. John Wiley & Sons. New York.

Klimov, Y. N. 1940. [Data on the biology of the ermine.] Trudy Biologischenkogo Instituta 7: 80-88. Also: *In* C. M. King (trans., ed.), pp. 108-17. 1975. Biology of Mustelids: Some Soviet Research. Brit. Libr. Lending Div. Wetherby.

Koford, C.B. 1978. The welfare of the puma in California. Carnivore 1(1): 92-96.

Kraft, V. A. 1966. [Influence of temperature on the activity of the ermine in winter.] Zool. Zhur. 45: 567-70. Also: *In* C. M. King (trans., ed.), pp. 104-7. 1975. Biology of Mustelids: Some Soviet Research. Brit. Libr. Lending Div. Wetherby.

Krebs, R. J. 1973. Behavioral aspects of predation. *In* P. P. G. Bateson & P. H. Klopfer (eds.), pp. 73-111. Perspectives in Ethology. Plenum. New York.

Krefting, L. W., J. W. Stoeckeler, B.J. Bradle, & W. D. Fitzwater. 1962. Porcupine-timber relationships in the lake states. J. Forest. 60: 325-30.

Krott, P. 1959. Der Vielfrass (*Gulo gulo* L. 1758). Monogr. Wildsäugeret 13: 1-159.

Kruuk, H. 1972. Surplus killing by carnivores. J. Zool. 166: 233-44.

Kurtén, B. 1971. The Age of Mammals. Columbia Univ. Press. New York.

Laberee, E. E. 1941. Breeding and Reproduction in Fur Bearing Animals. Fur Trade J. Can. Toronto.

Larsen, J. A. 1965. The vegetation of the Ennadai Lake area, N.W.T.: Studies in subarctic and arctic bioclimatology. Ecol. Monogr. 35: 37-59.

Latham, R.M. 1952. The fox as a factor in the control of weasel populations. J. Wildl. Mgt. 16: 516-17.

Leach, D. 1977a. The forelimb musculature of marten (*Martes americana* Turton) and fisher (*Martes pennanti* Erxleben). Can. J. Zool. 55: 31-41.

Leach, D. 1977b. The description and comparative postcranial osteology of marten (*Martes americana* Turton) and fisher (*Martes pennanti* Erxleben): The appendicular skeleton. Can. J. Zool. 55: 199-214.

Leach, D., & A. I. Dagg. 1976. The morphology of the femur in marten and fisher. Can. J. Zool. 54: 559-65.

Leonard, R. D. 1980a. *In* C. W. Douglas & M. A. Strickland (eds.), pp. 15-25. Trans. 1979 fisher conf. Ontario Min. Nat. Resources. Unpubl. report.

Leonard, R. D. 1980b. Winter activity and movements, winter diet and breeding biology of the fisher in southeast Manitoba. M.S. thesis. Univ. Manitoba. Winnipeg.

Litvaitis, J. A., & W. W. Mautz. 1976. Energy utilization of three diets fed to a captive red fox. J. Wildl. Mgt. 40: 365-68.

Litvaitis, J. A., & W. W. Mautz. 1980. Food and energy use by captive coyotes. J. Wildl. Mgt. 44: 56-61.

Llewellyn, L. M. 1942. Notes on the Alleghenian least weasel in Virginia. J. Mammal. 23: 439-41.

Lockie, J. D. 1959. The estimation of the food of foxes. J. Wildl. Mgt. 23: 224-27.

Lockie, J. D. 1961. The food of the pine marten in West Ross-shire, Scotland. Proc. Zool. Soc. Lond. 136: 187-95.

Lockie, J.D. 1964. Distribution and fluctuations of the pine marten, *Martes martes* (L.), in Scotland. J. Anim. Ecol. 33: 349-56.

Lockie, J. D. 1966. Territory in small carnivores. Symp. Zool. Soc. Lond. 18: 143-65.

Lund, H. M.-K. 1962. The red fox in Norway. II. The feeding habits of the red fox in Norway. Papers of the Norwegian St. Game Res. Inst. 2nd Ser. no. 2: 1-79.

MacArthur, R. H. 1972. Geographical Ecology. Harper & Row. New York.

McCord, C. M. 1974. Selection of winter habitat by bobcats (*Lynx rufus*) on the Quabbin Reservation, Massachusetts. J. Mammal. 55: 428-37.

McMahon, T. 1973. Size and shape in biology. Science 179: 1201-4.

Manville, R. H. 1948. The vertebrate fauna of the Huron Mountains, Michigan. Amer. Midl. Natur. 39: 615-41.

Markley, M. H., & C. F. Bassett. 1942. Habits of captive marten. Amer. Midl. Natur. 28: 604 -16.

Marr, J. W. 1948. Ecology of the forest-tundra ecotone on the east coast of Hudson Bay. Ecol. Monogr. 18: 117-44.

Marston, M. A. 1942. Winter relations of bobcats to white-tailed deer in Maine. J. Wildl. Mgt. 6: 328-37.

Mech, L. D. 1966. The Wolves of Isle Royale. Fauna Natl. Pks. U.S. Fauna Ser. 7.

Mech, L. D. 1970. The Wolf: The Ecology and Behavior of an Endangered Species. Nat. Hist. Press. Garden City, N.Y.

Mech, L. D. 1977a. Population trend and winter deer consumption in a Minnesota wolf pack. *In* R. L. Phillips & C. Jonkel (eds.), pp. 55-83. Proc. 1975 Pred. Symp., Montana For. Conserv. Exp. Sta., Univ. Mont. Missoula, Mont.

Mech, L. D. 1977b. A recovery plan for the eastern timber wolf. Natl. Pks. & Conserv. Mag. Jan.: 17-21.

Mendall, H. L. 1944. Food of hawks and owls in Maine. J. Wildl. Mgt. 8: 198-208.

Meyer, M., & B. G. Chitwood. 1951. Helminths from fisher (*Martes pennanti pennanti*) in Maine. J. Parasit. 37: 320-21.

Miller, F. W. 1931. A feeding habit of the long-tailed weasel. J. Mammal. 12: 164.

Moors, P. J. 1974. The annual energy budget of a weasel (*Mustela nivalis* L.) population in farmland. Ph.D. thesis. Univ. Aberdeen, Scotland.

Moors, P. J. 1977. Studies of the metabolism, food consumption and assimilation efficiency of a small carnivore, the weasel (*Mustela nivalis*). Oecologia 27: 185-202.

Morgan, B. B. 1942. New host records of nematodes from Mustelidae (Carnivora). J. Parasit. 29: 158-59.

Morgan. L. 1977. In Alaska, another wolf kill up against the wall. Natl. Wildl. 15(5): 6-8.

Morse, W. B. 1961. Return of the fisher. Amer. For. 64(4): 24-26, 47.

Mullen, R. K. 1970. Respiratory metabolism and body water turnover rates of *Perognathus formosus* in its natural environment. Comp. Biochem. Physiol. 32: 259-65.

Mullen, R. K. 1971a. Energy metabolism of *Peromyscus crinitus* in its natural environment. J. Mammal. 52: 633-35.

Mullen, R. K. 1971b. Energy metabolism and body water turnover rates of two species of free-living kangaroo rats, *Dipodomys merriami* and *D. microps.* Comp. Biochem. Physiol. 39A: 379-90.

Mullen, R. K., & R. M. Chew. 1973. Estimating the energy metabolism of free-living *Perognathus formosus*: A comparison of direct and indirect methods. Ecology 54: 633-37.

Murdoch, W. W., & A. Oaten. 1975. Predation and population stability. Adv. Ecol. Res. 9: 1-125.

Murr, E. 1929. Zur Erklarung der verlangerten Tragdaur bei Säugetieren. Zool. Anz. 85: 113-29.

Murr, E. 1931. Experimentelle Abkurzung der Tragdaur beim Frettchen (*Putorius furo* L.). Anz. der Akad. Wiss., Wien, s.: 265-66.

Nellis, C. H., S. P. Wetmore, & L. B. Keith. 1978. Age related characteristics of coyote canines. J. Wildl. Mgt. 42: 680-83.

van Nostrand, N. 1977. Nova Scotia reports: Fisher. Can. Trapper 6(2): 20.

Nyholm, E. S. 1959. [Stoats and weasels in their winter habitat.] Suomen Riista 13: 106-16. Also: In C. M. King (trans., ed.), pp. 118-31. 1975. Biology of Mustelids: Some Soviet Research. Brit. Libr. Lending Div. Wetherby.

Olson, H. F. 1966. Return of a native. Wisc. Conserv. Bull. 31(3): 22-23.

O'Meara, D. C., D. D. Payne, & J. F. Witter. 1960. Sarcoptes infestation of a fisher. J. Wildl. Mgt. 24: 339.

Ondrias, J. C. 1962. Comparative osteological investigations on the front limbs of European Mustelidae. Arkiv. för Zoologi 13(15): 311-20.

Papke, R. L., P. W. Concannon, H. F. Travis, & W. Hansel. 1980. Control of luteal function and implantation in the mink by prolactin. J. Anim. Sci. 50: 1102-7.

Parmalee, P. W. 1971. Fisher and porcupine remains from cave deposits in Missouri. Trans. Ill. Acad. Sci. 64: 225-29.

Parsons, G. R. 1980. In C. W. Douglas & M. A. Strickland (eds.), pp. 25-60. Trans. 1979 fisher conf. Ontario Min. Nat. Res. Unpubl. rep.

Parsons, G. R. 1980. In C. W. Douglas & M. A. Strickland (eds.), pp. 25-60. Trans. 1979 fisher Conf. Ontario Min. Nat. Res. Unpubl. rep.

Parsons, G. R., M. K. Brown, & G. B. Will. 1978. Determining the sex of fisher from lower canine teeth. N.Y. Fish & Game J. 25: 42-44.

Pearson, O. P., & R. K. Enders. 1944. Duration of pregnancy in certain mustelids. J. Exp. Zool. 95: 21-35.

Pennant, T. 1771. Synopsis of Quadrupeds. J. Monk. Chester.

Penrod, B. 1976. Fisher in New York. Conservationist 31(2): 23.

Petersen, L. R., M. A. Martin, & C. M. Pils. 1977. Status of fishers in Wisconsin, 1975. Wisc. Dept. Nat. Res., Rep. No. 92.

Petskoi, P. G, & V. M. Kolpovskii. 1970. [Neck glandular structure in animals of the family Mustelidae.] Zool. Zhur. 49: 1208-19.

Pittaway, R. J. 1978. Observations on the behaviour of the fisher (Martes pennanti) in Algonquin Park, Ontario. Le Naturaliste Canadienne 105: 487-89.

Pitts, J. L. 1977. Con: Alaska wolf kill, nonsense! Natl. Wildl. 15(5): 9.

Poole, T. B. 1970. The polecat. Grt. Brit. Comm. Forest. Rep. No. 76.

Powell, R. A. 1975. A model for raptor predation on weasels. J. Mammal. 54: 259-63.

Powell, R. A. 1976. Compact carnivore. Anim. Kingdom 78(6): 12-19.

Powell, R. A. 1977a. Hunting behavior, ecological energetics and predator-prey community stability of the fisher (Martes pennanti). Ph.D. thesis. Univ. Chicago.

Powell, R. A. 1977b. Return of the fisher. Field Mus. Nat. Hist. Bull. 48(2): 8-12.

Powell, R. A. 1978a. A comparison of fisher and weasel hunting behavior. Carnivore 1(1): 28-34.

Powell, R. A. 1978b. Zig! Zag! Zap! Anim. Kingdom 80(6): 20-25.

Powell, R. A. 1979a. Ecological energetics and foraging strategies of the fisher (Martes pennanti). J. Anim. Ecol. 48: 195-212.

Powell, R. A. 1979b. Mustelid spacing patterns: Variations on a theme by Mustela. Z. Tierpsychol. 50: 153-65.

Powell, R. A. 1979c. Fishers, population models and trapping. Wildl. Soc. Bull. 7: 149-54.

Powell, R. A. 1980a. Stability in a one-predator-three-prey community. Amer. Natur. 115: 567-79.

Powell, R. A. 1980b. Fisher arboreal activity. Can. Field-Natur. 94: 90-91.

Powell, R. A. 1981. Hunting behavior and food requirements of the fisher (Martes pennanti). Pp. 883-917. In J. A. Chapman & D. Pursley (eds.) Proc. 1st Worldwide Furbearer Conf. Worldwide Furbearer Conference, Inc. Baltimore, Md.

Powell, R. A., & R. B. Brander. 1977. Adaptations of fishers and porcupines to their preda-tor-prey system. *In* R. L. Phillips & C. Jonkel (eds.), pp. 45-53. Proc. 1975 Pred. Symp. Mont. For. Conserv. Exp. Sta., Univ. Mont. Missoula, Mont.

Powell, R. A., & R. D. Leonard. (submitted). Energy expenditure of a female fisher with kits.

Prell, H. 1927. Uber doppelte Brunstzeit und verlangerte Tragzeit bei den einheimische Ar-ten der Mardergattung *Martes* Pinel. Zool. Anz., 74, s.: 112-28.

Prell, H. 1930. Die verlangerte Tragzeit der einheimischen *Martes*-Arten. Ein Erklarungsver-such. Zool. Anz. 88, s.: 17-31.

Pringle, L. 1964a. Killer with a future — The fisher. Anim. Kingdom 67: 82-87.

Pringle, L. 1964b. Fisher vs. deer. N.Y. Fish & Game J. 11: 67.

Pringle, L. 1973. Follow a Fisher. Thomas Y. Crowell. New York.

Pringle, L. & D. Mech. 1961. The fascinating fisher. Field & Stream 66(August): 31, 106, 107, 109, 111.

Progulske, D. R. 1969. Observations of a penned, wild-captured black-footed ferret. J. Mam-mal. 50: 619-20.

Pyke, G. H. 1978. Are animals efficient harvesters? Anim. Beh. 26: 241-50.

Pyke, G.H., H. R. Pulliam, & E. L. Charnov. 1977. Optimal foraging: A selective review of theory and tests. Quart. Rev. Biol. 52: 137-54.

Quick, H. F. 1953a. Wolverine, fisher and marten studies in a wilderness region. Trans. N. Am. Wildl. Conf. 18: 513-33.

Quick, H. F. 1953b. Occurrence of porcupine quills in carnivorous mammals. J. Mammal. 34: 256-59.

Radinsky, L. B. 1968a. A new approach to mammalian cranial analysis, illustrated by ex-amples of prosimian primates. J. Morph. 124: 167-80.

Radinsky, L. B. 1968b. Evolution of somatic sensory specialization in otter brains. J. Comp. Neur. 134: 495-506.

Radinsky, L. B. 1971. An example of parallelism in carnivore brain evolution. Evol. 25: 518-22.

Radinsky, L. B. 1973. Are stink badgers skunks? Implications of neuroanatomy for mustelid phylogeny. J. Mammal. 54: 585-93.

Rand, A. L. 1944. The status of the fisher (*Martes pennanti* Erxleben) in Canada. Can. Field-Natur. 58: 77-81.

Rausch, R. A., & A. M. Pearson. 1972. Notes on the wolverine in Alaska and the Yukon Territory. J. Wildl. Mgt. 36: 513-33.

Reardon, J. 1977. Pro: Alaska wolf kill, good sense! Natl. Wildl. 15(5): 8.

Remington, J. D. 1952. Food habits, growth, and behavior of two captive pine martens. J. Mammal. 33: 66-70.

Roberts, W. K., & R. J. Kirk. 1964. Digestibility and nitrogen utilization of raw fish and dry meals by mink. Am. J. Vet. Res. 25: 1746-50.

Robinson, W. L., & G. J. Smith. 1977. Observations on recently killed wolves in Upper Michigan. Wildl. Soc. Bull. 5: 25-26.

Romer, A. S. 1966. Vertebrate Paleontology. Univ. Chicago Press. Chicago.

Rosenzweig, M. L. 1966. Community structure in sympatric Carnivora. J. Mammal. 47: 602-12.

Rudnai, J. A. 1973. The social life of the lion. Washington Square East Publishers. Wall-ingford, Penn.

Schaller, G. B. 1967. The Deer and the Tiger. Univ. Chicago Press. Chicago.

Schempf, P. F., & M. White. 1977. Status of six furbearers in the mountains of northern California. Calif. Reg., Forest Service, U.S.D.A.

Schmidt-Nielsen, K. 1971. Locomotion: Energy cost of swimming, flying and running. Science 177: 222-28.

Schoener, T. W. 1969. Optimal size and specialization in constant and fluctuating environments: An energy-time approach. Brookhaven Symp. Biol. 22: 103-14.

Schoener, T. W. 1971. Theory of feeding strategies. Ann. Rev. Ecol. Syst. 2: 369-404.

Schoonmaker, W. J. 1938. The fisher as a foe of the porcupine in New York state. J. Mammal. 19: 373-74.

Schorger, A. W. 1942. Extinct and endangered mammals and birds of the Great Lakes Region. Trans. Wisc. Acad. Sci., Arts & Letters 34: 24-57.

Scott, T. G. 1941. Methods and computation in fecal analysis with reference to the red fox. Iowa St. Coll. J. Sci. 15: 279-85.

Scott, W. E. 1939. Rare and extinct mammals of Wisconsin. Wisc. Conserv. Bull. 4(10): 21-28.

Selwyn, S. 1966. Kestrel catching weasel. Brit. Birds 59: 39.

Seton, E. T. 1926. Lives of Game Animals. Vol. 2. Doubleday, Doran & Co. New York.

Seton, E. T. 1937. Lives of Game Animals. Vol. 2. The Literary Guild of Am. New York.

Silver, H. 1957. A history of New Hampshire game and furbearers. N.H. Fish & Game Dept. Concord, N. H.

Sokolov, I. I., & A. S. Sokolov. 1971. [Some characteristics of locomotor organs of *Martes martes* L. associated with its mode of life.] Byull. Mosk. O-va. Ispt. Priv. Otd. Biol. 76(6): 40-51.

Spencer, R. F., J. D. Jennings, D. E. Dibble, E. Johnson, A. R. King, T. Stern, K. M. Stewart, & W. J. Wallace. 1965. The Native Americans: Prehistory and Ethnology of the North American Indians. Harper & Row. New York.

Statistics Canada. 1978. Fur production, Season 1976-1977. Can. Min. Indus., Trade & Comm. Ottawa.

Stevens, C. L. 1968. The food of fisher in New Hampshire. N.H. Dept. Fish & Game. Unpubl. rep. Concord, N.H.

Strickland, M. A. 1978. Fisher and marten study, Algonquin region, progress report no. 5. Ontario Min. Nat. Res. Unpubl. rep.

Strickland, M. A. 1980. *In* C. W. Douglas & M. A. Strickland (eds.), pp. 25-60. Trans. 1979 fisher conf. Ontario Min. Nat. Res. Unpubl. rep.

Strickland, M. A., & C. W. Douglas. 1978. Some predictions for fisher and marten harvests in 1978-1979. Can. Trapper (December): 18-19.

Strickland, M. A., C. W. Douglas, G. R. Parsons, & M. K. Brown. 1981(in press). Age determination of fisher by cementum annuli. N.Y. Fish & Game J.

Taylor, C. R. 1973. Energy cost of locomotion. *In* L. Bolis, K. Schmidt-Nielsen, & S. H. Maddrell (eds.), pp. 25-42. Comparative Physiology. North-Holland Publ. Co. Amsterdam.

Taylor, C. R., K. Schmidt-Nielsen, & J. L. Rabb. 1970. Scaling the energetic cost of running to body size in mammals. Amer. J. Physiol. 219: 1104-7.

Taylor, W. P. 1935. Ecology and life history of the porcupine (*Erethizon dorsatum*) as related to the forests of Arizona and the southwestern United States. Univ. Arizona Bull. Biol. Sci. 6.

Teplov, V. P. 1948. [The problem of sex ratio in ermine.] Zool. Zhur. 27: 567-70. Also: *In* C. M. King (trans., ed.), pp. 98-103. 1975. Biology of Mustelids: Some Soviet Research. Brit. Libr. Lending Div. Wetherby.

Travis, H. F., & P. J. Schaible. 1961. Fundamentals of mink ranching. Coop. Extension Serv., Mich. Agr. Exp. Sta. Bull. 229.

Vogt, B. 1977. Nobody's neutral about wolves. Natl. Wildl. 15(5): 4-5.

Watt, K. E. F. 1959. A mathematical model for the effect of density of attacked and attacking species on the number attacked. Can. Entomol. 91: 129-44.

Weckwerth, R.P., & V. D. Hawley. 1962. Marten food habits and population fluctuations in Montana. J. Wildl. Mgt. 26: 55-74.

Weckwerth, R.P., & P. L. Wright. 1968. Results of transplanting fishers in Montana. J. Wildl. Mgt. 32: 977-80.

Weise, T. F., W. L. Robinson, R. A. Hook, & L. D. Mech. 1975. An experimental translocation of the eastern timber wolf. Audubon Conserv. Rep. No. 5.

Welker, W. I., & G. B. Compos. 1963. Physiological significance of sulci in somatic sensory cerebral cortex in mammals of the family Procyonidae. J. Comp. Neur. 120: 19-36.

Welker, W.I., & S. Seidenstein. 1959. Somatic sensory representation in the cerebral cortex of the raccoon (*Procyon lotor*). J. Comp. Neur. 111: 469-501.

Williams, R.M. 1962. The fisher returns to Idaho. Idaho Wildl. Rev. 15(1): 8-9.

Wolff, J. O. 1975. The effects of over-winter food supply and habitat patchiness on seasonal movements and population densities of snowshoe hare (*Lepus americanus*). Abst. Tech. Papers, 55th Ann. Meeting Amer. Soc. Mammal: 17-18.

Wood, J. 1977. The fisher is: . . . . Natl. Wildl. 15(3): 18-21.

Wright, P. L. 1948. Preimplantation stages in the long-tailed weasel (*Mustela frenata*). Anat. Rev. 100: 593-608.

Wright, P. L. 1963. Variations in reproductive cycles in North American mustelids. *In* A. C. Enders (ed.), pp. 77-97. Delayed Implantation. Univ. Chicago Press. Chicago.

Wright, P. L., & M. W. Coulter. 1967. Reproduction and growth in Maine fishers. J. Wildl. Mgt. 31: 70-87.

Wunder, B. A. 1975. A model for estimating metabolic rate of active or resting mammals. J. Theor. Biol. 49: 345-54.

Yocum, C. F., & M. T. McCollum. 1973. Status of the fisher in northern California, Oregon and Washington. Calif. Fish & Game 59(4): 305-9.

Young, H. C. 1975. Pequam the fisher. Fur-Fish-Game 71(11): 16-17, 48-50.

Yousef, M.K., W. D. Robertson, D. B. Dill, & H. D. Johnson. 1973. Energetic cost of running in the antelope ground squirrel *Ammospermophilus leucurus*. Physiol. Zool. 46: 139-47.

Appendix

Mammals and Birds Mentioned in the Text and Tables

Mammals

armadillo, nine-banded	*Dasypus novemcinctus*
badger	
American	*Taxidea taxus*
European	*Meles meles*
stink	genera *Mydaus, Suillotaxus*
bat	
big-eared	*Macrotus waterhousii*
equatorial fruit	*Eidolon helvum*
Jamaican fruit	*Artibeus jamaicensis*
long-winged	*Miniopterus schreibersii*
bear	
black	*Ursus americanus*
brown or grizzly	*Ursus arctos*
polar	*Ursus maritimus*
beaver	*Castor canadensis*
bobcat	*Lynx rufus*
caribou	*Rangifer tarandus*
chipmunks	*Eutamias* spp., *Tamias striatus*
coatimundi	*Nasua* spp.
coyote	*Canis latrans*
deer	
black-tailed	*Odocoileus hemionus*
roe	*Capreolus capreolus*
white-tailed	*Odocoileus virgianus*
euro	*Macropus robustus*
ferret	
black-footed	*Mustela nigripes*
fitch	*Mustela putorius*

fisher	*Martes pennanti*
fox, red	*Vulpes vulpes*
hare, snowshoe	*Lepus americanus*
lemming, southern bog	*Synaptomys cooperi*
lynx	*Lynx lynx*
marten	
American pine	*Martes americana*
beech, house, or stone	*Martes foina*
European pine	*Martes martes*
Japanese	*Martes melampus*
yellow-throated	*Martes flavigula*
mink	*Mustela vison*
moles	family Talpidae
moose	*Alces alces*
mountain lion	*Felis concolor*
mouse	
meadow	*Microtus pennsylvanicus*
meadow jumping	*Zapus hudsonicus*
red-backed	*Clethrionomys gapperi*
western harvest	*Reithrodontomys megalotus*
white-footed	*Peromyscus* spp.
woodland jumping	*Napeozapus insignis*
muskrat	*Ondatra zibethicus*
otter	
Canadian or river	*Lutra canadensis*
Eurasian	*Lutra lutra*
giant	*Pteronura brasiliensis*
polecat, European	*Mustela putorius*
porcupine	*Erethizon dorsatum*
rabbit, cottontail	*Sylvilagus* spp.
raccoon	*Procyon lotor*
ratel	*Mellivora capensis*
sable	*Martes zibellina*
seal	
elephant	*Mirounga angustirostris*
gray	*Halichoerus grypus*
harbor	*Phoca vitulina*
northern fur	*Callorhinus ursinus*
southern fur	*Arctocephalus* spp.
shrew	
masked	*Sorex cinereus*
short-tailed	*Blarina brevicauda*
skunk	
western spotted	*Spilogale gracilis*
others	genera *Conepatus, Mephitis, Spilogale*
squirrel	
douglas	*Tamiasciurus douglasii*
eastern gray	*Sciurus carolinensis*
flying	*Glaucomys* spp.
fox	*Sciurus niger*

red	*Tamiasciurus hudsonicus*
western gray	*Sciurus griseus*
tayra	*Tayra barbara*
walrus	*Odobenus rosmarus*
weasel	
least	*Mustela nivalis*
long-tailed	*Mustela frenata*
short-tailed	*Mustela erminea*
wolf	*Canis lupus*
wolverine	*Gulo gulo*
woodchuck	*Marmota monax*

Birds

blackbird, red-winged	*Agelaius phoeniceus*
chickadee, black-capped	*Parus atricapillus*
crow	*Corvus brachyrhynchos*
ducks	family Anatidae
flicker, yellow-shafted	*Colaptes auratus*
grouse, ruffed	*Bonasa umbellus*
jay	
blue	*Cyanocitta cristata*
gray	*Perisoreus canadensis*
junco, dark-eyed	*Junco hyemalis*
nuthatch, red-breasted	*Sitta canadensis*
owls	order Strigiformes
quail, Coturnix	*Coturnix coturnix*
sparrows	family Fringillidae
starling	*Sturnus vulgaris*
thrushes	family Turdidae
woodpecker, downy	*Dendrocopos pubescens*